THE FRIEND OF THE BRIDEGROOM

THE FRIEND OF THE BRIDEGROOM

On the Orthodox Veneration of the Forerunner

Sergius Bulgakov

Translated by

Boris Jakim

WILLIAM B. EERDMANS PUBLISHING COMPANY
GRAND RAPIDS, MICHIGAN / CAMBRIDGE, U.K.

© 2003 Wm. B. Eerdmans Publishing Co.
All rights reserved

Wm. B. Eerdmans Publishing Co.
255 Jefferson Ave. S.E., Grand Rapids, Michigan 49503 /
P.O. Box 163, Cambridge CB3 9PU U.K.

Printed in the United States of America

08 07 06 05 04 03   7 6 5 4 3 2 1

Library of Congress Cataloging-in-Publication Data

Bulgakov, Sergei Nikolaevich, 1871-1944.
[O pravoslavnom pochitanii Predtechi. English]
The friend of the bridegroom: on the Orthodox veneration
of the Forerunner / Sergius
Bulgakov; translated by Boris Jakim.
p.   cm.
Includes bibliographical references and index.
ISBN 0-8028-4979-2 (alk. paper)
1. John, the Baptist, Saint. 1. Title.
BS2456 .B8513 2003
232.9′4 — dc21
2002035225

www.eerdmans.com

Contents

Translator's Introduction	vii
Author's Preface	xi
Introduction: St. John, Forerunner of the Lord	1
1. The Birth of the Forerunner	18
2. St. John the Forerunner, Preacher of Repentance	42
3. The Baptism of John	46
4. The Baptism of the Lord, Followed by the Testimony concerning the Lamb of God	51
5. The Friend of the Bridegroom	72
6. The Forerunner's Agony and the Savior's Testimony about Him	85
7. The Savior's Discourse about John the Forerunner	104
8. John and Elias	115
9. The Honorable Death of the Forerunner	119
10. The Glorification of the Forerunner	129

Excursuses

1. On the Interrelationship of the Angelic and Human Worlds   156
2. St. John the Forerunner and St. John the Divine   171
3. St. John the Forerunner and St. Joseph the Betrothed   177

Index   189

Translator's Introduction

I

John the Baptist is also John the Forerunner, the one who prepares the way for the Lord. John is a "humanized angel or an angelic man,"[1] a living and personal communion of the angelic and human worlds. "He had attained a perfect resemblance to the angels, a perfectly passionless state."[2]

The path of direct struggle against the flesh, of self-renunciation, is the monastic path, which is a "putting on of the angelic habit." This is the path of self-crucifixion and self-mortification, the path of liberation from the flesh, the path toward a glorified state. This is the supreme path, the path of departure from the sinful world about which it is said: "Love not the world, neither the things that are in the world ... the lust of the flesh, and the lust of the eyes, and the pride of life" (1 John 2:15-16). The Forerunner is the true founder of monasticism, of the putting on of the angelic habit. His extreme of self-renunciation led to glorification.

John is "the friend of the Bridegroom" (John 3:29). The Bridegroom is Christ; the Bride is the Church. John is present at this mysterious wedding. He sees it with the eyes of a prophet, and rejoices in it as a friend, the friend of the Bridegroom. The friend's joy is the triumphant joy of humility; in him the human nature is humbled to the point of total self-renunciation. In Bulgakov's words, "that which the Forerunner's soul had desired, that which had filled his entire life, is now before his eyes. . . . Filled with the joy of total self-renunciation in love, he pronounces his

---

1. See p. 131 of the present edition.
2. See p. 163 of the present edition.

Forerunner's profession of faith: 'he must increase, but I must decrease' (John 3:30). This is perfect joy."[3]

2

Father Sergius Bulgakov (1871-1944) is the twentieth century's most profound Orthodox systematic theologian. Born into the family of a poor provincial priest, Bulgakov had a strict religious upbringing and entered the seminary at a young age. But owing to a spiritual crisis, in the direction of materialism and atheism, he did not complete his seminary studies. He chose, instead, to follow a secular course of study, which led to his matriculation at the University of Moscow, where he specialized in political economics.

This marked the beginning of his relatively short-lived Marxist period. In 1901, after defending his master's thesis, *Capitalism and Agriculture* (1900), Bulgakov was appointed professor of political economics at the Polytechnical Institute of Kiev. During his years there (1901-6), he underwent a second spiritual crisis, this time in the direction of idealist philosophy and the religion of his youth.

Influenced first by the philosophies of Kant and Vladimir Solovyov, and then by the great Orthodox theologian Pavel Florensky, Bulgakov gradually began to articulate his own original sophiological conception of philosophy. This conception was first elaborated in his *Philosophy of Economy*, for which he received his doctorate from the University of Moscow in 1912. Later, in *The Unfading Light* (1917), he gave his sophiological ideas definite philosophical shape. Following this, Bulgakov's intellectual output was, for the most part, theological in character. Indeed, his personal religious consciousness flowered in the following year, and he accepted the call to the priesthood, receiving ordination in 1918.

These years of internal crisis and growth in Bulgakov's personal life paralleled the tumultuous period in Russian political and social life that climaxed in the October Revolution of 1917 and the subsequent Bolshevik ascendancy. In 1918, Bulgakov left Moscow for the Crimea to assume a professorship at the University of Simferopol. But his tenure was short-lived, owing to Lenin's banishment in 1922 of more than one hundred scholars and writers deemed incurably out of step with the official ideology.

Bulgakov left the Soviet Union on January 1, 1923, traveling first to

---

3. See p. 79 of the present edition.

Constantinople, and then to Prague. Finally, having accepted Metropolitan Eulogius's invitation both to become the Dean of the newly established Saint Sergius Theological Institute and to occupy the Chair of Dogmatic Theology, he settled in Paris in 1925. Here, until his death in 1944, he was to make his most fruitful and lasting contributions to Orthodox thought.

His finest accomplishment was the great trilogy *On Divine Humanity*, consisting of volumes on Christology (*The Lamb of God*, 1933), pneumatology (*The Comforter*, 1936), and ecclesiology and eschatology (*The Bride of the Lamb*, published posthumuously, 1945).[4] In the decade prior to the publication of *On Divine Humanity*, Bulgakov produced the so-called "little trilogy," *The Friend of the Bridegroom* (1927), *The Burning Bush* (1927), and *Jacob's Ladder* (1929). These works about saintliness and angelhood are efforts to capture the glory, the uncreated light streaming from John the Baptist, the Mother of God, and the holy angels.

3

In *The Friend of the Bridegroom*, we find a fusion of the glories of all three: of the Forerunner, of the Mother of God, and of the angels (of whom John is first). We find this fusion represented in the second row (sometimes the first) of the iconostasis (the sanctuary screen in Byzantine churches): The Savior is at the center, with the Mother of God and the Forerunner to each side. One angel, or two, follows on each side, followed by icons of human saints. The central part represents the heavenly or angelic world, which is followed by the human world. In this heaven, in this angelic surround, closer to the Lord than the angels, but in their midst, stand not only the Mother of God but also the Forerunner. He is therefore missing from the human saints and is closer than the angels themselves to the Lord's throne.

We find an even more striking image of glorification in the icon *Deisis*, which means "prayer." On this icon the Savior is represented in royal or high-priestly garments, in His power and glory, sitting on a throne and with the Mother of God and the Forerunner standing before Him, hands raised in prayer. They pray not for themselves (for those in a glorified state have nothing to ask for) but for the world and for the hu-

---

4. Published by Wm. B. Eerdmans Publishing Co., 2001, in Boris Jakim's translation.

man race. This is not only a presence together in prayer but a union in and through Christ in the fullness of the whole prayer of the Church. It is a high-priesthood in the Church, a liturgy celebrated in the name of the whole Church. Bulgakov calls the *Deisis* "the unification of the heavenly and the earthly, of the angelic and the human, in Christ's Divine Humanity, in the Church that is His Body. It is a veil of intercession spread over the world. It is the glorified humanity, praying to Christ for the humanity that is not glorified."[5]

And this is the key to this book: It is not a work of arcane scholarship intended solely for the academic reader interested in hermeneutical subtleties and disputes. Woven of the testimonies of Church iconography and hymnography, it is a work of prayer. In some passages, it captures, as it were, the glory of the Forerunner; and we can see his radiance. How human beings can approach the super-human glory — that is a perennial (perhaps the greatest) theme of Orthodox theology, and it is the theme of this book. It holds forth the hope that, by renouncing themselves, by detaching themselves from the travails of the world, human beings can attain the state that is proper to them.

* * *

I have eliminated, or shortened, some of Bulgakov's notes, particularly those which refer to patristic interpretations. I have also abridged some of the quotations from Church hymns. Quotations from the Bible are from the King James Version.

Here and there in untwisting some thorny passages I have used the excellent translation into French by Constantin Andronikof and Tatiana Maillard: *L'Ami de l'Epoux: De la vénération Orthodoxe du Précurseur* (Lausanne: Editions L'Age d'Homme, 1997).

---

5. See p. 144 of the present edition.

Author's Preface

My aim in this work is to provide a dogmatic interpretation of the veneration, in Orthodoxy, of the Forerunner and Baptist of the Lord. In addition to Gospel narratives, this interpretation is based on sacred tradition as it is embodied in the patristic literature, in liturgy, and in iconography. Given the nature of the material, I mainly had to use the data of liturgical theology, i.e., the content of liturgical texts and icons. It goes without saying that to my conjectures I can attribute only the significance of personal theological opinions, of dogmatic hypotheses, so to speak, for this domain of inquiry is a difficult one and one that has not been well explored. The present work (1925-26) is the second part, as it were, of my recently published book, *The Burning Bush* (on the Orthodox veneration of the Mother of God). Their common theme is a dogmatic interpretation of the Orthodox veneration of the Mother of God and the Forerunner taken separately and together. In other words, the subject of both books is the *Deisis*, the iconographic representation of the presence of the Mother of God and the Forerunner before Christ.

Paris
Easter, 1927

INTRODUCTION

St. John, Forerunner of the Lord

"St. John, Forerunner and Baptist of the Lord, pray to God for us!"

The holy Orthodox Church honors and venerates St. John, Forerunner and Baptist of the Lord, above all saints. In order of glorification in the Church he comes right after the Virgin Mary. The Church attests in a prayer to the Forerunner that "we know that, after the Mother of God, he is, before the Lord, greater than anyone born on earth." According to the Lord Himself, he is the greatest "among them that are born of women" (Matt. 11:11). The Church venerates him by celebrating not only his death but also his conception and birth, an honor that is bestowed upon no other human being except the Mother of God. The Church also celebrates the synaxis of St. John the Forerunner (7 January) soon after that of the Mother of God (26 December).[1] The holy Church not only places the Forerunner immediately after the Mother of God in order of veneration, but it also mystically *unites* the two of them. The Church places them together in immediate proximity to Christ the Savior, in, for example, the widespread *Deisis* icon, which is always present in the iconostasis, as well as in the icon of St. Sophia, Wisdom of God (the Novgorod school). "By natural kinship and harmony in prayer, you two are one, Mother of the King of all and divine forerunner; pray together [for us]." What is especially remarkable is that this placing of the two of them together in proximity to Christ has not a grain of evidentiary support in the Gospel narratives. This is not the case with icons depicting the

---

1. In addition, the Church celebrates the synaxis of the archangel Gabriel, on 26 March, after the Annunciation.

Mother of God together with John the Divine, the "beloved disciple," at the Lord's cross, which find support in John 19:25. By contrast, the Gospels give us no grounds to associate the Forerunner and the Mother of God, since they contain no indication of any meeting between them on earth except that which took place when the Forerunner was still in his mother's womb.

In the *Deisis* ("supplication"), the Mother of God and the Forerunner stand, interceding for the human race, in immediate proximity to the *Glorified Christ*, the King and High Priest, the Great Hierarch. This icon is, according to the Church, a representation of the Forerunner's heavenly glorification, a revelation of his heavenly glory. This glorification is indicated also by other iconographic features, namely his depiction with wings, making him, a human being, a participant in the angelic world, and especially his representation on certain icons as wearing a crown (there are such representations of the Mother of God as well). Also, at the divine *proskomide*,[2] a portion of John the Forerunner is extracted before that of any other saint, immediately after that of the Mother of God. Here too we have the same closeness to the Most Pure One.

What is the basis for this closeness between them? That is the first question that arises in pious reflections on the Forerunner. Even in the flesh they were in a certain kinship (Luke 1:36), although She belonged to the tribe of kings, Judah, whereas he belonged to the priestly Levite tribe. Profoundly kindred to each other are their spiritual feats, the model and foundation of every path of ascesis, whose perfect example is given to us in the Feat of the Archetypal Ascetic, our Lord Jesus Christ. Their feat consists in *humility* as the supreme fruit and as the basis and power of self-renouncing love. The Feat of the Son of God consists in the fact that, "being in the form of God, [He] thought it not robbery to be equal with God: But made himself of no reputation, and took upon him the form of a servant, and was made in the likeness of men: And being found in fashion as a man, he humbled himself, and became obedient unto death, even the death of the cross" (Phil. 2:6-8). Similar is the feat of the Mother of God, who bore witness to this by Her answer to the Archangel — "Behold the handmaid of the Lord; be it unto me according to thy word" (Luke 1:38) — and by freely taking upon Herself Her share of the bearing of Christ's cross. And She indicated that She was the receptacle of humility, the very personification of humility, when She said that the Lord "hath regarded the low estate of his handmaiden" (Luke 1:48).

---

2. In the Eastern Church the *proskomide* is the elaborate preparation, before the beginning of the service, of the bread and wine for the Eucharist. — Trans.

But John the Forerunner too is the bearer of humility *par excellence* and of the most profound self-renunciation. "He must increase, but I must decrease" (John 3:30) — such is the Forerunner's consciousness of himself and such is his feat. What is a forerunner? It is someone who, renouncing himself, devotes *all of himself, all of his life,* to *another,* to someone else, to one who comes after. The Forerunner's ministry is wholly determined and exhausted by active humility, by self-renouncing love. The Forerunner gives himself wholly to the One who comes, proclaiming: "There cometh one mightier than I after me, the latchet of whose shoes I am not worthy to stoop down and unloose" (Mark 1:7). To give one's life for the Other, to devote oneself wholly to the One who comes, to lose one's I in voluntary, sacrificial self-annulment — that is the feat of love that, in a spirit of humility, humbles itself as much as it is humanly possible. And this self-renunciation refers not to a particular act or moment but to life in its entirety, to the whole of one's inner path and self-determination. One must be the Forerunner not only outwardly but also inwardly, through an unceasing, uninterrupted feat of self-renunciation: "The friend of the bridegroom . . . rejoiceth greatly because of the bridegroom's voice: this my joy therefore is fulfilled" (John 3:29). This self-witness of triumphant humility manifests in all its magnificence the feat of the Forerunner, who knew not only the feat of humility and its cross but also its sweetness, glory, and joy. This is *triumphant* humility, its apotheosis.

To this let us add the following consideration: although the greatest of those born of women (cf. Matt. 11:11) united in his order the highest of accomplishments, he did not work miracles, as the Gospel of John underscores: "Many resorted unto Him, and said, John did no miracle" (John 10:41), except a single, unique one, for the sake of which he came into the world — the miracle of bearing witness to the Messiah: "But all things that John spake of this man were true" (John 10:41).

Thus, the closeness of the feats of the Mother of God and of the Forerunner consists in the fullness of their humility. Just as the Mother of God, the handmaid of the Lord, is wholly and only the Mother of God in all things and always, so John the Baptist is wholly and only the Forerunner. In Her, all movements and gestures of the soul that are personal, willful, sinful, not-Mother-of-Godly die away; and, in him too, there is nothing personal, nothing except his mission as the Forerunner. There can be no loftier mission, no fuller consecration to God or more perfect self-surrender to Him than that which we find in the Mother of God and the Forerunner. Manifested in them is the fullness of obedience that was violated by our progenitors in Eden. Despite the immeasurable difference between the Queen of heaven and earth, higher than all creation, and the Forerunner in terms of the holiness of their missions, they are similar in the *fullness* of their obedience. And it is this similarity in humility that allows the Church to bring the two of them into close proximity. If the new Eve, the Mother of God, fulfilled the obedience violated by the ancient Eve, then the Forerunner, as the prefigurer of the New Adam, who is to come to restore the darkened human image, pre-initiated that obedience to the Father that the Son of God and of man fulfilled in His human nature. The Forerunner anticipated, as it were, the human feat of Christ the Savior. Sinful, willful nature has died in him, giving place to God's will. In the Forerunner, as in the Mother of God, original sin is not yet overcome but is pre-overcome: the Adamic nature is pre-restored in them, the definitive restoration coming only with the Savior. In them, humanity experiences *self*-restoration and *self*-salvation in the measure that such experience is given to and therefore required of humanity. The fallen human essence is raised to the *highest* level that is accessible to it; the peak is attained but man's natural essence is thereby exhausted. The Old Testament is accomplished, and therefore overcome. The Forerunner, like the Mother of God, belongs by his origin to the Old Testament, but by his life of grace he belongs to the New Testament. "You were seen, O prophet, standing between the Old and New Testaments, manifesting their light" (Office of the Forerunner, canon of the 6th tone, 9th ode, 2nd tr.). "The law and the prophets were until John" (Luke 16:16), said the Lord. John is the living boundary, the crest of the watershed; he looks in both directions at the same time, and here once again he cannot be separated from the Ever-Virgin. In Her the law was fulfilled, having revealed its meaning and inner justification. In him it was accomplished in order to die into new life. Without measure is the obedience of the Forerunner-Baptist and of the Most Pure One Full of Grace. Without measure is their divinely bestowed humility and wisdom.

*　　*　　*

Who is the Forerunner of the Lord? What is his significance? We know his ministry: he was a preacher of repentance, a baptist and prophet; he was also an evangelist and the first martyr, an angel in the flesh and a preacher of Christ to those in hell. To prepare the way for Christ, that was his mission. But his significance consists not only in this; it consists, first and foremost, in himself, in his person. The Forerunner's work was necessary for that of Christ; the coming of the Forerunner was necessary for that of Christ. In other words, not only John's mission but also his person was necessary. *If not for John, Christ the Savior could not have come into the world.* John and Christ are personally and indissolubly linked like the great and small celestial lights to which the Church hymn compares them.[3]

Christ's link to the Mother of God is clear and easy to understand; without Her the Nativity would not have taken place: the divine incarnation presupposes and implies divine motherhood. Less apparent but not less indissoluble is the link between Christ and the Forerunner, for the Lord's Baptism, which corresponds to His spiritual birth and His reception of the Holy Spirit, presupposes the Baptist. And so, the place he occupies in relation to Christ is correlative to that of the Mother of God.

In the Gospel of Matthew, the genealogy of Christ the Savior, son of David, follows the royal branch of Judah, but it also embraces, in a side branch, through the blood relation between the Most Pure Virgin and Elisabeth (Her "cousin"), the priestly branch of the Levites, out of which the Forerunner came. (One knows that there was no special prophetic branch, for prophets arose by God's will in all tribes and in all situations.) The Forerunner and, in his person, the priestly branch are linked by blood kinship to the Lord, although not in the direct genealogical line. But it is not this that expresses the necessary connection between the coming of the Forerunner and that of Christ. This connection is more profound and essential than a mere blood relationship. It consists in the fact that Christ could not have come into the world if He had not been preceded by the Forerunner. The coming of the Forerunner constitutes, if not the direct condition, as in the case of the Mother of God, then the indirect, yet necessary, condition of Christ's incarnation. This connection is indisputably indicated by Scripture, though this is usually done not directly but through hints and allusions. To define this connection must be our first order of business.

One's attention is captured first of all by the fact that the coming of the Forerunner is prophesied in the Old Testament as one of the events through which our salvation is built. The Forerunner's birth and his coming are events that God uses in building our salvation. The Forerunner, like the Mother of God, figures from all eternity in God's thought about the salvation of the world; and his coming, like that of the Mother of God, is prepared from all eternity. Let us try to understand the whole depth and significance of this prophecy concerning the Forerunner, which all

---

3. "All creation is illuminated by solar rays, for, O Forerunner, you appeared like a radiant star of the spiritual sun" (tone 7, canon, ode 2, tr. 1).

three synoptic Gospels so insist upon and which is confirmed by the Lord Himself (Matt. 11:10; Luke 7:27). These prophecies do not belong to the realm of the external foretelling of the future. To satisfy human curiosity about the future in its contingent and secondary aspects is not their goal. That which these prophecies announce is *internally necessary* to the economy of our salvation. They are an anticipation of salvation: they announce the salvation that has already started. And in this sense, the coming of the Forerunner is part of this economy of salvation.

Among the great prophets, Isaiah announces the coming of the Forerunner in chapter 40, which he begins with words of comfort and glad tidings: "Comfort ye, comfort ye my people, saith your God" (40:1). Further, he describes the coming of salvation, the appearance of the Glory of God, the coming of the Lord in all His power. And the first stage of this coming is here indicated to be the coming into the world of the Forerunner: "The voice of him that crieth in the wilderness, Prepare ye the way of the Lord, make straight in the desert a highway for our God" (40:3). All four evangelists attest to the special significance of this prophecy when they speak of the coming of the Forerunner: Matthew 3:3, Mark 1:3, Luke 3:4, John 1:23 (in the Gospel of John the Forerunner himself bears witness to the prophecy). It would be hard to find many other Old Testament prophecies that receive such attention and confirmation in the Gospels — an obvious sign of the great importance of this prophecy.

A second prophecy concerning the Forerunner is contained in the book of the prophet Malachi: "Behold, I will send my angel,[4] and he shall prepare the way before me" (Mal. 3:1). In the New Testament we have a variant of the second part of this verse: "who shall prepare thy way before thee." These words are referred by the Lord Himself directly to the Forerunner (Matt. 11:10, Luke 7:27); Mark also uses them in connection with the Forerunner (Mark 1:2). This prophecy announces not only the appearance itself of the Forerunner in the fullness of messianic times but also the fact that he is *sent by God into the world* for a task necessary on the pathways of our salvation.

It is worthy of note that this idea of the express sending of the Forerunner by God is found in the Gospel of the beloved disciple, in the solemn announcement of the Incarnation of the Word, as one of the conditions of this Incarnation. In the prologue of the Gospel of John it is written: "There was a man sent from God, whose name was John" (1:6).

---

4. The King James translation is modified here to conform with the Russian Bible. — Trans.

Aside from the direct testimony concerning the sending of John into the world, the context in which this is said is remarkable and worthy of the most profound attention. After proclaiming the supra-eternal Word of God (1:1-5), the Evangelist announces His Incarnation; but before doing so, as if in anticipation of the Incarnation, the Evangelist mentions John, who "came for a witness, to bear witness of the Light" (1:7). And after reaching the triumphant crescendo "and the Word was made flesh" (1:14), the Evangelist returns to the Forerunner and his witness. In so doing, he establishes a necessary and indissoluble connection between the coming of Christ and that of the Forerunner, between the accomplished Incarnation and the witness borne to it.

This connection is implicitly but nevertheless expressively attested to by the other evangelists as well. Each does so in his own particular manner; Mark and Luke express it the most clearly. The Gospel of Mark has the clearest schema though one that is brief; it is meager in detail but does not leave out anything significant. It also expresses the most universal and the most ancient consciousness of the primitive Church, as reflecting the preaching of the apostle Peter. It does not include an introductory chapter, such as the narrative of Christ's Nativity in Matthew, or a historical prologue such as we find in Luke, or a theological prologue such as we find in John. Right at the outset Mark proclaims "the beginning of the Gospel of Jesus Christ, the Son of God" (1:1). And what does this beginning consist of? It consists of the story of the Forerunner, who is thereby introduced into the very heart of the Gospel, as a necessary condition or part of the latter.

This connection is expressed with less salience in the more extensive narrative in Matthew. However, it contains a detail that can also be interpreted in this sense: The Forerunner's preaching here is almost identical to that of Jesus: "Repent ye: for the kingdom of heaven is at hand" (Matt. 3:2; cf. 4:17). This nearly identical language is not accidental, of course; it attests that the coming of the Forerunner betokens that the kingdom of heaven is nigh. Again, it attests to his indissoluble union with the Savior.

Luke expresses the same idea in his own manner, also indirectly but very expressively, in an extensive narrative. It is sufficient to note that his Gospel opens with the appearance of an angel to Zacharias and the birth of the Forerunner, which Luke directly and deliberately links with the Annunciation and the birth of Christ. This is the only place where we find the story of the Mother of God's visit to Elisabeth and the leaping of the Forerunner in her womb (which will be discussed later). In general, the fact that the sending of the Forerunner into the world was announced by the very same Archangel Gabriel who brought the glad tidings of the Nativity to the Mother of God provides a direct confirmation of our thesis. Moreover, this is presented as a fulfillment of the other Gospel narratives, a task openly set for himself by Luke. The name of the Forerunner, John ("homonym of grace," as the Church calls him in a prayer that it addresses to him), *Iehova hanan*, signifies: "God gives grace."[5]

Of essential importance here is the fact that the *name* of the Forerunner is given to him by the archangel before his birth and even before his conception: "and thou shalt call his name John" (Luke 1:13; cf. 1:60, 63). In order to assess the significance of this fact, it is sufficient to mention that, in the Annunciation to the Virgin Mary, the same archangel tells Her in the same words: "and shalt call his name JESUS" (Luke 1:31). Both sacred names, in different senses but preestablished from all eternity, figure in the same context, in the narrative of the sending of the archangel Gabriel to the earth, and within the limits of the same chapter (the first) of the Gospel of Luke. (According to tradition, the name of the Mother of God was also told in advance by the angel to Joachim and Anna, although in the Gospel of Luke, in the same chapter, the first, it is merely said, with special emphasis: "The virgin's name was Mary" [Luke 1:27].) This forenaming has the same significance as the Old Testament prophecy of the coming of the Forerunner. Of course, the Lord knows *all* the names before the appearance of their bearers in the world. Not only people but even animals had names, which Adam gave them. As far as people are concerned, the prophets repeatedly bear witness to this, e.g., Isaiah 43:1: "I have called thee [Israel] by thy name; thou art mine"; or Isaiah 45:3 (concerning Cyrus): "I, the LORD . . . call thee by thy name."

What then is the significance of the Forerunner, whose coming into the world is closely linked with the coming of the Messiah Himself and the Incarnation? The coming of the Forerunner is associated with the "fullness of time," *to plērōma tou chronou* (Gal. 4:4; cf. Eph. 1:10), which must be fulfilled before the Son of God, the Son of man, can come into the world. This fullness — which is the fullness of the whole of the Old Testament holiness, and in general that of the holiness that is attainable by man — consisted not only in the appearance of the Most Pure Virgin who was worthy of being the Mother of God but also in the appearance of a man worthy of meeting the Lord as a *friend*, of becoming the *friend of the Bridegroom*. Becoming man signified for God not only being born of the Virgin, becoming incarnate, but also being received by the human race in the person of

---

5. This name is encountered several times in the Old Testament: *Jehochanan, Iochanan*. The Septuagint translates it as *Ioanan*, or *Iona, Ioanes*.

the Forerunner. Once born, the Lord was not to remain solitary among men. Not even His Most Pure Mother could free Him from solitude, for in Her divine maternity She was one with Him as it were and for this reason could not have entered into a relationship of otherness to Him, could not have become His friend (a "third person," as we tend to say). Such an "other" in relation to the Savior, capable of meeting and receiving Him before and on the part of all humankind, and worthy of being called the friend of the Bridegroom, should naturally be the *greatest of those born of women*. For there is no higher calling and no higher dignity for a man than to be the *friend of the Bridegroom*. The Lord wishes to find in man a friend who would be a god according to grace, a creaturely image and likeness of God. But since the fall, when man stopped being God's friend and became a child of wrath (see Eph. 2:3), his return to God's friendship, his reconciliation with God, has become the express task of the divine economy of our salvation. And just as the long history of the Old Testament Church was the condition of the blossoming of the Edenic lily of the Mother of God on the trunk of this tree, so the fullness of the Old Testament holiness was the condition for the blossoming alongside Her of the Forerunner of the Lord, "like a fragrant bud, like a sweet-smelling cypress" (Canon of the Forerunner, 9th ode, 2nd tr.).

At the Last Supper, at the threshold before accomplishing His redemptive act, the Lord calls His disciples "friends," "not servants" (John 15:14-15), although they had yet to become worthy of the vocation to which the Lord called them. But when He came into the world the Lord needed a friend who was worthy of meeting Him. One could *become a friend of the Lord* only by virtue of Christ's redemptive sacrifice and the grace of the Holy Spirit, making us sons of the Father by adoption and crying in our hearts: "Abba Father." The New Testament Church is separated from the Old Testament Church by the *divine* fact of the redemptive sacrifice: "this is My blood of the New Testament" (Matt. 26:28). And this frontier cannot be crossed by any human effort. Nevertheless, there remains the path of human *ascent*, of human approach to God's friendship. This path has its beginning in Moses, about whom it is said: "And the LORD spake unto Moses face to face, as a man speaketh unto his friend" (Exod. 33:11). It is followed to the end by the Forerunner, who represents in this sense, together with the Mother of God, the peak of human holiness and therefore of human self-renunciation: In him the *sinful* human nature is crucified and dies, and awaits a new, divine-human life, a life of grace. Therefore he is a servant of *redemption*, but only of redemption; a servant of preparation, not of new birth; a servant of the present, not of the future. He is a call to the heavens, an open mouth, the dry earth thirsting to receive the rain of heaven. He is the dying of the old man; he is redemption, *metanoia*. In him, there remains not even the possibility of natural life, of this life that surged even in the righteous of the Old Testament, in patriarchs, judges, kings, and prophets, until the Old Testament reached its end — in the Forerunner.

The Forerunner no longer has a life of his own. He is entirely the friend of the Bridegroom, entirely outside himself. He no longer belongs to himself; he no longer lives for and by himself. He is not himself but other than himself, the friend and only the friend of the Bridegroom, whereas the Bridegroom is not yet his friend, and will not even become his friend within the bounds of earthly existence. This represents his limit but also the greatness of his mission and the power of his self-renunciation. He himself will not follow the Lord, will not become His disciple, will not hear from His lips those words so sweet that He addressed to His disciples: "Ye are my friends [*philos*]" (John 15:14). The Forerunner is like the moon that pales at sunrise and is extinguished in the sun's shining. He is only the Forerunner, who bears a freely accepted, fully understood cross, the cross of the ministry of the one who precedes the One who comes.

This enables us to understand the Lord's words concerning the Forerunner, which with an eternal chisel express the essence and nature of the Forerunner's ministry. It enables us to understand the words which, at first glance, seem severe, almost cruel, and contradictory: "Verily I say unto you [this opening underscores the importance of the subject being discussed], Among them that are born of women there hath not risen a greater [*meizōn*] than John the Baptist: notwithstanding he that is least [*mikroteros*] in the kingdom of heaven is greater than he" (Matt. 11:11; Luke 7:28). John is the greatest amongst human beings because, for himself, he is no longer a human being. But even that which is humanly highest remains *qualitatively* different from divine life. That is why even he who is least is, by virtue of his participation in this divine life, greater than he who is highest according to the natural human essence. (There is here, of course, no consideration of the question of what John the Forerunner himself will be in the Kingdom of God. But we have the Church's answer to this question: In the Kingdom of God too, the Forerunner is the greatest, the first after the Mother of God.)

*　　*　　*

Nowhere else in the New Testament does the antinomy of man's sinful nature attain such an acuteness and intensity: in order to assert his genuine human essence, in order to save his soul, man must surrender himself entirely, must allow his soul to perish. All forms of human feat are therefore united in the Forerunner: "O preacher of Christ and Baptist, angel, apostle, martyr, prophet, forerunner, priest, close friend, seal of the prophets, the most honorable of all those born" (Sticheron to St. John the Forerunner).

However, we are considering now not the ministry and saintliness of the Forerunner but the mission to which he was called, that of preparing a way for the Lord. Without this preparation the Lord could not have come into the world. What did this preparation consist in? In the preaching of repentance and in the softening of hearts? This, of course, was important, but its importance was not decisive; at the very least the Gospel does not speak of it as decisive. The Forerunner prepared the coming of the Lord, first and foremost, not through others but in himself, by the very fact of his existence. *The Lord was met in the world.* He did not find Himself alone in the world, for a *friend, prepared and worthy to receive Him,* had come to meet Him. In this meeting, this friend represented *all humankind*, or rather, the whole Old Testament Church, which, in his person, was coming to an end, surpassing its limited holiness. In meeting the New Adam, John was the worthy descendant of the old Adam who, by his obedience, was prepared not to repair (for man does not have the power to do so) but to efface to some degree Adam's disobedience, even as the New Eve, by Her humility and obedience, effaced the disobedience of the first Eve. Together with the holiness of the Woman, who manifested herself as the *handmaid of the Lord,* worthy of receiving God, there also blossomed the righteousness of a male worthy of meeting God.

Numerous were those who, judged worthy of being close to Him, awaited Him on earth: the righteous Joseph, the betrothed; the righteous Simeon and Anna the prophetess; the future apostles, the twelve as well as the seventy. But neither these elders who were departing the world, who had already completed their lives before Christ's coming into the world, nor the future apostles could *meet* Him in the true and precise sense of the word, that is, in such a way as to withstand the meeting, to recognize Him, to manifest Him to the world, and to be worthy of this. The apostles were worthy of being called by the Master and, through a long period of instruction, through falls and tribulations, of participating in the mysteries of the Kingdom of God and in the faith in the Savior. But, strictly speaking, prior to the Resurrection they had not yet attained the apostolic dignity: they received it fully only in the Pentecost. Therefore, one can say that, at the beginning of the Savior's earthly ministry, they did not know the Lord and thus could not meet Him worthily. Besides the Mother of

God, only the Forerunner knew the mystery of the Incarnation and was also capable of withstanding the meeting with the Lamb of God. Therefore, in the person of the Forerunner, the Savior was received on earth, and this reception constitutes the Forerunner's participation in the work of the Incarnation. In him was *accomplished* the Incarnation for the Church, and he and the Mother of God represent the Church, he in his own way and She in her own way, but the two inseparably, near Christ the Savior: the Mother-Bride of God and the friend of the Bridegroom at the marriage feast of the Lamb.

The role of the Forerunner in the Incarnation and in the redemption of the world can also be clarified from another angle: John is not only the Forerunner but also the Baptist. Although the Nativity of Christ is truly the birth of God and the Most Pure One is truly the Mother of God, God's becoming man is not yet fully accomplished in the Nativity. It is fully accomplished in the Lord's Baptism, which is accompanied by the descent of the Holy Spirit upon His human essence; and this is Christ's Pentecost. After the latter, He becomes truly *Christos,* the Christ, the one anointed by the Holy Spirit. Just as in humankind fleshly birth is distinguished from that by water and by the spirit, so, for the fullness of divine kenosis and in-humanization, not only the Nativity but also the Baptism of Christ had to occur. In this light, Christ's Baptism must be viewed as completing the Nativity, and thus it needs a spiritual "birthgiver," or Baptist. The Baptism is a necessary aspect of the Incarnation. Since the Lord could not baptize Himself without violating the fullness of His in-humanization, He needed the Baptist for this fullness of His Incarnation, just as He needed the Mother for His Nativity.

The Baptist's providential preparation acquires a significance that is similar to that of the Mother of God. The Baptist had to become *worthy* of his mission and his work. He had to become capable of meeting face to face the God who was to be baptized, of seeing in the opening heavens the descending Holy Spirit, of hearing the Father's voice, of witnessing the mystery of the Theophany. Such a capability and power could not be attributed to any of the Old Testament saints, even the greatest; only the Forerunner was able to withstand the presence of Christ and accomplish the Baptism. This expresses, we repeat, the Baptist's participation in the building of our salvation. The Bridegroom found a worthy friend. He did not find Himself in the world alone; He was received by the one who "came for a witness, to bear witness of the Light, that all men through him might believe" (John 1:7). This "all" must, of course, be understood not in a quantitative but in a qualitative sense. John the Forerunner came as a living representative of all humankind. In his person was accomplished the meeting of the God-man with humanity, of the Sole Sinless One with sinful humankind, which, in Him, overcame its alienation.

If it is true that the Forerunner's mission, like that of the Mother of God (though in a different, special sense), is necessary and essential for the Incarnation, then to participate in this feat, to have inner knowledge of it, and to follow it are necessary if we are to be saved, if we are to assimilate Christ's sacrifice. It is indisputable that every member of the Church, insofar as he lives by the life of the Church, spiritually participates in the divine maternity, uniting the voice of his soul with the voice of the one who said: "Behold the handmaid of the Lord" (Luke 1:38), and spiritually giving himself to the divine Nativity. Every Christian soul, according to St. Augustine, gives birth to Christ in its heart, joins the "synaxis of the Mother of God," the feast solemnly celebrated by the Holy Church the day after Christmas. On this day the Church celebrates not only the feast of the Mother of God but also the divine maternity that is common to all of us, about which the Church sings: "we [that is, the whole human race] offer to Thee the Virgin Mother."

The aforesaid in no wise diminishes the significance of the personal feat and holiness of the One who is more honorable than the cherubim and higher than all creation. She, and only She, and precisely She, is the Mother of the Divine Son. She is Mary, who gave birth to Jesus Emmanuel. But she is not thereby separated from all creation and the human race. Rather, she remains the Edenic flower on Adam's tree (see the evangelical genealogy in Luke) and calls all human beings to come to Her. She is the personal realization of the divine maternity common to all humanity, and the Son of God did not call Himself the Son of Mary but the Son of man. Jesus addresses Her personally on two occasions, both recorded in the Gospel of John, and both times He calls Her "woman," a collective impersonal term designating the whole human race taken in its female manifestation. And the entire human essence received by Him participates in this divine Nativity.

One can even say that every human being, insofar as he is truly a human being, not distorted by sin or enslaved by the price of this world, is a member of the Body of Christ, belongs to the Church, and, in the Church, participates in the supra-eternal divine Nativity. That is why there can be no true Christianity if the Mother of God is not venerated, inwardly known, honored, and followed. It is impossible to venerate the Son in separation from His Mother, to adore the Divine Infant in isolation from the Mother of God. Knowledge and veneration of the Mother of God are not only a dogma of faith but also an internally necessary condition of salvation.

And a Christian must know not only the birth but also the reception of God, not only the feat of the Virgin Mary but also that of John the Forerunner. In John was accomplished the voluntary, loving, conscious self-renunciation of the human essence before the presence of the Divine essence. Man rendered *proper* adoration and obedience to God, which he refused Him in Eden. Man recognized the insignificance before God of the creaturely, human essence and joyously offered it in sacrifice, in the joy of love. In the Forerunner was realized that love of man for God and that love of a human person for Christ the God-man without which there is no true liberation from the prison of spiritual selfhood, from self-assertion in oneself, that is, in nothingness, for the fullness of all being is only in God. Only he will save his soul who loses it for Christ, who desires not his own life but only Christ's, as the apostle says: "not I, but Christ liveth in me" (Gal. 2:20).

And this path on which the egotistical human essence, ossified in its self-assertion, is dissolved in Christ's love was first followed to the end by the Forerunner: He was the Forerunner precisely because he completely renounced himself, transferred the center of his *own* being into the *Other*. He arrived at a humility so perfect and genuine that he felt himself unworthy of unloosing the latchet of Christ's shoes (see Mark 1:17); and when he met Him he diminished himself in the joy in the Other. In John, as well as in Mary, human egotism was vanquished; and in this central point there was already overcome the personal sinfulness that is a consequence of the universal original sin, the sin of egotism and self-delusion: "ye shall be as gods" (Gen. 3:5). John was liberated from this self-deification, for in his heart he rejoiced in God, His Savior, and adored Him as the true God. This was precisely *repentance* as inner change, *metanoia*, and John was its preacher. Even before he began his preaching, he had made repentance an inner part of himself. He is its living personification. He is the threshold that cannot be avoided on the way to the kingdom of heaven: "Repent ye: for the kingdom of heaven is at hand" (Matt. 3:2). And conversely, this kingdom is now at hand for men because, among other reasons, it has *already* been realized in the Forerunner. The latter thereby received the power to approach the King himself who brought the Kingdom of God to earth. And one can approach Christ only in John's way; only through repentance can one meet the Christ who has come.

Human self-liberation has taken place in John. Therefore, he was, after the fall, *the first man* who was prepared for salvation, who was ripe for the Kingdom of God, who repented of Adam's sin. He had transferred his center from himself into God. He became *other* for himself and therefore he became a friend, the friend of the Bridegroom.[6] And his soul became open to the *joys* of this friendship, as the fiery words of the Gospel of John attest: "The friend of the bridegroom, which standeth and heareth him, rejoiceth greatly because of the bridegroom's voice: this my joy is therefore fulfilled" (John 3:29).

This joy of the friend of the Bridegroom is the joy of every Christian soul in the approach of Christ, to Whom this soul dedicates its human essence. It was given to John to accomplish on earth his unique, personal mission as the Forerunner; and this feat of prophet, preacher of repentance, and Baptist is, of course, one that cannot be repeated. Nevertheless, there is in this feat a universally human significance and a universally Christian content that is necessarily experienced by every human being on the path to Christ: namely repentance and self-renouncing love, the love of the friend of the Bridegroom. All those who approach the heavenly Bridegroom and bring their human essence to Him like a bride (the liturgical hymn of 27 June calls the Forerunner "the bringer of brides") will become in their hearts friends of this Bridegroom.

There are two modes of relation of the soul to Christ as the Bridegroom. In the Church, every soul that surrenders itself to Christ and lives by His life has with respect to Him the relation of a "bride"-church that receives its life from Him. This is the feminine mode of relation to Christ. But there is another mode, if not of communion with Him, at least of striving toward Him: in it we renounce ourselves because of our love for Christ. The soul knows then the sweetness of friendship for the Bridegroom, this mode and way of the Forerunner, which is the mode of male love, of the male relation to the Bridegroom. These two modes of relation do not exclude one another but are joined together in an indissoluble unity. Love is both self-renunciation and communion as love in the other; love is the unity of the life of two. As the Bride of Christ, the Church has and gives communion of life, this unity; and this unity is the principle of divine maternity in the Church's self-definition.

As a multi-unity of hypostases, in the image of the trihypostatic unity of God, the Church is unceasing self-renunciation, dying for the other, friendship for the Bridegroom. Love is sacrificial self-mortification and resurrection, union and friendship. The fullness of ecclesial love,

---

6. In this passage Bulgakov plays on the words *drugoi* (other) and *drug* (friend). — Trans.

communion with Christ, is given in the *union* of the love for Christ of the Mother of God and the Forerunner, standing together before Him in the *Deisis*.

That is why the figure of the Forerunner is not one of many figures of saints venerated by the Church, but is unique in its significance. He is greater than the apostles; greater even than the greatest of the apostles, whom the Lord instructed, preparing them for their apostleship, battling against their limitations, and sometimes even against their sinful weaknesses — despite which, seized with fear, they abandoned Him before His death on the cross, and remained in anguish and confusion until the appearance of the Resurrected Christ and the pouring forth of the gifts of the Holy Spirit. When the Forerunner begins his ministry, he is fully prepared, mature, fully formed. He follows the path of his ministry without being darkened or tainted by the slightest sin. He is the light of the loftiest holiness that is accessible to man prior to and outside of Christ. The greatest of those born of women, he is superior to all men according to their human nature. He can be compared only to the Virgin Mary, who, as the Mother of God, is superior to all creatures, including him. But, in her human nature, in Her human holiness, She is more akin to the Forerunner than to anyone else.

This kinship consists in the absence of all voluntary personal sin, in personal sinlessness, which, of course, in no wise signifies freedom from original sin, a freedom that is given to human beings only by the Savior. (That is why the least in the Kingdom of God is greater than the greatest of those born of woman; in this are manifested the weakness of all human nature and its insufficiency for salvation.) The Church eloquently confirms this kinship by celebrating the synaxis of the Mother of God right after Christmas (26 December) and the synaxis of the Forerunner (7 January) the day after celebrating the baptism of Christ. The Mother of God and the Forerunner each have a separate synaxis; they unite the Church around themselves; they summon all members of the Church to this synaxis, which thereby becomes essential in the life of the Church for the salvation of the faithful.[7]

This also indisputably bears witness to the fact that the Forerunner's feat is by no means annulled by the New Testament. It belongs also to the essence of New Testament piety. Like the divine maternity, this feat remains a foundation of the Church's life, for in it is revealed the *human*

---

7. In contrast to these human synaxes, the celebration of the synaxis of the archangel Gabriel (26 March) refers to the angelic world, to the celestial orders.

side or precondition of communion with God. John stands at the boundary between the Old and New Testaments, between the old and new man. He is this very boundary; in or by him this boundary is overcome in the human soul. That which was once realized in and with him is even now being realized in the human heart.

Thus, the Forerunner, together with the Mother of God, finds himself in special, exclusive proximity to Christ the Savior. They form His immediate entourage in His icons: in these icons the human race in its loftiest holiness and devotion to God is represented not by the apostles, martyrs, or saints, and not even by the angels or archangels, but by the Mother of God and the Forerunner, this mystical dyad. And one is struck by the fact that this primary human dyad is traditionally represented on the chalice that contains the precious and life-giving Blood of the Lord: the medallion icon of Christ the Pantocrator is here always framed by medallion icons of the Mother of God and the Forerunner. There is no stronger and more profound expression of the exceptional proximity of the Forerunner to the Lord than this icon of his presence, together with the Mother of God, at the awesome mystery of the transmutation of the sacred gifts. He who was given to touch with his hand the "crown of the head of the One Baptized," is given, through the intermediary of his icon, to touch and always to be present at the precious blood of the "Lamb of God, which taketh away the sin of the world" (John 1:29), at the blood of the One Whom he himself announced and preached to the world.

CHAPTER 1

The Birth of the Forerunner

By celebrating the venerable conception of the Forerunner (24 September) and his venerable birth (24 June), the Holy Church puts him into close proximity with the Mother of God, whose glorious conception (9 December) and glorious birth (9 September) she also celebrates. The Church does not accord such veneration to any other human beings. The Church generally commemorates saints on the day of their death or the day of their glorification. How does she justify the exception made here? What thought does the Church express in this commemoration of the Forerunner and the Mother of God? This thought is profound and significant: for every human being, life is a path of salvation, a possibility of liberation from sin, of finding the grace of the Holy Spirit. Therefore, the essential and decisive moment of a life can only be its conclusion, the death of a righteous one: "Precious in the sight of the Lord is the death of his saints" (Ps. 116:15). The death of a saint is a victorious liberation from sin, the fulfillment of a feat. "I have fought a good fight, I have finished my course, I have kept the faith: Henceforth there is laid up for me a crown of righteousness" (2 Tim. 4:7-8). Therefore, the Church does not generally celebrate the birth of saints, for it represents the initial state of their captivity, their subjugation by sin. Every human being is born in sin, and "there is no man who lives and does not sin," even if his life lasts but a single day. Secular biographers may characterize the birthdays of eminent people as joyous and festive, but the Church celebrates only the victory over sin, the realized feat. Moreover, owing to the instability of human nature, there can be no certainty, as long as a life has not yet ended, that a man has been saved from sin or even from depravity. "Brethren, I count not myself to have apprehended: but this one thing I do, forgetting those things which are behind, and reaching forth unto those things which are before, I press toward the mark for the prize of the high calling of God in Christ Jesus" (Phil. 3:13-14).

But if that is the case, the Forerunner occupies a special, exceptional place by virtue of the fact that the Church celebrates his conception. The Church attests that his saintliness began at the moment of his conception, the authoritative text being the Archangel Gabriel's proclamation to Zacharias: "and he shall be filled with the Holy Spirit, even from his mother's womb"[1] (Luke 1:15). That which for all men is the crown and fulfillment of a life in its entirety is given to the Forerunner in his mother's womb, from his conception. That is why the Church summons people to exult in this event: "Today, in an unfruitful womb, the fruit of prayer led to the conception of John the Forerunner! Rejoice, wilderness, and exult, humankind! For the preacher of redemption is coming; he is becoming flesh in his mother's womb" (Office of 24 September). "Creation rejoices in your conception, prophet and Forerunner, John the Baptist, for your birth prefigures for us the birth of the Lord" (sticheron in praise). "God's prophet, elder, rejoice! For you have begotten a son who is the greatest among men, John the Forerunner of the Lord. Rejoice, Elisabeth! Rejoice, the whole earth, praising God, the creator of all things."

Just as in the case of the Mother of God, there inevitably arises in relation to the Forerunner the question of *whether he is free of sin* from his conception and birth. But what freedom can it be a question of here? In any case, not of freedom from original sin. As far as the Forerunner is concerned, this is attested to by the Lord, who said that the least in the Kingdom of God is greater than he, the greatest of those born of women. But it is precisely original sin that separates one from the Kingdom of God. And, in general, there is no basis to conclude that John the Baptist, preacher of repentance and of baptism for the remission of sins, was free from sin prior to the coming into the world of the Savior (this is equally applicable to the Virgin Mary, contrary to the Catholic dogma of Her immaculate conception). There is no and can be no liberation from original sin outside of or prior to the sacrifice of the Savior on the cross; and even the Forerunner remains subject to original sin. He is redeemed from original sin by our Lord together with the whole of the human race.

Nevertheless, the Church celebrates his conception; that is, from his very conception the Church venerates him as a saint: the grace of the Holy Spirit rests upon him even in his mother's womb, thereby attesting to his

---

1. Here, and throughout the book, the King James' "Holy Ghost" has been changed to "Holy Spirit." — Trans.

saintliness. Human saintliness can coexist with original sin, which is sufficiently demonstrated by examples of the righteous of the Old Testament, some of whom, like Enoch and Elijah, were translated into heaven while alive. This saintliness has a preliminary character, so to speak. It was confirmed and perfected by the Lord's redemption and preaching in hell. The Forerunner can therefore be a saint at the highest level of Old Testament saintliness, which consisted not in liberation from original sin (which is impossible for human powers) but in freedom from personal sins.

Original sin is the universal sickness of the human essence, which becomes mortal and subject to sin. Original sin is actualized through human freedom in a series of personal sins, in personal sinfulness, in which it is manifested in the life of every human being. And there can be more or less of this *personal* sinfulness; it can be reduced to zero, to pure potentiality, that is, to *personal* sinlessness, as in the case of the Most Pure and Most Immaculate Virgin Mary, who is free of all personal sin and even of any sinful inclination. And in the view of the Church, which venerates his saintliness from the moment of his conception, the Forerunner too is free of personal sin. For this, there is no need to imagine a *deus ex machina* that would arbitrarily return to a specific person, namely to Mary, the supernatural grace taken away from Adam because of his fall, as the Catholic dogma of the immaculate conception of the Mother of God teaches. To be consistent, Catholic theology would have to extend its dogma of the immaculate conception to the Forerunner, which it does not do for some reason (although it is disposed to extend it to Joseph).

Because they participate in the human essence, the Mother of God and the Forerunner also possess in a fundamental property or state of this essence: they are subject to original sin and death. But this condition that is common to the whole human race, *hamartēma*, is not actualized in them by particular, personal sins, *parabaseis, paraptōmata*. It is suppressed and vanquished by their personal freedom. This freedom from sins if not from the sin or sinfulness inherent in human nature is a wholly special and exceptional phenomenon in the life of humankind, which corresponds to another special and exceptional event: the coming of the God-man into the world. The world and sinful humanity are subject to the prince of this world. Satan has gained dominion over the world and keeps it by force (as is attested, for example, by the prayer of exorcism that, during baptism, expels Satan from the newborn). But is it permissible to think that Satan could, even for a moment, possess the body and soul not only of the Most Pure Mother of God but even of the Forerunner? Is such a possession compatible with the fact that the Holy Spirit touched the Forerunner in his mother's womb? Obviously not.

One must recognize that the power of Satan over fallen humanity has its limits and degrees (this is revealed to us already in the Book of Job). The power of the "prince of this world" over creation is not equal to that of God; it is not all-powerful and all-penetrating. Satan is a usurper who has ravished what does not belong to him and what, in the end, he does not have the power to control. His power has a natural limit to it and is always limited in general. Satan never had any power over the Lord Jesus, even when he did not know Him: "If thou be the Son of God," Satan asks in order to tempt Him (Matt. 4:3). Satan did not fathom the mystery of the seedless conception and the divine incarnation, even though it was demons who called Jesus the "Son of the most high God" (Mark 5:7; cf. Luke 8:28) even before the apostle Peter's profession of faith. Otherwise, Satan would not have attempted to triumph over Him by the crucifixion, to take Him by means of his victim, Judas Iscariot. The Lord says: "the prince of this world cometh, and hath nothing in me" (John 14:30). Satan had "nothing" in the Lord, in the sense that both personal sin and original sin were absent in Him.

But it is possible to be free of personal sin while remaining subject to original sin. And it follows, among other things, that there is no need to have recourse to the idea of immaculate conception, i.e., freedom from original sin, in order to exclude the power of the devil, which is incompatible with the dignity and purity of the Mother of God and the Forerunner.

In general, Satan is limited by human freedom to the extent it is realized in human saintliness, which attracts God's grace not only in the New Testament but even in the Old Testament (though, prior to the Pentecost, only in anticipations). And Satan *never* had power over the *persons* of the Forerunner and the Most Pure Mother of God; he did not encroach upon their freedom, for he could not pierce the fiery circle of their radiance. Their personal sinlessness, which is combined with the subordination to original sin of their human essence, is due to their human freedom, their feat, their merit. It is not the result of a mechanical return to them of a gift lost or taken away, as Roman Catholic doctrine teaches.

But this saintliness, although personal, is not exclusive to a single person. It is the accumulated saintliness of the generations of the Old Testament Church. The genealogy of Christ the Savior, which is that of Joseph and Mary, enumerates the "forefathers and fathers" who accomplished the feat of faith (Heb. 11), who in their sacred lineage gathered and transmitted their merits. Every descendant inherited the richness and saintliness of his forefathers, as is attested concerning the Forerunner's parents: "they were both righteous before God, walking in all the commandments and ordinances of the Lord blameless" (Luke 1:6). To this is added the general piety of the priestly tribe to which they belonged: "A certain priest named Zacharias, of the course of Abia: and his wife was of the daughters of Aaron, and her name was Elisabeth" (Luke 1:5). A spirit that comes into the world is sent by God into the body appropriate to it from the appropriate parents. There is a certain preestablished harmony between the one who is born and where and how he is born. Although this harmony is usually hidden from human eyes, Scripture sometimes gives us a glimpse of it,[2] as in the present case.

John was announced by the prophets and sent by God into the world to accomplish his work. In its supra-eternal self-determination in God, his spirit was already that of the Forerunner, as the archangel Gabriel's words to Zacharias (Luke 1:13-17), as well as John 1:6-7, clearly attest. Elisabeth gave birth not merely to an infant who later became the Forerunner; she gave birth precisely to the Forerunner, who had to begin his mission in his infancy. (The same thing must be said about the Mother of God: Joachim and Anna gave birth not merely to the infant Mary, who later became the Mother of God; they gave birth precisely to the Mother of God, who still had to pass through Her infancy.)

This mystery of supra-eternal self-determination, one of the most unfathomable mysteries for man, concerns his creation and the origin of his soul in God. Without posing this question in all of its scope, here we must only establish the fact that, in a certain sense, the Forerunner, announced by the prophets and the angel, existed *prior to* his birth. In God, who foretells future events through prophets, there is no time, no present and future. The Forerunner, like the Mother of God, has been called from all eternity, for in creating the world and man, the Lord predetermined the incarnation and in-humanization of His Son for the salvation of fallen humanity. Consequently, He predetermined that both the Forerunner and the Mother of God would appear on earth at a certain time. God's thought is also God's deed: all things that exist in God from eternity bear the imprint of eternity. But this does not annul the freedom of the creaturely spirit. In particular, the Forerunner is the Forerunner according to his own self-determination and free will, not through an external predestination.

---

2. "For I was a witty child, and had a good spirit. Yea rather, being good, I came into a body undefiled" (Wis. Sol. 8:19-20).

The Birth of the Forerunner

In creating man to be free, God allows him, as it were, to participate in his own origin,[3] receives from him his agreement to be. A spirit that becomes incarnate in a specific body acquires its qualities by virtue of its freedom.

Therefore, at his birth the Forerunner is not some indeterminate thing that contains various possibilities of movement upward or downward. No. He is a great light, a bearer of the divine flame, come into the world so determinate that he received the Holy Spirit in his mother's womb. We have an Old Testament example of such sanctification in the mother's womb in the prophet Jeremiah, to whom the Lord said: "Before I formed thee in the belly I knew thee; and before thou camest forth out of the womb I sanctified thee" (Jer. 1:5). Of course, one cannot equate the *degrees* of this sanctification, but characteristic is this fact of being known by God prior to birth and of sanctification while still in the womb. "God is no respecter of persons" (Acts 10:34); and this election corresponds to the spiritual essence, to self-qualification and self-determination of the spirit that is born. The Forerunner is already the Forerunner by his very idea.

The saintliness of the Forerunner over the course of his life is not *directly* attested to in the Gospels. However, not only does he not possess any traits that contradict such a saintliness but he possesses a number of traits that indirectly confirm it:

a. Prior to his birth, his saintliness is attested to by his leaping in his mother's womb at the approach of the Mother of God, announcing Christ before either of them was born. And this testimony of his was given voice by his mother, Elisabeth, who was also filled by the Holy Spirit through this leaping, and said: "Whence is this to me, that the mother of my Lord should come to me?" (Luke 1:43). This episode obliges us to take into account a particular aspect of the spiritual development of the Forerunner. While still in his mother's womb, prior to full bodily development, he was already conscious of his existence; he possessed a power of knowledge to which was revealed the approach of Christ, conceived in the Mother of God's womb. Corresponding to this power of knowledge is a saintliness that is actively realized in the movements of his spirit toward Christ. The Forerunner's feat, ministry, and saintliness clearly begin at this point.

---

3. This, of course, is not Origen's preexistence of souls, which is condemned by the Church; for there is no "pre" here referring to a time before birth. This is a contraposition not between different times, preceding and following, but between eternity, supratemporality, and temporality. In God everything is eternal and supratemporal, but everything manifests itself in time.

b. Let us now consider the saintliness of the Forerunner at the beginning of his preaching. Nothing is known about the Forerunner's childhood and youth, but when he begins to preach baptism and repentance, he is already worthy of baptizing the Lord (about this more below) and of being a witness to the Theophany, of seeing the descent of the Holy Spirit and hearing the Father's voice. This clearly could not have been possible for anyone infected with sin and gripped, in the presence of the Most Holy Lord, by the terror inherent in the state of sin. The baptism required of the Baptist the same personal sinlessness that the birth of Christ required of His Mother.

c. The sinlessness and saintliness of the Forerunner prior to his martyrdom are attested to by Christ in His conversation on the subject of the Forerunner with His disciples (Matt. 11) and in His speech to the people (Luke 7). In the latter the Lord proclaims that the Forerunner is the greatest of those born of women, that he is greater than the righteous Enoch, raised into heaven while alive; greater than Abraham and Moses, both of whom are called "friends of God"; greater than Elijah, who rose to heaven in a fiery chariot; greater than all the righteous of the Old Testament. And his whole life is crowned by the martyrdom of a righteous one. In this way, the Gospel bears witness to the saintliness of the Forerunner at the beginning, middle, and end of his life. At what point, where and how, could sin enter in?

Only this saintliness and sinlessness, this election that distinguishes him from the rest of humankind, can explain the place that the narrative of his birth, as well as the different features that characterize it, occupies in the Gospel. This place, in the first chapter of Luke, is intertwined with the narrative of the Annunciation. The Forerunner's conception and birth, announced by the appearance of the Archangel Gabriel, who is then sent to Nazareth to the Virgin Mary; the Mother of God's visit to Elisabeth after the Annunciation; the leaping of John in his mother's womb and Elisabeth's prophetic words; and the Forerunner's birth — all this forms a single narrative. It is the Gospel's *earthly prologue,* just as the first chapter of the Gospel of John is its heavenly prologue. Luke sets for himself the task of describing things "in order" (1:3); and he begins this order with what preceded Christ's Birth (chapter two) but was necessarily connected with it: the Forerunner's birth and the Annunciation. From this point of view, the plan of the first chapter of Luke is revealing:

vv. 1-4: introduction;
vv. 5-25: the appearance of the Archangel to Zacharias and the conception of the Forerunner;

vv. 26-38: the appearance of the Archangel to the Virgin Mary and the conception of Jesus Christ;

vv. 39-56: the meeting of the two mothers and the two infants; the Forerunner's testimony concerning Christ and Elisabeth's testimony concerning the Mother of God;

vv. 57-80: the birth of the Forerunner; followed by 2:1-20, describing the birth of Christ.

The Gospel of Luke begins with the birth of the Forerunner. We have already indicated the significance of the *place* occupied by this event in the Gospel: the Incarnation begins with the Forerunner's birth. In contrast to the other synoptic Gospels, Matthew and Mark, Luke puts the events of this Gospel story in a broader connection with the events preceding and conditioning the birth of Christ. Only in Luke do we have the narrative of the Annunciation and of the Mother of God's visit to Elisabeth; and in connection with this narrative, also in the first chapter of the Gospel, we have the story of the Forerunner's birth. This serves as the frame for the narrative of the Annunciation: the latter event is directly linked to the birth of the Forerunner. Indeed, in his Annunciation to Mary, the Archangel Gabriel directly refers to the Forerunner's conception, which had already taken place (Luke 1:36-37). Thus, according to the plan of the Gospel of Luke, the two events essentially constitute a single event, the common principle for "the certainty of those things, wherein thou hast been instructed" (Luke 1:4).

One must fully assess the significance of the place of the story of the Forerunner's birth in the prologue of the Gospel of Luke in its connection with the Annuciation and the meeting of the two mothers, which, prior to the Nativity, truly anticipates the coming of Christ and of His Forerunner. Equally important here are the fact that the Annunciation was indissolubly linked with the Forerunner's conception and the interpretation of the significance of this fact that is given in the prologue of the Gospel of Luke. The interdependence of these two events is underscored by the fact that both were announced by the same heavenly messenger, the Archangel Gabriel (Luke 1:1-26). Appearing to Zacharias, he names himself: "I am Gabriel, that stand in the presence of God; and am sent to speak unto thee, and to shew thee these glad tidings" (Luke 1:19). To Mary he does not name himself, perhaps because he was known by Her when She lived at the temple, according to the church hymns. Therefore the text merely says: "in the sixth month [i.e., after the conception of the Forerunner] the angel Gabriel was sent from God unto a city of Galilee"

(Luke 1:26). This precision with regard to the date of the Annunciation in relation to the Forerunner's conception establishes, once again, the interdependence and unity of these two events.

The *place* given to the Forerunner's conception in the prologue of the Gospel of Luke has a direct parallel in the Gospel of John. Immediately after the heavenly prologue in John, the prologue to the earthly events opens thus: "There was a man sent from God, whose name was John" (John 1:6). The Gospel of John speaks neither of the birth of Christ nor of the birth of the Forerunner, but only of the coming into the world of the Lord with His Forerunner. Therefore, the term "sent" stands for the whole of Luke's narrative, while retaining its place in the general plan of the prologue.

Luke begins with a chronological indication: "There was in the days of Herod, the king of Judæa . . ." (Luke 1:5). In the Gospel of Matthew, which, in contrast to Luke, begins directly with Christ's birth, this indication refers to Christ Himself: "Now when Jesus was born in Bethlehem of Judæa in the days of Herod the king" (Matt. 2:1). Of course, this chronological indication increases the importance of what is being reported. The Evangelist indicates the name of the Forerunner's father (and mother): the priest Zacharias, of the course of Abia (Luke 1:5). David had established twenty-four "courses," of which the eighth was that of Abia (see Neh. 12:17), destined for the successive performance of the priestly functions. The name Zacharias signifies "he who is remembered by God." Aside from the first chapter of Luke, nothing more is said about Zacharias in the Gospels. But the tradition of the Church has preserved other information about him. First of all, the Church venerates him not as a mere priest but as a high priest. Scripture sometimes calls even a high priest a priest (see Acts 5:24). In the office of St. Zacharias, he is in fact called a high priest: "The tiara has been placed on your head, O prophet, possessing, in figuration, the true divine consecration." "Creation rejoices in your birth, high priest, for you have caused the preacher's repentance to flower" (Canon, str. 5, tr. 1, 2). "When you offered the censer of the office, O archpriest, you received the prophecy of the Forerunner" (str. 3, tr. 1).

Tradition represents him as the high priest who greeted the Virgin Mary as She entered the temple; that is what the Holy Church calls him in the office of the Presentation in the temple. During the celebrations of the vigil (20 November) and of the feast itself (21 November), Zacharias is invoked as the priest who led the Virgin Mary into the temple. He is also called "Zacharias, the high priest" (sticheron of the little vespers) and

"Zacharias, the elder, father of the Forerunner" (lithia). Inspired by the Holy Spirit, he led Her into the Holy of Holies. A certain tradition (this time embodied not in an office but rooted in church writings, e.g., in Origen) proclaims that Zacharias was the high priest who, on the fortieth day after the birth of the Savior, received the Mother with Infant in the temple and led Her to the place reserved for virgins, thus provoking the indignation of the scribes. Here, Zacharias professed that the Virgin, having become a mother, did not stop being the Most Pure Virgin.

Church tradition usually identifies Zacharias with the son of Barachias, about whom the Savior says: "that upon you may come all the righteous blood shed upon the earth, from the blood of righteous Abel unto the blood of Zacharias . . . whom ye slew between the temple and the altar" (Matt. 23:35). The Church marks this tradition in the office of "the saintly prophet Zacharias, father of John the Forerunner" (5 September). "The temple was living and animated by the Divine Spirit; you also were in the middle of the temple, glorious one, serving God with pure heart; and you were unrighteously slain, accomplishing unto martyrdom your glorious divine course" (sticheron). "A pure priest, you entered the holy of holies, and clothed in priestly vestments, you served God immaculately, like Aaron laying down the law and like Moses leading the people of Israel. . . . And then you were slain. But your righteous blood is a saving cure for us, and like fragrant myrrh it leads us into everlasting life" (sticheron). "You were slain by the sword in the temple of God. O prophet, pray with the Forerunner that our souls be saved" (troparion).

According to Origen, Zacharias's murder between the sanctuary and the altar was motivated by the fact that he placed Mary among the virgins at the Presentation of the Lord in the temple. In the thirteenth canonical rule, St. Peter of Alexandria connects Zacharias's murder with a wholly different circumstance and attributes it to Herod. "The bloodthirsty Herod saw that he was insulted by the magi. Seeking to kill along with them another boy born before Him, and not finding him, he had his father, Zacharias, killed between sanctuary and altar, while the infant escaped with his mother, Elisabeth."

About Elisabeth (Elisheba means "God is my vow") we learn in Luke (1:5) that she "was of the daughters of Aaron." The wife of a priest does not necessarily have to belong to the Levite tribe; she can descend from other tribes of Israel. Her descent not only from the Levites but even from the high priest Aaron attests to the purity of the priestly blood received by John. It also attests to the fact that the Mother of God had the same blood, evidently on the maternal side, for Elisabeth was Her "cousin," and, according to tradition, the sister of Anna, the wife of Joachim, who were the parents of the Virgin Mary.

The Church commemorates the saintly prophet Zacharias and the saintly and righteous Elisabeth on 5 September, celebrating their feat in two offices: the first is dedicated to Zacharias alone, while the second is dedicated to the two of them together. St. Zacharias is venerated as a priest and prophet ("having served God as a priest according to the law and having prophesied that Christ would be born from a Virgin, made incarnate by the action of the Holy Spirit, you appeared to the universe like a pillar of light") and, as we have seen, as a martyr. The two are venerated for their righteousness: "Blessed Elisabeth, the Holy Spirit called you righteous with Zacharias, proclaiming that you were righteous before God" (canon, ode 3, tr. 1). "Not every living being is justified before God. But you Elisabeth, worthy of memory, are so justified" (tr. 2). "Just as God said about His Church: beautiful are you who are close to me, and immaculate, you too are immaculate, righteous Elisabeth" (ode 8, tr. 1).

The righteous Elisabeth is also celebrated as the first person to announce the Glad Tidings: "We hear you as the first proclaimer when, the Messiah having already become incarnate, you said in fear and trembling to the divinely chosen young woman who had visited you: 'whence is this to me, that the mother of my Lord should come to me?'" (Luke 1:43). The righteous Elisabeth is called Mary's cousin, first in the Gospel (Luke 1:36), and then in the office. As we have already said, she is honored as the sister of Anna, the mother of the Virgin Mary (Nicephorus, bk. 2, ch. 3).

On the subject of the righteous Elisabeth and Zacharias, the Evangelist informs us that "they had no child, because . . . Elisabeth was barren, and they both were now well stricken in years" (Luke 1:7). The Virgin Mary too was born to parents who were very old and considered barren. The passion and lust proper to human beings had faded before these two conceptions, which were miraculous works of piety and prayer. The sinfulness about which the prophet David speaks ("I was shapen in iniquity; and in sin did my mother conceive me" [Ps. 51:5]) is paralyzed and disappears, as it were, in these two holy conceptions. These conceptions do not differ from human conception, but they are accomplished differently: without sinful ardor or passion. In this one cannot fail to see a special design of God, who protects from passion and lust the sacred fruit which, from its very conception, is filled with the Holy Spirit. It is in the sense of such a paralysis of original sin in its manifestation or actualization — and only in this sense, and not in the sense of a victory over it — that one can speak of an immaculate conception, not only of the Mother of God but also of John the Forerunner.

Thus, between the conceptions of the Forerunner and the Mother of God, celebrated by the Holy Church, there is a qualitative resemblance but also a *quantitative* difference, so to speak. If there can exist different degrees of righteousness and saintliness, one is compelled to presume that the conception of the Mother of God (and, accordingly, the righteousness of the saintly and righteous Joachim and Anna) is more pure and spotless than that of the Forerunner, without being immaculate (in the sense of a formal exemption from original sin as a *privilegium*, as the Catholic dogma postulates). The Church celebrates the saintly and righteous Joachim and Anna in the following terms (in the office of 9 September):

> O blessed dyad, you surpass all parents, for you have conceived the one who is superior to all creatures. (sticheron) Having produced from your barren loins the scepter, the holy Mother of God, from whom Christ the God, light of the salvation of the world, appeared; conjugal dyad, shining with the purity of dawn, which adorned a barren human nature with the divine light of virginity, thus you have engendered Her, Joachim and Anna, agreeable to God. (ode 5. tr. 1) Joachim the righteous and Anna the chaste, bursting with an abundance of virtues, gave birth to the virgin queen, strong with divine glory. (ode 8, tr. 1, 2)

The circumstances of the Forerunner's conception are described in the Gospel of Luke. The Archangel Gabriel appeared to the priest Zacharias in the sanctuary. We have already noted that this messenger was the same archangel Gabriel who was sent to the Virgin Mary for the Annunciation. This attests to the importance of the annunciation of the Forerunner's birth, which is described in connection with the Annunciation to Mary. The birth of the Forerunner, preacher of repentance, is announced by the Archangel as "joy and gladness; and many [*polloi*] shall rejoice at his birth" (Luke 1:14). These words about joy are made even more significant by the fact that the angel who announces the Birth of Christ to the shepherds tells them: "Fear not: for, behold, I bring you good tidings of great joy, which shall be to all people" (Luke 2:10). Joy in the birth of the Forerunner will be, first of all, a joy for his father, and then for all. The Archangel also communicates the name of the son who is not yet born: "thy prayer is heard; and thy wife Elisabeth shall bear a son, and thou shalt call his name John" (Luke 1:13). This mention of the name by

God's messenger signifies that the coming of John was foreseen from all eternity in the ways of the Lord. A name is not a simple appellation; it is an essence, *nomen omen*. Such a signification is attested to by the fact that the archangel's annunciation, in which every word has its special weight, introduces the Forerunner's name. This becomes particularly clear if these words are compared with the Archangel's words to Joseph concerning the Savior's birth: "She shall bring forth a son, and thou shalt call his name Jesus" (Matt. 1:21). This naming acquires an even greater significance by virtue of the circumstances of the Forerunner's birth — by virtue of the *dispute* that took place concerning the name of the new-born and with the resolution of which Zacharias's muteness was cured: "On the eight day they came to circumcise the child; and they called him Zacharias, after the name of his father. And his mother answered and said, Not so; but he shall be called John. And they said unto her, There is none of thy kindred that is called by this name. And they made signs to his father, how he would have him called. And he asked for a writing table, and wrote, saying, His name is John. And they marvelled all. And his mouth was opened immediately, and his tongue loosed, and he spake, and praised God" (Luke 1:59-64).

Further, the Gospel bears witness to the fact that the Forerunner is great, saintly, and full of grace: "He shall be great in the sight of the Lord, and shall drink neither wine nor strong drink [that is, he will be an ascetic]; and he shall be filled with the Holy Spirit, even from his mother's womb" (Luke 1:15). Then, the Gospel speaks about his activity as a preacher of repentance: "And many of the children of Israel shall he turn to the Lord their God" (Luke 1:16). Finally, he is announced as the Forerunner: "And he shall go before him in the spirit and power of Elias, to turn the hearts of the fathers to the children, and the disobedient to the wisdom of the just; to make ready a people prepared for the Lord" (Luke 1:17). This verse is a paraphrase of the prophecy of Malachi about the Forerunner as "Elijah the prophet," which is clarified here as "in the spirit and power of Elias" (about which see below, chapter eight): "Behold, I will send you Elijah the prophet, before the coming of the great and dreadful day of the Lord: And he shall turn the heart of the fathers to the children, and the heart of the children to their fathers, lest I come and smite the earth with a curse" (Mal. 4:5-6). Applying this ancient prophecy to the Forerunner, the Archangel's words attest, once more, that his coming was foreseen in the divine plan of the Incarnation.

In his human frailty Zacharias could not hear this annunciation without being shaken and troubled: the whole of the Old Testament righteousness and purity was insufficient in the face of the New Testament that was approaching. "And Zacharias said unto the angel, Whereby shall I know this? for I am an old man, and my wife well stricken in years" (Luke 1:18). When we hear this, we immediately think of the Most Pure Virgin's answer at the Annunciation, which contains no doubt but only a question: "How shall this be, seeing I know not a man?" (Luke 1:34). To Zacharias the Archangel responds by revealing his name to him and by imposing muteness upon him "until the day that these things shall be performed, because thou believest not my words, which shall be fulfilled in their season" (Luke 1:20).

In celebrating the conception of the Forerunner by a special office, the Holy Church represents this event in the following sticheron:

> I am an archangel of the omnipotent God, my name is Gabriel, said the incorporeal one to the old man. You will now become deaf and you will learn silence, not having believed my words. And when your spouse gives birth for you the trumpet of the Word, you will very clearly proclaim, opening your tongue to the spirit: O infant, you will be called prophet of the Most High, in order to prepare His ways by grace. (sticheron, tone 6)

Let us also cite the following troparion (canon, ode 6): "Prophet of God, exult, old man, you have engendered a son greater than whom there is none among men: John, Forerunner of the Lord. Rejoice, Elisabeth! Exult, the whole earth, bringing the praise of all to God the Creator."

The Archangel Gabriel announces the conception of the Forerunner not only to Zacharias but also to the Virgin Mary: "And, behold, thy cousin Elisabeth, she hath also conceived a son in her old age: and this is the sixth month with her, who was called barren. For with God nothing shall be impossible" (Luke 1:36-37). We have already indicated the significance of this mention, which links the two annunciations. And this link becomes stronger and is revealed in what follows. After the Archangel had departed and the mysterious virginal conception had taken place, "Mary arose in those days, and went into the hill country with haste, into a city of Judah, And entered into the house of Zacharias, and saluted Elisabeth" (Luke 1:39-40). This visit was, as it were, Mary's response to the archangel's words and to his silent invitation. In the Mother of God's knowing heart it became clear who was being born of the barren one, and for what purpose. Here, a new and mysterious interweaving of the two annunciations is accomplished.

In his narrative, Luke places the meeting of the two future mothers between the Forerunner's conception and birth. This passage refers to both the Mother of God and the Forerunner. For the first time the Mother of God is greeted on earth as the *Mother of the Lord*. Even before his birth the Forerunner bears witness to the coming Savior. Since any crudely mechanical interpretation of the Forerunner's leaping in his mother's womb must be rejected in advance, one must acknowledge that the Forerunner's spirit, illuminated by the Holy Spirit, knew the Savior even in His Mother's womb, and rejoiced in His approach with the joy of the friend of the Bridegroom. The power and significance of this leaping were such that his mother was filled with the Holy Spirit and pronounced her prophetic speech concerning the Mother of God: "And it came to pass, that, when Elisabeth heard the salutation of Mary, the babe leaped in her womb; and Elisabeth was filled with the Holy Spirit" (Luke 1:41). From his very conception and before his birth the Forerunner was the Forerunner of the Lord and manifested himself as such.

In order to accomplish his ministry he still had to follow a long path of ascesis and growth, just like the Divine Infant, but there was not a moment of his existence when he was not already the Forerunner. In this respect too one must draw an analogy with the Mother of God: She, of course, actualized Her divine maternity only after the Annunciation and the birth of Christ, but She was already conceived and born as the receptacle agreeable to God, as the Mother of God. What distinguishes the Forerunner from the Mother of God here results from the difference in the positions of the Forerunner and the Mother of God in relation to Christ the Savior: the Mother of God's virgin life had to unfold over a period of years until the conception without male seed took place, whereas the Forerunner's first meeting with the One who comes took place six months after his conception. In response to Elisabeth's salutation, the Mother of God said: "My soul doth magnify the Lord" (Luke 1:46). This marvelous hymn, by which the Holy Church never stops magnifying Her, comprises not only the reception of Elisabeth's prophecy and the direct application of it to Herself (Luke 1:46-49), but also the messianic hymn, the proclamation of the salvation come in Israel, and the appearance of the power of God and the Kingdom of God (Luke 1:50-55). With the lips of the Most Pure One the Old Testament Church renders glory to God, Who received His servant Israel, "as He spake to our fathers, to Abraham, and to his seed" (Luke 1:55). We find a similar testimony in the hymn of Zacharias.

After telling of the meeting of the two mothers, illuminated by heavenly light, the Evangelist relates the birth of the Forerunner. The miraculous healing of Zacharias's muteness caused a commotion in the land: "And fear came on all that dwelt round about them: and all these sayings were noised abroad throughout all the hill country of Judæa. And all they that heard them laid them up in their hearts, saying, What manner of child shall this be!" (Luke 1:65-66). The Forerunner's coming into the world provoked in hearts a holy trepidation. In solemnly celebrating the birth of the Forerunner (24 June), the Holy Church praises him in the following manner:

> The last of the prophets and the beginning of the apostles, earthly angel and heavenly man, voice of the word, warrior and forerunner of Christ, who in advance leaped from joy because of the promise and preached the sun of justice before His nativity, today Elisabeth gives birth to him and rejoices. And Zacharias marvels in his old age, freed from the bonds of his muteness; and as the voice of the father he prophesies most clearly: "Infant, you will be called a prophet of the Most High and you will walk before Him to prepare His way. Thus, angel, prophet, apostle, warrior, forerunner, preacher of repentance and teacher, as the voice of the light of the Word, pray unceasingly for us who with faith celebrate your memory!

The Evangelist adds: "the hand of the Lord was with him" (Luke 1:66). In the Old Testament this expression sometimes signifies God's wrath, but this is clearly not applicable here. It can also signify the prophetic illumination by the Holy Spirit, especially in Ezekiel: "the hand of the Lord was strong upon me" (Ezek. 3:14). Applied to the Forerunner, this Old Testament expression signifies, of course, the fact that he was born a *prophet*, and the infant's size of his body did not correspond to the maturity of his spirit, which was already capable of bearing the weight of God's hand (which clearly should be understood not in a mechanical sense but in the sense of the spiritual intensity of the human essence).

The prophetic spirit of the Forerunner was so mighty that it was transmitted from him to his father, Zacharias, who also became a prophet. Such was the abundance of gifts of grace in this obscure Judæan town (Jutte according to some; Hebron, according to others), in the hill country in which the greatest of men was born. "And his father Zacharias was filled with the Holy Spirit, and prophesied" (Luke 1:67). Let us try to understand the content of this prophecy. The whole prophecy, from verses 68 to 79 with the exception of verses 76-77, which directly refer to the new-born Forerunner, constitutes a messianic hymn. "Blessed be the

Lord God of Israel; for he hath visited and redeemed his people. And hath raised up an horn of salvation for us in the house of his servant David: as he spake by the mouth of his holy prophets, which have been since the world began" (Luke 1:68-70). Here, it is clearly a question not of the birth of the Forerunner, who, as we know, was a member of the Levite tribe, the tribe of priests, but of the "horn of salvation" (Ps. 18:2), of the house of David, that is, of Christ, of the "holy covenant," of "the oath . . . to . . . Abraham" (Luke 1:72-73). This whole hymn, composed in the Old Testament style, with expressions borrowed from prophecies of the Messiah, is analogous to that part of the hymn of the Mother of God which also has a messianic character (see above). Why, on the occasion of the birth of his son, does Zacharias bear witness to the coming of the Messiah? Manifestly because the first birth, that of the Forerunner, anticipates the other, which is the coming of Christ, because it bears witness to the approach of the Kingdom of God.

The participation of the Forerunner in the accomplishment of our salvation and the inseparability of his work from that of Christ are implicitly attested to in this prophetic speech: the Forerunner's birth already initiates Christ's coming into the world, for the Bridegroom is preceded by the friend of the Bridegroom. The salvation and the emancipation of His people, that is, the Incarnation with all its salvific fruits, is spoken of here as a work already accomplished from its very beginning, which is the birth of the Forerunner. This birth is therefore placed in a close and inseparable connection with the Incarnation, as we clarified above. This idea is expressed by the very construction of the speech: it is entirely, in its beginning and in its end, an Old Testament hymn to the Christ who is becoming incarnate. In this sense, this speech is directly parallel to the Old Testament hymn of Simeon (Luke 2:29-32), with the difference that the former speech was pronounced under the inspiration of the Holy Spirit during the presentation at the temple of the Forerunner, on the day of his circumcision (Luke 1:59), whereas the latter was sung during the holy Presentation of the Lord Himself, also on the day of His circumcision, equally under the inspiration of the Holy Spirit (Luke 2:22). To this one can add that the former speech was sung by a righteous priest, or even by a high priest, whereas the latter was sung by a righteous man.

In the middle of his hymn, Zacharias directly addresses the infant, whose birth was the sign of the salvation that had come, as the Forerunner of the Lord: "And thou, child, shalt be called the prophet of the Highest: for thou shalt go before the face of the Lord to prepare his ways; To give knowledge of salvation unto his people by the remission of their sins"

(Luke 1:76-77). (In the context of the exposition of the Gospel of Luke, these words are entirely analogous to those that the elder Simeon addresses to Mary concerning the Infant: Luke 2:34-35.) These words show that Zacharias was convinced of the truth of the Archangel's prophecy, which he had not yet understood at the altar of incense; and that is why his lips — now opened to proclaim his faith — were then sealed. He speaks now with the words of the ancient prophecies about the Forerunner (Isaiah and Malachi), which are repeated in the Archangel's speech (Luke 1:17). This represents the reception of the Forerunner by the Old Testament Church in the person of its priesthood.

Thus, the essential idea of Zacharias's prophecy can be summarized as follows: the salvation of Israel has been accomplished, and the horn of salvation has been raised in the house of David, for the Forerunner has been born. This interpretation places the Forerunner's birth into a living and essential connection with Christ's birth, which is described in the following narrative, in the second chapter of Luke. But the first chapter adds a few more words about the childhood of the Forerunner (Luke 1:80), about which the other evangelists do not speak at all. Here is what Luke says: "*the child grew, and waxed strong in spirit,* and was in the deserts till the day of his shewing unto Israel." The first half of this verse, italicized here, has an intentional parallel in Luke 2:40: "*the child* [Jesus] *grew, and waxed strong in spirit,* filled with wisdom; and the grace of God was upon him." This parallel implicitly confirms the general idea of the unique and exclusive closeness of the Forerunner to the Lord and to His work of salvation. (But there is an important difference: the addition in Luke 2:40 of "filled with wisdom; and the grace of God was upon him.")

The Gospel of Luke has only a single phrase about the Forerunner's life before he began his mission of preaching: "[he] was in the deserts till the day of his shewing unto Israel" (Luke 1:80). What desert this was, Luke does not say. Most probably, it was the stony desert to the east of the Jordan. The Evangelist wishes to give here not a geographic but a spiritual datum, to establish the fact that John was a desert-hermit. It was in the desert that God's call, for which he was preparing himself, came to him: "Annas and Caiaphas being the high priests, the word of God came unto John the son of Zacharias in the wilderness" (Luke 3:2). It was in the desert that he first preached: "In those days came John the Baptist, preaching in the wilderness of Judæa" (Matt. 3:1). It was also in the desert that he began his mission of baptism: "John did baptize in the wilderness" (Mark 1:4). This circumstance is so essential for the Forerunner's life and activity that it is predicted in the prophet Isaiah: "the voice of him that crieth in the wilderness" (Isa. 40:3). And as we already know, this prophecy is mentioned by all the evangelists (Matt. 3:3; Mark 1:3; Luke 3:4; John 1:23). In connection with this, Matthew 3:4 and Mark 1:6 also describe his fasting and asceticism: "The same John had his raiment of camel's hair, and a leathern girdle about his loins; and his meat was locusts and wild honey." (John's great fasting is also indirectly attested to in the Lord's speech to the people: "For John the Baptist came neither eating bread nor drinking wine" [Luke 7:33]).

The Church lovingly celebrates John's desert-hermitage and asceticism[4] as well his entire spiritual feat: "You have accomplished your life on earth like an angel, O all-blessed one!" (7 January, canon, ode 6, tr. 2). "You rejoice with the angelic orders, having demonstrated a life like that of the incorporeal ones" (ode 9, tr. 3). "We honor you with joy, John, the all-blessed one, you who, on earth, manifested yourself as equal to the angels by a life transfigured and superior to all" (ode 8, tr. 1).

It is necessary to remark that neither the Old nor the New Testament mentions the feat of desert-hermitage and fasting except with reference to John. In this sense he is the founder of the ascetic life that is "equal to that of angels" (as monks say). The mortification of the flesh is a constant theme of iconography: the emaciated figure of John the Forerunner became one of the favorite subjects of Orthodox and particularly Russian icons.

However, of significance in this passage of Luke is not only the feat of desert-hermitage but the *desert* itself as such: "You went from swaddling clothes to living in the desert. You fled, prophet, to the uninhabitable desert" (Office of the Forerunner, tone 1, canon, ode 8, tr. 3). Filled with the Holy Spirit from his mother's womb and preparing to meet and baptize the Lord, he had preserved himself from the breath of sin and its contamination. The *desert*, as a place which is inhabited neither by man nor by the sin that inheres in him, was that pure place in which it was natural for one called to freedom from personal sin to preserve himself from falls. To be sure, the desert too is not free from spirits of evil. But one should not exaggerate their knowledge. They could have failed to know who was being preserved in the deserts of Israel until he was ready to appear to the people. They did not know and did not fathom the mystery of the Incarnation. This is clear from the fact that only after the Lord's bap-

---

4. "Beautiful swallow, precious nightingale, virtuous desert-loving dove, baptist of the Lord, fruit of the desert" (tone 1, canon, ode 9, tr. 4). "Angel, you came out of barren loins, O Baptist! From your very swaddling clothes you lived in the desert" (24 September, office of the conception of the Forerunner, sticheron to Glory).

tism and Theophany did the tempter, in order to try Him, approach Him in the desert with the uncertain words: "If thou be the Son of God" (Matt. 4:3). Therefore, a special divine providence could have protected John from Satan's malice, and in any case he was not exposed to it as the Forerunner, for this mystery was then not yet known to Satan.

The role of the desert in the Forerunner's life is comparable to that of the temple in the life of the Virgin Mary as a young child and adolescent: She was brought into the temple; and there, served by angels, She was preserved from all evil. The Forerunner, on the other hand, removed himself into the desert, the temple of nature. To be sure, there is an essential difference here, naturally resulting from their different ministries and vocations. But despite this obvious difference it is important to establish the similarities too. It is important to note that the temple plays no role in the life of the Forerunner: in him, who stands at the threshold between the Old and New Testaments, the Old Testament temple loses its significance. John stands before God in the desert, listening to the call of the new priesthood according to the order of Melchizedek. Belonging to the priestly class, John could and should have been a priest. But the Gospel, which emphasizes his belonging to the priestly class, contains no information about any relation he might have had to the temple. John, a priest by blood, did not perform the priestly functions in the Old Testament temple; and nothing indicates that he ever entered a temple. And even if one supposes that he had, this would not have gone beyond the ritual obligations to which all the Jewish faithful were held.[5]

The Forerunner's life "in the deserts" until the day of his appearance to the world has another meaning besides that of his distancing himself from sinful life. It was a kind of voluntary death with regard to people, a great monastic "habit" of consecration to God. To live in the desert is not only to live without people, outside of human society, but also to live with God and for God. This is such a fullness of living in God and knowledge of God that no concession is made for human feelings and attachments. The Forerunner, whose whole spiritual feat consisted in total self-surrender, in the sacrifice of his life for another, begins this path and feat of his from his swaddling clothes. He dies for everything that is human in order to become the Forerunner and only the Forerunner, the friend and only the friend of the Bridegroom, in order to preserve the integrity of his feelings and the fullness of his powers for this feat.

---

5. On this theme see the reflections of S. Vishniakov in his book, *St. John: Great Prophet, Forerunner, and Baptist of the Lord* (Moscow, 1879), pp. 65-66.

The Friend of the Bridegroom

On certain icons the Forerunner is represented as not yet beheaded but with his head in his hands. This might mean that self-beheading, a sacrificial death, took place in him before his bodily death, and that this self-beheading was his "life in the deserts."

This desert-hermitage before the face of God is enshrouded in profound mystery and silence; only its fruits are revealed in preaching and baptism. The Baptist's energy, strong enough to withstand the Lord's Baptism and Theophany, was accumulated, then, "in the deserts." This energy is spiritual integrity, chastity, the incorruptibility by sin of the original human nature. This purity and freedom from personal sin give the wisdom, integrity, and chastity that characterize the one whom the Church venerates as a "teacher of purity" and even as an "angel." This energy is *virginity*; the Forerunner, equal to angels, is a virgin, and the desert, which separates him from people, is chastity. The Church also venerates St. John the Divine as a virgin, this John who was judged worthy of receiving in his home the Ever-Virgin and of being adopted by Her. However, the virginity of John the Divine is the result of ascesis; it is a state, not the essence of his nature, as it is with the Forerunner, who is the greatest of those born of women and who stands in immediate proximity to the throne of God.

The Forerunner's virginity is more than a factual state as it is defined in Revelation: "These are they which were not defiled with women" (Rev. 14:4). This is, in a certain sense, already a liberation from sex and its ardors. This does not mean, of course, that the difference between the male and female essences has been abolished: These essences are primordial, and only their union expresses the fullness of God's image in man: "God created man in his own image ... male and female created he them" (Gen. 1:27). This difference is affirmed and eternalized by the Divine Incarnation, where the Woman gives birth to the male Infant. And John, as a bearer of virginity, also did not stop having the male essence, just as the Ever-Virgin did not stop having the female essence. But these differences became subjugation to sex only as a consequence of sin, when the luminous bodies of our progenitors were clothed in coats of skins after the fall. And just as the Virgin Mary in Her ever-virginity is a woman (Gal. 4:4) in the sense that She has a female essence, but is not a woman in the sense of sexuality,[6] and just as the Lord is of the male sex (Luke 2:23), but also not in the sense of sin-shackled nature, so the Forerunner of the Lord was of the male sex, but he was not a male in the fleshly sense, for he was

---

6. See my study on the Mother of God: *The Burning Bush: On the Orthodox Veneration of the Mother of God* (Paris, 1927).

clothed in virginity. It is in this sense (though not only in this), that he is called an *angel* in prophecies (Mal. 3:1) and in church hymns.

The Forerunner's virginal nature must be understood precisely in relation to the virginity of the Mother of God, to Whom the Church links him in the *Deisis*, in a relation both of similarity and difference. Original sin corrupted the nature of human beings precisely by destroying virginal innocence in them and thereby casting them into sex. And although virginity is possible for human beings as a factual state, as a fruit of ascesis, it is not possible as liberation from original sin. However, by the feat of ascetic chastity, even the fallen human being is capable of approaching virginity by liberating himself from sex, by becoming an "angel" (like the Forerunner). But he can never attain virginity by this feat alone, for this is possible only by virtue of redemption, by the action of God's grace. That is why, in this sense too, although the Baptist was the greatest of those born of women, it is fair to say that the least in the Kingdom of God, i.e., after *redemption*, is greater than he.

But this approach to virginity has its limit or fullness, after which it becomes possible for a human being to receive a divine energy that restores the lost virginity and transforms fact into ontology, virginity into ever-virginity. This peak of *human* virginity or saintliness was attained by the Virgin Mary, who was therefore judged worthy of becoming the Mother of God. But this peak was attained not only by Her but also by John, who was therefore judged worthy of becoming the Forerunner and Baptist of the Lord. The virginity of the female essence in Mary corresponds to the virginity of the male essence in John. The analogy and correspondence are complete here. It is this analogy that fully justifies the placing of the Mother of God and the Forerunner together in prayer before Christ's throne in the *Deisis*, at the Dread Judgment, and (what is especially interesting here) on icons of Sophia, the Wisdom of God (of the Novgorod school), where a fiery angel, sitting on a throne, is framed on the right by the Mother of God and on the left by the Forerunner. Sophia is Virginity *par excellence*, as the energy of spiritual integrity, or chastity, and for this reason it is natural that she be represented by bearers of virginity (but about this more below).

It would be inappropriate and even impossible to attempt to measure and compare the degrees of virginity and spiritual integrity, as a force of saintliness, in the Mother of God and the Forerunner. It is sufficient to indicate that the Mother of God is superior even to the Forerunner (which iconography visibly expresses by placing Her to the right of Christ, while the Forerunner is placed to the left), for She, and only She, was called to be the Mother of God, and, after being overshadowed by the Holy Spirit, to become the Ever-Virgin, that is, to perfect and fully deify Her nature. Herein lies the mystery and power of the divine maternity and glorification of the Mother of God as the Queen of heaven and earth. Even the Forerunner cannot follow Her here.

Nevertheless, he, the greatest of those born of women, also attained this supreme degree of human virginity and saintliness, beyond which begins the reign of grace, the Kingdom of God. And he, having accomplished all that he was judged worthy of accomplishing, possessed the whole human power of virginity that it is humanly possible to possess. He was a virgin in his personal being, although he could not attain ever-virginity, could not liberate himself from original sin. He was not given ever-virginity during his life, but he too was given the grace of the Holy Spirit, corresponding to his ministry as Baptist. And he could receive and assimilate this grace only by achieving the fullness of virginity and saintliness. The Forerunner was *prepared* for his ministry, but this means that he had attained the supreme degree of virginity, or (what is the same thing) saintliness. In both Mary and John, *all human possibilities* are fulfilled in the sense of personal freedom from sin, but original sin is not yet overcome.

Thus, the Forerunner cannot be equated with the Ever-Virgin, who is more honorable than the cherubim and incomparably more glorious than the seraphim, although he is equal to the angels, and even surpasses them by his proximity to Christ. But we are justified in comparing them, as both of them were clothed in virginity and, in their personal paths, overcame the power of sex.

This mystery of the virginity of John, of this "angel," is expressed by this one term: "in the deserts" (Luke 1:80).

* * *

And none of the people knew then that they were living at the same time as the "greatest born of women," nor that precisely in their historical epoch a work of the purification of the sinful human essence was being accomplished that it is impossible for man to surpass. The world was intoxicated and deafened by its own grandeur. Tiberias reigned on the world's throne. The hosts of Rome controlled the universe. Roman law held the universe in its iron grip. Horace was writing his odes, Tacitus his history, Vergil his *Aeneid*, and Seneca and Epictetus their philosophical works. Greece was surrendering itself to the sweet luxuriousness of its aesthetic and philosophical contemplation. The waves of the human ocean were rising and falling. Great political events, international wars, cataclysms were ripening and taking place. The world was living with all the intensity of the life of human genius and creativity, of sin and vice. But it did not know — no one in the world knew — that the fullness of human maturity had been fulfilled, that, in the Jordan desert, the greatest of those born of women was waiting for his hour to come. The ways of God are unfathomable for man.

CHAPTER 2

St. John the Forerunner, Preacher of Repentance

"In those days" (Matt. 3:1) when the time came for Christ's appearance to the people, the Forerunner suddenly burst forth out of obscurity and made himself known as a prophet-preacher. The years of preparatory ascesis, prayer, silence, fasting, contemplation, and immersion in Scripture had come to an end. The Forerunner was called to accomplish his mission: "The word of God came unto John the son of Zacharias in the wilderness" (Luke 3:2). What did God's word reveal to John? Besides his mission as the preacher of repentance, it revealed the mystery of his vocation, as he himself bears witness: "He that sent me to baptize with water, the same said unto me, Upon whom thou shalt see the Spirit descending, and remaining on him, the same is he which baptizeth with the Holy Spirit" (John 1:33).

John's preaching is reported in the three synoptic Gospels (Matt. 3:1-12; Mark 1:1-8; Luke 3:1-18), as well as in the Gospel of John (1:15-17, 19-28), and the narratives agree. The story of the preaching is incorporated in the story of the coming of the Lord Jesus Christ as "the beginning of the gospel" (Mark 1:1). Even though the Forerunner's preaching has its own significance and independent content, he chiefly announces the One who is to come, combined with testimony about himself (contained in all four Gospels): "And [he] preached, saying, There cometh one mightier than I after me, the latchet of whose shoes I am not worthy to stoop down and unloose. I indeed have baptized you with water: but he shall baptize you with the Holy Spirit" (Mark 1:7-8; see also Matt. 3:11; Luke 3:16; John 1:26-27). The Forerunner's preaching proclaims the coming Christ: it is centered around this expectation and meeting. It prepares the way of the Lord, according to the prophecy of Isaiah (Isa. 40:3), in the light of which all the Evangelists present the coming of the Forerunner. And he himself presents his coming in these terms (John 1:30). When John comes, he is fully conscious of his ministry and of his vocation as Forerunner. Messianic times were about to begin. The world had grown silent and was on the alert, listening to the voice crying in the wilderness. And so powerful, so startling, so imposing was the appearance of the Forerunner that unto him, "in the wilderness of Judæa" (Matt. 3:1), "there went out . . . all the land of Judæa, and they of Jerusalem" (Mark 1:5).

After three centuries during which the prophetic voice was silent, it thundered once again in the Jordan desert. And it spoke of *repentance, metanoia:* "Repent ye: for the kingdom of heaven is at hand" (Matt. 3:2), with the same words that opened the preaching of Christ Himself (see Matt. 4:17). The appearance of the Forerunner already anticipates the Kingdom of God; it speaks of its coming as that of the King Himself: these two planes merge into a *single* event.

In announcing the One who represents the accomplishment of all of Israel's yearnings and in applying to himself Isaiah's prophecies about this Kingdom, the Forerunner, nevertheless, speaks of *repentance* as of a fundamental change in thoughts and feelings. This was that essential preparation of human souls without which the Messiah's coming was impossible. The Forerunner was sent into the world precisely to "prepare . . . the way of the Lord, make straight . . . a highway for our God" (Is. 40:3; cf. Matt. 3:3; Mark 1:3; Luke 3:4).

The Kingdom of God, which, with Christ, was approaching the world, was so different from earthly Judaic conceptions that a *metanoia* had to take place. This change had to involve not only opinions but also works, not only beliefs but also practical conduct. "Bring forth therefore fruits meet for repentance" (Matt. 3:8; also Luke 3:8). In the face of the New Testament that was approaching men, less significant became the Old Testament superiority of the chosen nation, the "sons of Abraham," of which the Hebrews were proud and which they considered decisive for salvation: "And think not to say within yourselves, We have Abraham to our father: for I say unto you, that God is able of these stones to raise up children unto Abraham" (Matt. 3:9; also Luke 3:8).

The Gospel only *indicates* the theme, content, and goal of John's preaching: "repent ye." It does not, of course, present the preaching itself, its fiery, triumphant, startling words. This is not necessary for the purposes of the evangelist, who merely remarks briefly: "Many other things in his exhortation preached he unto the people" (Luke 3:18). But it is necessary to linger over those particulars of John's preaching that are preserved in the Gospel. According to Matthew and Luke, he reprimanded and threatened those (the Pharisees and Sadducees) who did not repent truly, though they came to be baptized by him. "O generation of vipers, who hath warned you to flee from the wrath to come? . . . And now also the axe is laid unto the root of the trees: therefore every tree which bringeth not forth good fruit is hewn down, and cast into the fire" (Matt. 3:7, 10; also Luke 3:7, 9). "[His] fan is in his hand, and he will thoroughly purge his floor, and gather his wheat into the garner; but he will burn up the chaff with unquenchable fire" (Matt. 3:12). These apocalyptic images, pronounced with a prophetic power, express the idea of an approaching judgment: "Now is the judgment of this world" (John 12:31).

Luke also presents other features of John's preaching, which refer to various circumstances: "And the people asked him, saying, What shall we do then? He answereth and saith unto them, He that hath two coats, let him impart to him that hath none; and he that hath meat, let him do likewise. Then came also the publicans to be baptized, and saith unto him, Master, what shall we do? And he said unto them, Exact no more than that which is appointed you. And the soldiers likewise demanded of him, saying, And what shall we do? And he said unto them, Do violence to no man, neither accuse any falsely; and be content with your wages" (Luke 3:10-14). These simple and practical answers reveal John the Baptist as a prophet, who, among other goals, is pursuing moral rehabilitation and improvement of conduct. Within certain limits John does not refrain from being a teacher of life, a rabbi.

Moreover, these questions illustrate the degree of his influence on different strata of the population and the powerful impression made by him. John's words melted hearts; people were set into motion, left their homes in search of the object of desire inspired by him. Repentance led them to a search for new life. They gathered round this new and great prophet: "The people were in expectation, and all men mused in their hearts of John, whether he were the Christ, or not" (Luke 3:15).

But he rejected this expectation, indicating the One mightier than he, who was to come after him. The Gospel, saying much in these few words, bears witness once again to the Forerunner's feat, to his self-renouncing humility. How great was the temptation for the sinful human essence, with its self-love and pride, to refer to itself, to trap within itself, without transmitting it, at least one ray of the glory and power that the Forerunner radiated in his preaching! And how heavy and irreparable would have been the consequences if he had given in to that temptation! The Forerunner's life and preaching, his work, form an integral part of the ministry of the Lord Jesus Christ, its prologue, just as the life and feat of the Mother of God form an integral part of it, though in their own special sense. Here, there must be no contamination with sin, not the slightest temptation; everything must be irreproachable and perfect. And just as in the chamber in Nazareth the fate of the world was being decided by the Virgin Mary's answer to the archangel's annunciation, so in the Jordan desert, in the Forerunner's awareness about himself, in the hidden movements of his heart, when he was asked whether he was Christ (John 1:19-20), the same question was being decided: Was the world ready to receive Christ? Could He appear to the people? Or — and this is horrible to say — will the world fail to receive the already-born Christ? John represented then all of humankind, whose fate was being decided in his heart. And the favorable decision could be made, the absolute answer could be spoken, the absolute self-determination could be realized only if John's feat was pure and holy. And Christ's Forerunner showed himself worthy of his calling.

That which seems natural and self-evident, as it were, in brief and schematic exposition, signifies, in reality, the fact that temptations, inevitable in his position for any other human being, had no power over John. *The Forerunner perfectly fulfilled his task.*

CHAPTER 3

The Baptism of John

John's ministry was not limited to the preaching of repentance; he was also sent to *baptize* with water (John 1:33), which is why he is called the Baptist. This baptism was "the baptism of repentance for the remission of sins" (Mark 1:4). "And [the people] were baptized of him in Jordan, confessing their sins" (Matt. 3:6). "All the people were baptized" (Luke 3:21). And this baptism was performed not through cleansing (cf. Lev. 13-14), and not through sprinkling with purifying water, which was habitual in the rituals prescribed by Mosaic law (see Num. 19:13-20), but through immersion in water. That is why it was usually performed in rivers, and in the deepest places (e.g., "In Ænon near to Salim, because there was much water there" [John 3:23]).

What is the significance of this mysterious act, for which John was sent by God? (Cf. in Matt. 21:25, the Lord's question to the high priests and elders, which, of course, implies only one answer, an affirmative one: "The baptism of John, whence was it? from heaven, or of men?") Human beings cannot fully fathom the mystery of the baptism of John, for it is also the mystery of Christ's baptism ("that he should be made manifest to Israel, therefore am I come baptizing with water" [John 1:31]). And the economy of our salvation is not entirely knowable by creaturely reason.

The baptism of John implied, first of all, the confession of sins: it was the outward expression of an inner decision — the decision to change one's life.[1] In this sense, it had, first of all, the significance of a sign for the one being baptized; and it thus possessed a personal, subjective significance.

---

1. Luke 3:3: "And he came into all the country about Jordan, preaching the baptism of repentance for the remission of sins."

But apart from this personal element, which could depend on any external sign, confession, prayer, or solemn promise, there was a public rite: baptism with water. This was a new rite that did not figure in the Old Testament prescriptions: John appears here as a new law-giver. In this too, he leaves behind the Old Testament and its ritual law, just as he leaves behind the Old Testament temple and piety.

To be sure, this novelty was not originally felt as a novelty, as the beginning of the abolition of the purification sacrifices and the ancient law. Rather, it was considered as the pious fulfillment of the latter. We can see this in the fact that all came to John, including the Pharisees, the defenders of the law, and the Sadducees (Matt. 3:7). And only in the end was it the case that they did "not ... believe him" (Matt. 21:25). But, in reality, the baptism of John came not to fulfill but to surpass the Old Testament law. The final words ("your house is left unto you desolate" [Matt. 23:38]) had not yet been pronounced; and the veil of the temple had not yet been rent in twain from the top to the bottom (Matt. 27:51). But the fullness of time for both the temple and the law had been achieved: John, a priest's son and hereditary Levite, was celebrating a *new* rite *outside* the temple.

This rite is baptism with water. Water, the transparent and clear element, is already given in nature for this purpose, as something incontestable. But baptism by immersion also has another significance: the one immersed in baptismal waters leaves, in a certain sense, this world, into which he returns when he emerges from the water. If the immersion continues, the person drowns and no longer returns to the world. If the immersion is accompanied by a spiritual catastrophe, by a regeneration, the person returns different; he is resurrected, as it were; he is the same, but not the same; he is new. It was this renewal, this new birth, *palingenesia*, that was sought in vain by the pagan mysteries. It was this kind of renewal that was the object of the baptism of John. Was it really such? What exactly did it confer? There was indisputably one thing it did not confer and did not have the power to confer: the remission of sins and especially the remission of original sin, for it was only *baptism with water*. John himself constantly emphasized this, proclaiming the powerlessness of his baptism and opposing it to true baptism: to birth from water and the Spirit (John 3:5). "I indeed baptize you with water unto repentance; but he that cometh after me ... shall baptize you with the Holy Spirit, and with fire" (Matt. 3:11; also Mark 1:8; Luke 3:16; cf. John 1:33).

To be sure, baptism with water and only water is powerless compared with this baptism with water and the Spirit or directly with the Holy Spirit and with fire. But was this baptism then a baptism at all? If not, what was it? This is a difficult and mysterious question. Indisputably, it cannot be understood on the basis of itself, just as the Forerunner cannot be understood on the basis of himself: he himself explains himself with reference to the One who comes after him. According to the patristic interpretation,[2] the baptism of John was an introduction to and a preparation for the baptism of Christ. The Gospel preaching begins and ends with baptism: it begins with the baptism of John (in all four Evangelists) and ends with the Savior's commandment that all be baptized (Matt. 28:19). Baptism with water is devoid of meaning if it is not the form for a future, true baptism.

However, until the time of that true baptism arrives, this form has an independent meaning as a preparation for that which is to come, as a human question which receives a divine answer. In order to be baptized, a person must feel the need for baptism, must go out to meet it, into the desert, even if that means leaving the ancient temple behind. As long as people lived in the piety of the temple and remained satisfied with this piety, as long as they did not seek baptism for the remission of sins, they could not receive baptism. A *thirst* for baptism had to be awakened in Old Testament Judaism. It was John the Baptist who awakened it — not by word but by deed: he called people to baptism and he baptized.

What did such baptism confer, and did it confer anything? From the fact that it was not a perfect baptism, it does not follow that it was not a baptism at all and did not confer anything. It was not a sacrament conferring the supernatural gift of the grace of the Holy Spirit, but it was, so to speak, a natural sacramental act: all the best energies of the human soul, implanted in it during its creation, were exerted, were awakened, were concentrated in prayer, repentance, faith. The *natural* side of baptism, that which is required from human beings for the reception of its *grace*, was present here. This is not nothing and even not a little.

After the coming of Christ and the descent of the Holy Spirit, the baptism of John had clearly become an outdated vestige and a cause of misunderstandings, as we can see in Acts 18:24-28 and 19:1-17. Here it is told how in Ephesus a certain Apollos taught the rudiments of faith, although he knew only the baptism of John and his disciples knew nothing of the Holy Spirit. The apostle Paul, who had just come to Ephesus, told them: "John verily baptized with the baptism of repentance, saying unto the people, that they should believe on him which should come after him,

---

2. St. Basil the Great, *Hom.* 13; St. John Chrysostom, *Commentary on the Gospel of John*, ch. 1.

that is, on Christ Jesus. When they heard this, they were baptized in the name of the Lord Jesus" (Acts 19:4-5). That which had been incomplete was now made complete without any difficulty, and the difficult misunderstanding was removed: it became clear that baptism with water, without the gifts of the Holy Spirit, was, in the light of Christian baptism, not a true baptism. It was, rather, a baptism directed at the Old Testament, at Judaism under the law: the voice crying in the wilderness called Judaism to new life through repentance. It is remarkable that this baptism of repentance retained its initiatory significance, so to speak, even after the baptism of Christ and His appearance to the people. According to the Gospel of John, John the Baptist remained in the places proper to him by the Jordan, first in Bethabara beyond the river (John 1:28) and then in Aenon near Salim (John 3:23); and he continued to baptize. John thus remained the Baptist up to the time of his imprisonment (John 3:23-24).

But it is even more remarkable that baptism — and evidently only the baptism of repentance — was also received by Jesus' disciples when He came with them into the land of Judæa "and there he tarried with them, and baptized" (John 3:22). True, the Evangelist clarifies this unexpected report by saying that "Jesus himself baptized not, but his disciples" (John 4:2). Nevertheless, the Evangelist directly opposes two groups of baptizers: Jesus and His disciples and John and his disciples (John 3:22, 25-26), so that a sense of competition arose among John's disciples: "They came unto John, and said unto him, Rabbi, he that was with thee beyond Jordan, to whom thou barest witness, behold, the same baptizeth, and all men come to him" (John 3:26). But this provoked John's unforgettable answer, the testimony about himself of the Forerunner, "the friend of the Bridegroom" (John 3:27-36). "When . . . the Lord knew how the Pharisees had heard that Jesus made and baptized more disciples than John . . . He left Judæa, and departed again into Galilee" (John 4:1, 3). There is no other information in the Gospel about the baptismal activity of Jesus' disciples. This certainly was not the baptism of the New Testament, in the death of Christ. This baptism was impossible before Christ's redemptive death. Rather, it was a contribution to the redemptive movement that was concentrated around John, which is why the great success of Jesus' disciples was met with surprise and with a certain jealousy by John's disciples. And it was also a sign of respect for the Baptist's work, which did not end with the fulfillment of his mission, but continued in a limited way until his imprisonment and death. It was not finished until his death, although it persisted for a time as a spiritual survival.

Just as the coming of the Forerunner preceded that of Christ, so his baptism was a preparation for the New Testament baptism. In particular, one can say that it prepared the sacred element, water, for the New Testament baptism; for the baptismal waters are the waters of the Jordan, and the baptismal water-blessing is made effective by the baptism and Theophany of Christ (see the office of the sacrament of baptism). John had knowledge of the mystery of the water; he revealed the waters of the Jordan, not in the geographic but in the mystical sense. He chose and indicated the waters into which the Lord's most pure body was immersed and upon which the Holy Spirit descended. And thereby the sacramental mystery of baptism was preaccomplished once and for all; the baptismal font, the sacred grave, was prepared into which the baptized are placed in memory of the Lord's three-day death. The baptismal waters are twice prefigured in the Old Testament: first in the waters of the Deluge (1 Pet. 3:20-21), in which humankind was buried, but with its living branch preserved in the family of Noah; and then in the waters of the Red Sea (1 Cor. 10:2), through which the Israelites passed but in which the Egyptians drowned. But these are prefigurations only of the death of some and of the salvation of others. They do not imply the death and resurrection of the same person, which constitutes Christian baptism. In the broadest sense, baptism signifies the salvific death and transfiguration of the whole world, which comes at the end of time when a new heaven and a new earth will appear.

John baptized neither anonymously nor in his own name; as the Forerunner, he baptized in the name of the One who was coming after him. According to the apostle Paul, "John verily baptized with the baptism of repentance, saying unto the people, that they should believe on him which should come after him, that is, on Christ Jesus" (Acts 19:4). This is also the predominant opinion of the holy fathers (St. Ambrose, St. Jerome, and others).[3] This also determines the *power* of this baptism: it was not powerless, for it was already performed in the Name that is worshipped by all heavenly, earthly, and netherworld creatures. It was, in any case, an effective blessing, associated with repentance, by the Name; it was a New Testament blessing but still in the Old Testament. But it did not have the power possessed by the New Testament "in the Name," as it unfolds in the invocation of the entire Holy Trinity — the Father and the Son and the Holy Spirit. But this revelation of the Name of God as the Name of the Holy Trinity was accomplished within the baptism of John in the Theophany, when the fullness of Christ's baptism and of Christian baptism was realized once for all ages.

---

3. S. Vishniakov, *St. John* (Moscow, 1879), p. 13.

CHAPTER 4

The Baptism of the Lord, Followed by the Testimony concerning the Lamb of God

Everything we have said so far about baptism and its significance is only the fruit and consequence of the baptism of the Lord. John's supreme mission, the main reason he was sent to baptize, was the baptism of the Lord by his own hand: "That he should be made manifest to Israel, therefore am I come baptizing with water" (John 1:31; cf. 32-34). The baptism of Jesus took place together with and in the midst of the baptism of all the people: "Now when all the people were baptized, it came to pass, that Jesus [was] also being baptized" (Luke 3:21). Outwardly, Jesus' baptism was one of many, without a sign by which the people could know it; and only John, together with Jesus Himself, knew what was taking place.

We have already said that, in his own way, the Baptist, precisely as the Baptist, occupies in the Incarnation a place just as necessary and inalienable as that of the Mother of God. In other words, the baptism is as essential in the Incarnation as the birth of Christ. It is His spiritual birth.

The Evangelists describe the baptism of Christ as something simple, natural, and clear: "Then cometh Jesus from Galilee to Jordan unto John, to be baptized of him" (Matt. 3:13; cf. Mark 1:9; Luke 3:21). To be sure, such an event in Jesus' life could not be accidental or arbitrary; it could only be internally necessary. Even less can it be understood only as an *image of humility*, manifested in the baptism of repentance. The Sole Sinless One had no sins, just as he had no need for repentance, as the Evangelist implies when he says that "Jesus, when he was baptized, went up straightway out of the water," that is, without taking time for repentance and the confession of sins. The same thing is proclaimed by the liturgical hymn: "I do not require you, Baptist, to surpass the limits. I do not say to you: speak to me the way you would to those without law and the way you do when you teach sinners. Do nothing but baptize me in silence, waiting for that which results from the baptism" (2 January, canon, ikos).

Although an image of humility is shown, the reception of baptism for the sake of a fictitious repentance would not accord with the truth and would lead to an erroneous interpretation. The Lord came to John to be baptized, but not for repentance and for the remission of sins. Rather, he came to receive the Holy Spirit. The latter descended upon Him during the baptism of John, with water, which then became baptism with the Holy Spirit. John was instructed about this in advance by God, for this event constituted the essence of his ministry, in relation to which everything else was subordinate and secondary: "I knew him not: but he that sent me to baptize with water, the same said unto me, Upon whom thou shalt see the Spirit descending, and remaining on him, the same is he which baptizeth with the Holy Spirit" (John 1:33).

This does not contradict what is reported in Matthew: "John forbad him, saying, I have need to be baptized of thee, and comest thou to me?" (Matt. 3:14). First of all, this is in full accord with the truth: the Lord, the Savior of the whole human race and the Redeemer from original sin, communicates the power of this redemption, i.e., the power of baptism, to John as well as to all others after His death and descent into hell. In this sense, He is the baptist of His Baptist. Also, here John trembles with the holy trepidation of human weakness, to which trepidation the office of baptism (7 January) bears such copious witness:

> Seeing you approach, Christ, and asking for baptism, the Forerunner cries out with trepidation: What do you command me to accomplish, O omnipotent Lord, beyond my powers? How will I touch you with my hand, you who contain all? It is rather for you to baptize your servant.
>
> The entire man has presented Himself now. He has become accessible to you now, He who is by nature inaccessible. Voluntarily impoverished, He is rich in order that I enrich the impoverished one by incorruptibility and redemption. Advance, baptize the one who is inaccessible to corruption and who takes the world out of corruption.
>
> God the Word appeared in the flesh to the human race, standing in the Jordan to be blessed. And the Forerunner said to Him: how can

I extend my hand and touch the head of the one who holds all things? Even though you are the child of Mary, I know who you are, supra-eternal God. You walk on the earth glorified by the seraphim, and the servant is not authorized to baptize the Master. Unfathomable Lord, glory to thee!

When John the Forerunner saw you, Lord, coming toward him, he was frightened; and, like a just servant, he cried out in fear: what humility, what salvific poverty you have clothed yourself in! By the riches of grace, O great good one, you have elevated the humbled man, for it is he you have clothed yourself in!

You announced to the Forerunner: come to me to accomplish the mystery of salvation; serve it with fear! I come to save all; and do not be in fear! Renewing the one who is overwhelmed by the sin of Adam, I will be baptized like a man, although pure by nature, in the waters of the Jordan, where, as you see, I have come.

John contradicts Him: among those who are of the earth, who has ever seen the bared sun, who inhabits the heaven of clouds, and who created sources and rivers enter into the waters? I marvel at the ineffable sight of you, Lord. Do not charge your servant with terrible commands!

The Forerunner was filled with a trepidation of humility, without which he could not assimilate the Lord's words. And there was neither doubt nor objection in those words of his that were followed by the Lord's: "Suffer it to be so now: for thus it becometh us to fulfill all righteousness [*pasan dikaiōsunēn*, i.e., lawful righteousness, justification, that which is necessary for justification]" (Matt. 3:15). And John obeys; he humbles his humility, surrenders himself to the accomplishment of the terrible command: "He [John] suffered Him" (Matt. 3:15). Having humbled Himself to the point of taking the form of a servant, the Lord comes to the Baptist together with all the people, from whom, as one of those being baptized, He does not differ outwardly.

Was Jesus baptized only in order to manifest His humility? Or did He require baptism and, therefore, also the Baptist, in order to fulfill all righteousness, which, otherwise, would have been unfulfilled? That is an essential question. To be sure, this righteousness consisted not in repentance for the remission of sins, of which the Sole Sinless One was completely free, as He Himself says about Himself: "The prince of this world cometh, and hath nothing in me" (John 14:30). It consisted in something else altogether: in the fullness of divine condescension.

The Friend of the Bridegroom

This merits reflection. The Incarnation is always understood as the reception by the Second Person of the Holy Trinity of human flesh from the Most Holy Mother of God, that is, as the birth of Christ. But this alone is insufficient for the fullness of the divine condescension, for this fullness requires not only the Lord's birth but also His baptism.

It is noteworthy that, in the early church, these two feasts were celebrated together under the name *Epiphaneia,* that is, the Theophany. This referred to one or the other of the events, as well as to the two taken together. This tradition is still preserved in the Armenian church. The convergence of the two feasts is also expressed in the liturgical structure of their offices. This structure exhibits intentional parallels and astonishing analogies, especially in the pre-feast offices (22-24 December and 2-5 January). Their triodes, canons, and stichera, deliberately similar to those of the offices of Holy Week, make one feast nearly completely the same as the other. Of course, the events celebrated are different, as are the persons who are venerated: the Mother of God in the first case, and the Forerunner in the second. Let us also mention that these two feasts are, respectively, accompanied by the synaxis of the Mother of God (26 December) and the synaxis of the Forerunner (7 January).

Epiphany, that is, the manifestation of the Son of God in the flesh, signifies that, having adopted the human nature in addition to the Divine nature, the Divine Hypostasis of the Son of God also became a human hypostasis. God became man, in whom "dwelleth all the fulness of the Godhead bodily" (Col. 2:9). Only the Second Hypostasis becomes hypostatically incarnate. The mystery of the incarnation of only one of the hypostases of the consubstantial and inseparable Trinity surpasses, of course, the human understanding. But this inseparability is inviolable: the Son is inseparable from the Father who engenders Him and whom he reveals in the world, just as He is inseparable from the Holy Spirit, who reposes upon Him. This inseparability is realized from all eternity in His divine nature. But it must be effective even in His human nature. Even as the Son receives from all eternity the Holy Spirit who proceeds from the Father and who, reciprocally, reveals the Son to the Father and the Father to the Son, so His human nature must receive the Spirit of filiation, in order that the Son of man truly become the Son of God. Christ's human nature is united in Him without separation and without confusion with the divine nature, and the fullness of the Incarnation requires that this human nature be united with the life of the entire Holy Trinity in the same way that the hypostasis of the Son in its divine nature is united with it. Otherwise, either the Incarnation will remain incomplete and external or a separation will be admitted in the Holy Trinity, and that is blasphemous.

In order to be the perfect God-Man, the Son must receive as Man that which He possesses as God. In order that the fullness of Divinity dwell in Him, it is necessary that the Son's human nature too be adopted by the Father by the descent of the Holy Spirit upon it. In the Holy Trinity the Son is born of the Father; but, in His birth as the Son, He is shown to the Father by the Holy Spirit, who proceeds from the Father and descends upon the Son and reposes upon Him. The Holy Spirit, the Spirit of filiation, renders the Son the son of the Father and manifests the Father to the Son. The Father engenders, but the Spirit realizes the filiation, gives possession of the one who is born. The procession of the Holy Spirit from the Father upon the Son must be understood in connection with birth, fatherhood, and sonhood: in the Spirit, the Father acquires, has the Son who is born, whereas the Son has the Father who engenders. This relationship exists from all eternity in the Holy Spirit, and it belongs from all eternity to each of the hypostases, linked to the other hypostases by its hypostatic self-determination. But this relationship must also be accomplished in time during the Incarnation, in the human nature received by the Son.

How is that possible? If the Holy Spirit reposes from all eternity upon the Son and renders Him the Son of the Father, He must also repose upon His human nature in the same manner as He reposes upon the Son of God by virtue of His divine nature. Otherwise, there would be no conformity between the two natures, and the Incarnation would be incomplete. In other words, Jesus must be Christ, the Anointed of the Holy Spirit. When and how can this anointment be accomplished? At the moment of His birth or later? The Lord's conception was the work of the Holy Spirit and of the Virgin Mary: "The Holy Spirit shall come upon thee, and the power of the Highest shall overshadow thee: therefore also that holy thing which shall be born of thee shall be called the Son of God" (Luke 1:35). The Holy Spirit descended upon the Virgin Mary at the moment of the Incarnation to such an exceptional degree that She was able to conceive without seed the Divine Infant. Therefore, the one born had, even in His human aspect, such a measure of holiness that He could be called the Son of God.

But this descent of the Holy Spirit upon the Virgin Mary does not imply an identical descent of the Holy Spirit upon the One to be born, for it must be an independent and separate act. The descent of the Holy Spirit upon the Virgin Mary protects the birth against sin and makes it *holy*, graced by the gifts of the Holy Spirit, but not by the Holy Spirit's hypostatic presence. The Gospel says it clearly: "The child grew, and waxed strong in spirit, filled with wisdom: and the grace of God was upon him" (Luke 2:40). It is a question, of course, of the gifts of grace of the Holy Spirit, given to the Infant's human nature in proportion to its growth and spiritual strengthening, whereas these gifts were proper from all eternity to His divine nature.

His growth and development, now as an adolescent, are shown a second time in the Gospel: "Jesus increased in wisdom and stature, and in favour with God and man" (Luke 2:52). This indicates that His human nature was incomplete and imperfect in some sense, which would be impossible if the Holy Spirit, the fullness of Divinity, had hypostatically reposed upon this nature. This fullness was realized only in the baptism, when the Holy Spirit descended upon the Lord's human nature in the form of a dove, and the Lord became the Anointed one, Christ, *Christos*, which implies *hupo tou Pneumatos Hagiou:* the Name of the Holy Spirit is tacitly implied in the name of Christ. It is pronounced at the same time as that of Christ. The hypostatic descent of the Holy Spirit upon Christ's *human* nature, His two natures being without confusion and without separation, took place at the baptism, when Jesus became the perfect God-Man. The time of His growth and strengthening having been concluded, He entered "into the fullness of Christ's age." But just as in the supra-eternal life of the Holy Trinity the procession of the Holy Spirit upon the Son makes Him the Son of the Father, so in the Incarnation the hypostatic indwelling of the Holy Spirit in the human essence makes Him the God-Man. It was by virtue of this indwelling of the Holy Spirit that He could work miracles, which, according to His own testimony, were due to the Holy Spirit, just as He could send the Holy Spirit upon the apostles by breathing upon them: "Receive ye the Holy Spirit" (John 20:22).

The baptismal theophany is therefore a new and definitive filiation: in descending to the earth upon the Son of God who is being baptized, the Holy Spirit bears witness before the Father to this sonhood and realizes it. And that is why, attesting to this, the response from the Father follows immediately: "And lo a voice from heaven, saying, This is my beloved Son, in whom I am well pleased" (Matt. 3:17; also: Mark 1:11; Luke 3:22). All three synoptic Gospels report this narrative (there is also an allusion to it in John 5:37). It is interesting to note that this convergence between Christ's birth and baptism is implicitly confirmed in one of the ancient variants of the Gospel text concerning baptism: In some of the fathers, the text of Luke 3:22, "Thou art my beloved Son," is followed not by "in thee I am well pleased" but by a verse from Psalm 2:7: "this day have I begotten thee." This version also bears witness to the Godsonhood but with a clear reference to the birth of Christ. These words do not represent a new, additional revelation; what they reveal is already contained in the very fact of the descent of the Holy Spirit. This is this very same fact in all its power as it exists in God. The one in whom the Father is "well pleased," i.e., the one upon whom He has poured forth His love (and the hypostatic love of the Father and of the Son is the Holy Spirit), is therefore the Son. The same words are pronounced, as we know, at the Transfiguration: "This is my beloved Son, in whom I am well pleased; hear ye him" (Matt. 17:5; cf. Mark 9:7; Luke 9:35). This voice signified for the disciples a *manifestation* of the preexistent sonhood, not the establishment of the divine sonhood itself. This voice came out of a cloud, which, according to the Old Testament, represents the Glory of God. It was the manifestation of Divinity in Jesus Christ, which in fact constituted the essence of the Transfiguration. In this sense one can say that the transfiguration has at its basis the baptism and, of course, the birth of Christ. Meanwhile, the baptism is called the Theophany because it is the revelation — through and in the Incarnation — of the entire Holy Trinity: "When you were baptized in the Jordan, Lord, the adoration of the Trinity was manifested. For the voice of the Father bore witness about you in naming you the beloved Son; and the Holy Spirit, in the form of a dove, attested to the affirmation of what was said." In contrast, at the Office of the Transfiguration, one simply sings: "You were transfigured on the mountain, O Christ our God, manifesting your glory to your disciples, to the extent they were capable of receiving it."

Thus we arrive at the conclusion that the Lord's Baptism truly constitutes Christ's spiritual birth, as it were: the Son of man is truly and fully glorified as the Son of God, as the voice from heaven attests (and let it be noted that God's word is, of course, already deed, already accomplishment). But here we might ask in perplexity: Does this conclusion not diminish the role of the Mother of God? Does it not revive the heresy of Nestorius, who taught that the Virgin Mary gave birth to a man who subsequently became Christ and the Son of God — this heresy which makes Her not the God-bearer *(Theotokos)* but the Christ-bearer *(Christotokos)*?

This blasphemous heresy, condemned by the Third Ecumenical Council, is directed against the dogma that the hypostasis of the Son of God is identical to that of Jesus Christ, and that the Logos was made incarnate and born of the Virgin Mary from the first instant of His conception, from the Annunciation. According to this heresy, Jesus was never, not in a single moment of His existence, a mere human being, and it was not the Holy Spirit that descended upon Christ at the Baptism but the Logos, who then inhabited this man for the first time. Not subordinating but opposing the Baptism to the Nativity, this theory has nothing in common with the idea developed here that the Baptism is directly and indissolubly linked with the Nativity and that it is only an unfolding or demonstration of the latter.

The Mother of God is truly the Theotokos, for the One She conceived and gave birth to is the true Son of God, the supra-eternal Word, the Second Person of the Holy Trinity. But the true Incarnation presupposes the development of the human nature into the fullness of maturity: The Lord passed through infancy, boyhood, and youth before arriving at full maturity. And one cannot, of course, say that the *fullness* of His human nature and therefore the fullness of the Divine-humanity were achieved from the very birth of Christ. However, this does not contradict the fact that the one born is the true God, even if He is as yet only the Divine Infant. The Divine Infant already possesses *all* the possibilities and, in this sense, the whole fullness of the God-Man; however, these possibilities are realized only in the course of time, in different times and seasons. And the most important of these possibilities was the one realized in the Baptism, by the descent of the Holy Spirit, by the *anointing* of Christ, after which He could apply to Himself the words of Isaiah's prophecy: "The Spirit of the Lord is upon me . . . he hath anointed me" (Luke 4:18).

But the question arises: Why did the Holy Spirit not descend in the form of a dove at the instant of His birth upon the one upon whom He reposes from all eternity in virtue of His Divinity? Why was a whole life needed before His full maturity could arrive and the Holy Spirit could descend upon Him? It is because the Lord had become truly incarnate, that is, had assumed full and true humanity. And the human nature possesses, as an indestructible property of the image of God in man, the freedom to accept or to reject God. God's grace precedes and accompanies man, cooperates with him and fills him with strength; but it does not coerce him, does not violate his freedom, does not reduce him to a machine or robot. The first word, the question, belongs to man, to his freedom, to his spiritual self-determination. Therefore, before the baptism could be accomplished, it was necessary for Jesus to come to the Baptist to be baptized by him. And this took place when Jesus "began to be about thirty years of age" (Luke 3:23), that is, after He had reached full maturity. The freedom and fullness of His *human* self-determination did not admit a premature, an insufficiently weighed decision to dedicate Himself to God, to devote

Himself to God's service. And the external sign that this decision had been made was the fact that Jesus went to the Jordan — to John.

The Baptism of the Lord is the *beginning* of His public ministry. It was after being baptized that He was led by the Spirit into the desert to be tempted, thereby definitively bearing witness about Himself. And it is after this that He began to preach about Himself as the Messiah (Luke 4) and about the Gospel of the Kingdom (Matthew 4). But, from the beginning, His ministry led to Golgotha. His coming to John already implied the decision He had made to do God's will to the end, a decision to which the descent of the Holy Spirit and the proclamation that He was the Son of the Father were the response. The immersion in the waters of the Jordan prefigured the death on Golgotha and the three days in the grave, as it did the Christian baptism in the death of the Savior. That which was accomplished in Gethsemane prior to the passion — "O my Father . . . thy will be done" (Matt. 26:42) — had already been preaccomplished in the Jordan.

But once again we are faced with the question: What is John doing here? Why do we need a baptist? Could the consecration to God and even the descent of the Holy Spirit not have taken place without his participation? Is it absolutely and internally necessary that precisely the Baptist be present at the Baptism and participate in it? The answer to this question must clearly be an affirmative one, as is evident from the following reflections.

The feat of sacrificial submission, of obedience to the will of the Father, accomplished by the new Adam and instigating the descent of the Holy Spirit upon Him, was not meant to be a solitary act, an act performed in isolation from people: That which is accomplished for humankind must be manifested to humankind, must be accomplished with and amongst people. The obedience of the Son of man was manifested in the form of human submission to God. And according to God's design, this human submission, as repentance, *metanoia,* was accomplished by the baptism of John, in the waters. And the Omnipotent one, come in the image of humility, humbled himself to the point of receiving baptism from a "servant," together with other men, with and amongst the people, as Luke 3:21 says: "When all the people were baptized, it came to pass, that Jesus also . . . [was] . . . baptized." With and amongst the people — this was essential for the One who took upon Himself the likeness of the flesh of sin, who came to summon to repentance not the righteous but sinners.

In order to "fulfill all righteousness," in order to express the readiness to do the Father's will, the Son of man, one might think, could still have offered a sacrifice by means of the Old Testament priesthood after the order of Aaron. But that would have been impossible, for the Old Testament had already fulfilled all its righteousness, and the priesthood after the order of Aaron had been replaced by the priesthood after the order of Melchizedek. The Lord could not have received baptism — or an equivalent grace-bestowing act — from the Old Testament priesthood, since He Himself was, for all eternity, the High Priest of the New Testament, after the order of Melchizedek. That is why the path chosen, that of the baptism of John, is, if not outside the Church, in any case outside the temple. John himself was a priest by blood, but he performed his priestly function outside the temple.

To receive the baptism the Lord needed a Baptist. Self-baptism would have contradicted the attestation of humility and obedience that was needed. Such an elimination of a baptist would have signified self-elevation, a rejection of the whole human race as unworthy or unnecessary. On the contrary, the Lord wished to humble Himself not only before God but also before the people whom He had chosen as His brothers, and to become for them a model of humility. But this was possible *only through another, through the Baptist*, not through self-baptism. At this critical point of His earthly path the Lord *needed* a baptist.

But not just anyone could be the baptist; if the baptist were a sinner and unworthy of his role, humility could become a humiliation and a temptation. Someone was needed who was pure of sin and who could withstand, without trepidation, the sight of the heavens opening at the baptism. There was but one member of the human race who was worthy of serving the Son of man's need, of baptizing Him. And the Lord, in His ways, prepared him from all eternity to stand in his place when the Lamb of God, who takes away the sin of the world, would approach to bend His neck and incline His head beneath the baptizing hand. Without him there would have been no baptism; the heavens would not have opened up; the Holy Spirit would not have descended upon the Son of man; the voice from heaven would not have sounded. It is terrifying for the human mind to think of *such* responsibility, but the Lord chooses and elevates a man after His heart. The Church sings with zeal and love this feat of the Forerunner in its baptismal offices.

It was given to the Baptist to be the seer of the mystery of the Holy Trinity in the Theophany. In purity of heart, the possessors of which will see God, he had foreknowledge of this mystery, which had already been partly unveiled in the Old Testament. And how could this knowledge not be revealed to the one who stood at the junction of the two Testaments!

But now this mystery was visible to his eyes. And the baptist became the Baptist. His spirit withstood what not one of the ancient prophets, not one of the ancient righteous men could withstand — the seeing of God face to face: "And John bare record, saying, I saw the Spirit descending from heaven like a dove, and it abode upon him. And I knew him not: but he that sent me to baptize with water, the same said unto me, Upon whom thou shalt see the Spirit descending, and remaining on him, the same is he which baptizeth with the Holy Spirit. And I saw, and bare record that this is the Son of God" (John 1:32-34).

Where among the ancient prophets will we find such words about God? Even the appearance of the angel of God cast the Old Testament prophets into the fear of death. God revealed only His "back" to his friend, the prophet Moses. Isaiah's lips were purified by a seraph with a burning coal taken from the altar of God after he had the vision of His Glory. John too saw and bore witness to what he saw. And he saw how his baptism, the baptism of repentance by water, became the baptism by the Holy Spirit.

It is noteworthy that neither the Gospels nor the tradition of the Church report anything about the participation of the Mother of God in the baptism, or even anything about Her presence at the baptism. To be sure, one cannot accept that, in her God-knowing heart, She had no knowledge of the mystery of the baptism and of the Theophany, or that She did not know that they had been accomplished. But here too She recedes into shadow, surrendering Her place to the Baptist: the Mother according to the flesh temporarily cedes, as it were, the Son to the Baptist, who gives birth to Him by water and the Spirit.

But in the baptism one finds united not only the Theophany, the descent of the Holy Spirit, and the affirmation that the Son of man is the Son of the Father in heaven, but also His appearance to the people, His *meeting* with the human race. The Lord had to be met, received, recognized, and proclaimed as such on the day when He came to the people. Here too He was not meant to remain in solitude, far from the human race: this meeting had to be *truly* a meeting. And it is John, as the Forerunner and friend of the Bridegroom, who accomplishes this meeting in the name of the whole human race. He speaks for humanity; he is humanity's voice, humanity's heart, which desires the Savior.

This meeting marks the beginning of the Gospel story, the first movement toward Jesus and the first call. There also comes to the fore the significance of John as a *witness*, which constitutes the main theme of the narrative about him in the Gospel of John, in contrast to the other Gospels: "The next day John seeth Jesus coming unto him, and saith, Behold the Lamb of God, which taketh away the sin of the world" (John 1:29). With these words the Forerunner expressed a knowledge and understanding of the mystery of the Incarnation so perfect that he could now depart with this knowledge to preach in hell: *he had understood everything*. These words, a clear reflection of the images of the 53rd chapter of Isaiah, fully and exhaustively express the idea of Christ's redemptive work: "Again the next day after John stood, and two of his disciples; And looking upon Jesus as he walked, he saith, Behold the Lamb of God!" (John 1:35-36). And what followed? "And the two disciples [Andrew and John] heard him speak, and they followed Jesus" (John 1:37). Thus, this was their first inner call, which occurred even before the Lord called them.

It was in John, and in the Baptism, that Christ manifested Himself to the world and to the human race. The Baptist and Forerunner became the friend of the Bridegroom. And again: if the Forerunner had not been there, or if he had not recognized the Lord and had not borne witness about Him, then the chasm that separated the Messiah from sinful men would have remained unbridged; there would have been no intermediary, no witness; and the preaching of the Gospel of the Kingdom would not have begun as it did begin. But the Forerunner accomplished his task; he appeared as the true Baptist of the Lord. To meet the Divine Infant, God had prepared Simeon; to meet the Messiah, God had prepared John the Forerunner.

* * *

After the Baptism:
The Testimony concerning the Lamb of God

John's task was to be the Lord's Forerunner, to prepare the way for the Lord and to meet Him. But he also had to be the Baptist and see the fulfillment of the baptism — the heavens opening and the Holy Spirit descending in the form of a dove; he had to hear the voice of the Father and be present at the manifestation of the entire Holy Trinity. But it was incumbent upon the Forerunner not only to recognize Christ for himself but also to testify about the recognized Christ. It was incumbent upon him to be an *apostle* of Christ. That is indeed how the Holy Church venerates him, for he had received the grace to preach and confess Christ the Savior. In this too he is the Forerunner, since his preaching about Christ precedes Christ's own testimony about Himself and, of course, that of His apostles.

This ministry of the Forerunner as a witness is mainly described in the Gospel of John, which in this respect, as in many others, aims to complete the other Gospels while implicitly presupposing them. In particular, on the subject of the Forerunner the Gospel of John says nothing about the preaching of repentance or about baptism; it speaks only of the Forerunner himself as a witness of Christ. This indisputable difference in presentation, or point of view, gives rationalistic criticism a pretext to dispute or even to reject the significance of the narrative concerning John in the Fourth Gospel. For the Church's understanding such a question does not even arise: it is empty and artificial. It is important to understand the inner and necessary connection between the synoptic representation of the Forerunner and that of the Gospel of John; the two representations complement each other, of course. The synoptic Gospels describe, so to speak, the *historical* appearance of the Forerunner; they represent the Forerunner himself, though in indissoluble connection with the One for whom he is preparing a path. In contrast, the Gospel of John represents him as the companion and witness of the Other; he is only the satellite of the Sun of truth and his light is extinguished in the beams of this Sun.

The Gospel of John, here as in many other cases, represents the supratemporal, supra-eternal relation between events, and in particular, the relation between the coming of the Forerunner and the Incarnation. This relation is already established in the prologue, where what is said about John is interwoven with what is said about the Word and His incarnation: "There was a man sent from God, whose name was John. The same came for a witness, to bear witness of the Light, that all men through him might believe. He was not that Light, but was sent to bear witness of that Light" (John 1:6-8). Thus is elucidated the sending of John as a witness, *martys:* "all men" must believe "through him," that is, thanks to him and his testimony. This means, of course, not that he will preach to all men but that his testimony will have significance for the whole human race: without John, Christ would not have been recognized (or He would have been incorrectly recognized).

But this part of the Gospel does not yet present the content of his testimony. The pericope that follows describes the coming of the Light into the world, and when the Evangelist arrives at the triumphant declaration that "the Word was made flesh" (John 1:14) he again, for the second time, refers to John as the witness to this: "John bare witness of him, and cried, saying, This was he of whom I spake, He that cometh after me is preferred before me: for he was before me [*prōtos mou*]" (John 1:15). It is here that the content of the Forerunner's testimony is revealed, although the Evangelist does not situate it in time or indicate the place where it was given. Rather, he marks the general content of the Forerunner's preaching, its *theme*, as it were. Immediately after the prologue, the Evangelist speaks a third time about the Forerunner, and here the Evangelist's words are more concrete. It is noteworthy that, with the exception of the prologue, which to a certain degree represents an independent whole, the story of the Gospel of John begins, like that of the synoptics but in its own way, with the Forerunner. But the Gospel of John considers the Forerunner not as Baptist and prophet but solely as *witness*.

The Forerunner's testimony necessarily becomes a testimony about himself. "And this is the record of John, when the Jews sent priests and Levites from Jerusalem to ask him, Who art thou?" (John 1:19). This evidently took place toward the middle of John's mission, when many-voiced rumor always had John on its lips, and the authorities, although they were hostile to him, had not yet decided to wage open warfare against him, for they feared the people. Instead, they preferred to trap him by his own words, in the same way they attempted to trap the Lord. But the questions themselves imply the answers that were uttered, expressing the people's hopes and the impression produced by the Forerunner. All the questions have a single content: Is John not the Messiah? Or, at the very least, does his coming not announce the beginning of the messianic times? "He confessed, and denied not; but confessed [clearly, the questions were repeated insistently], I am not the Christ [*ho Christos*, the awaited Christ]" (John 1:20).

With this answer the Forerunner overcomes the temptation proper to him and that he alone had the strength to vanquish — the temptation of being seduced by the glory of the Forerunner, of appropriating for himself the light of the One who comes, of putting himself in His place. In a word, it was his humility that was being tested. Other questions naturally flow from this negative answer: "And they asked him, What then? Art thou Elias? And he saith, I am not" (John 1:21). This is a question not about the Messiah but about the messianic time. The prophecy of Malachi (Mal. 4:5), as the Church interprets it, links the return of Elias (Elijah) to earth to the second and dread coming of the Lord Jesus Christ, whereas the scribes link it to the first coming (cf. Matt. 17:10). It is clearly in *this* sense that the Forerunner gave his negative answer. But this answer does not exclude the possibility that John comes in the spirit and power of Elias and has a certain mysterious kinship with him, as the Lord Himself attests (see Matt. 17:11-13). (About this more below.) In any case, the Forerunner cannot be directly identified with Elias; this identification was perhaps suggested by the doctrine of metempsychosis that later spread among the Jews (through the Kaballah).

This is followed by the question: "Art thou that prophet [*ho prophētēs*]? And he answered, No" (John 1:21). Of course, according to the testimony of the Lord Himself, John was the greatest of the prophets, but here it is a question not of the prophetic ministry in general, of *prophētēs*, but of a specific ministry, of *ho prophētēs*, of the prophet announced by Moses in Deuteronomy 18:18, who is precisely the Messiah: "I will raise them up a Prophet from among their brethren, like unto thee, and will put my words in his mouth; and he shall speak unto them all that I shall command him." John responded negatively to this question, because he was not the Prophet-Messiah, nor the special messianic prophet, the companion of the Messiah, awaited by certain Jews (according to St. Cyril of Alexandria and St. John Chrysostom). Nor was he one of the former prophets, either as their personal incarnation or as a member of their order; for he is distinguished from the order of the Old Testament prophets: "The law and the prophets were until John" (Luke 16:16; Matt. 11:13). Although John has the prophetic gift, his mission surpasses the prophetic ministry: "But what went ye out for to see? A prophet? yea, I say unto you, and more than a prophet" (Matt. 11:9; Luke 7:26). For he is the prophet-Forerunner; it is given unto him to see and to know; all the prophets belong to the Old Testament and therefore they are "until John." In contrast, he belongs both to the Old Testament and to the New Testament, to the former because he is a prophet and to the latter because he is the Forerunner: "You were seen, Prophet, standing between the Old and the New, accomplishing the baptism for the two and manifesting their light" (Office of the Forerunner, tone 5, ode 9, tr. 2).

Having exhausted all the hypotheses that came to their minds to explain the coming of the Forerunner, those who were sent "said . . . unto him, Who art thou? that we may give an answer to them that sent us, What sayest thou of thyself? He said, I am the voice of one crying in the wilderness, Make straight the way of the Lord, as said the prophet Esaias [see Isa. 40:3]" (John 1:22-23). Fully in agreement with the synoptics, the Evangelist John defines the specific character of the coming of the Forerunner by referring to the biblical prophecy that we are already familiar with. There is the difference, however, that, in all the synoptic Gospels, the prophecy is applied to him in the third person, whereas in the Gospel of John it is the Forerunner himself who bears witness about himself using the words of the prophecy, which therefore express, in the first place, the awareness he has of himself. He did not become the Forerunner only after the meeting with Christ; he was the Forerunner even prior to it. This state was for him not an external fact but his inner self-determination and the awareness he had of himself. Those who were sent obviously did not understand this answer, just as they did not understand the prophecy itself. For the Forerunner is revealed only through Christ, whose Forerunner he is. But first they did not know Christ, and then they did not wish to believe in Him. Remaining deaf to his answer, those who were sent (they were experienced in the law — "they which were sent were of the Pharisees" [John 1:24] — and knew that, for Jews, the baptism with water was, in any case, an incomprehensible innovation) continued interrogating him, undeniably in order to test him: "Why baptizeth thou then, if thou be not that Christ, nor Elias, neither that prophet?" (John 1:25).

This element in the narrative about the Messiah — the questions of the Pharisees — is absent in the synoptic Gospels; the evangelist John thus *completes* their narrative. This element is totally convincing: the Pharisees were dismayed when they saw the influence of the preacher of repentance and could not counteract his preaching. And they tried to tempt the Forerunner with their habitual method, that of insidious interrogation. It was not by chance that, in response to their tempting questions, the Lord answered them with a question about the power of John's baptism (see Matt. 21:25-26; Mark 11:30-33; Luke 20:4-8). The Pharisees were hoping to receive an answer that would ruin John. Instead they heard from him the confession of the Forerunner that, according to the synoptic Gospels (see Matt. 3:11; Mark 1:8; Luke 3:16), the people had already repeatedly heard from him. He had already solemnly proclaimed — "cried out [*kekragen*]" (John 1:15) — his confession to the people, according to the same Fourth Gospel: "John answered them, saying, I baptize with water: but there standeth one among you, whom ye know not; He it is, who coming after me is preferred before me, whose shoe's latchet I am not worthy to unloose" (John 1:26-27).

The Evangelist so values the fullness and concreteness of the narrative of this event that he specially mentions the place where this occurred: "These things were done in Bethabara [*en Bethania*] beyond Jordan, where John was baptizing" (John 1:28).

This serves as the point of departure for a new narrative, the third, about the testimony of John, still in the first chapter: "The next day John seeth Jesus coming unto him, and saith, Behold the Lamb of God, which taketh away the sin of the world" (John 1:29). The Evangelist John speaks as an eyewitness here, for he was one of the Forerunner's disciples who were present at what was taking place and were astonished by what they heard. This explains the great concreteness and (contrary to the rationalistic critique) the historical authenticity of the Evangelist's narrative. It is noteworthy that this Evangelist-theologian, this seer of mysteries, whose theology soars as high as the eagle, tells us not only about the supraeternal Word but also about the Forerunner, precisely as the servant of the Word. While the other evangelists tell us about the Forerunner, the Evangelist-theologian shows us the Forerunner himself in the hidden recesses of his soul. It is this that constitutes the distinctive character of the Fourth Gospel as far as the Forerunner is concerned. It contains the confession of the latter. And these words of the Forerunner about Christ: "Behold the Lamb of God which taketh away the sin of the world," express a knowledge of Christ so perfect, such an understanding of his redemptive deed on the cross, that one can say that these few words contain the *whole Gospel*.

The Forerunner *knew* the mystery of the redemptive Passion, the mystery of the cross, and he proclaimed it. He proclaimed it with the words of that "Old Testament evangelist," that prophet, to whom it was given, out of the dark of the ages, to see and understand Golgotha. Chapter 53 of Isaiah, this miracle of miracles in the prophetic books, is, of course, wholly contained in the words of the Forerunner, but now as fulfillment: the paschal lamb, the prefiguration of the Lamb of God, is sacrificed as food for the faithful. The Forerunner is manifested here as the true Deutero-Isaiah. Isaiah's prophecy is miraculous not only because it fully fathoms the mystery of the redemptive passion but also because it contradicts the traditional expectation of the Jews, who are awaiting a Messiah who will be a king, not a suffering Messiah whose kingdom will be not of this world.

In his testimony, the Forerunner is truly an evangelist, which in fact is what the Holy Church calls him ("You are a preacher of Christ, an angel, an apostle"). The four Gospels do not contain a more concise and complete formula to express Christ's redemptive work than these words of the Forerunner (John 1:29). And the Forerunner continues his testimony: "This is he of whom I said, After me cometh a man which is preferred before me: for he was before me. And I knew him not: but that he should be made manifest to Israel, therefore am I come baptizing with water. And John bare record, saying [this repetition reinforces the importance of these words], I saw the Spirit descending from heaven like a dove, and it abode upon him. And I knew him not: but he that sent me to baptize with water, the same said unto me, Upon whom thou shalt see the Spirit descending, and remaining on him, the same is he which baptizeth with the Holy Spirit. And I saw, and bare record that this is the Son of God" (John 1:30-34).

This expresses both a complete Christology and the Forerunner's full awareness about himself, about his role. He proclaimed twice that he did not know the Messiah. By no means should this proclamation be understood in the sense that he never met and never saw his Relative, whom he recognized even when he was still in his mother's womb, during the Mother of God's visit. "Filled with the Holy Spirit" (Luke 1:41), Elisabeth attested that the Mother of the Lord had come to visit her. It is difficult to accept that, knowing that he was the Forerunner, the Forerunner did not pay exceptional attention to the One who, in secret in Nazareth, was increasing "in wisdom and stature, and in favour with God and man" (Luke 2:52). Although his stay in the desert made relations with other people difficult or impossible, John had an exceptional sensitivity, filled with grace, to the One whose Forerunner he was. Therefore, it is completely possible and even probable that the Forerunner *knew* Jesus of Nazareth. That is why when Jesus came to him to be baptized, he did not receive Him like a stranger, but instead met him with the words: "I have need to be baptized of thee, and comest thou to me?" (Matt. 3:14). Even if this were a prophetic illumination, it would show that Jesus was not unknown to him. The Forerunner was awaiting Jesus; he was filled entirely with this expectation of Jesus, as he himself said about himself: "That he should be made manifest to Israel, therefore am I come baptizing with water" (John 1:31).

However, the mystery of the Annunciation, of which even the angels were ignorant (1 Pet. 1:12; 1 Tim. 3:15), could not be accessible to any human being except to Her Who was the God-bearing womb. Nor could this mystery be known to the Forerunner, however much in his humility he might have bowed down before the Unknowable One who was to come, however much the expectation of Him might have filled his life, his thought, his heart, and his will. Another reason the Incarnation remained a mystery was that knowledge of Him was also knowledge of the Holy Trinity, of the Father, of the Son, and of the Spirit, and this to a degree of fullness that was never accorded to the Old Testament, which had only an obscure idea of the Trinity.

The Divine Incarnation is also a theophany, a manifestation of the entire Holy Trinity, of the Son who becomes incarnate, of the Father who sends Him into the World, and of the Holy Spirit who from the Father descends upon Him. And no human being had a revelation of this, except, of course, the Cause Herself of the Incarnation, who knew the Spirit that descended upon Her, the Son born of Her, and the Father revealed in Them. It is true that this revelation is not explicitly mentioned in the Gospels, but it is shown by the deed itself.

The other human being who, by reason of his role in the work of salvation, was chosen to receive this knowledge was the Baptist. By the baptism that he conferred, the Holy Spirit descended upon the One being baptized; and, in baptizing, the Baptist had to learn the mystery of the Incarnation and that of the Holy Trinity.

Before the Baptism, the Forerunner, to be sure, did not know that Jesus was "one of the Holy Trinity," that He was the Son of God; he could not attain such knowledge by his human powers alone; for him to gain such knowledge, the heavens had to open, the Holy Spirit had to descend, and the voice of the Father had to bear witness to His Beloved Son. True, John had a certain preliminary, Old Testament knowledge, and more than Old Testament knowledge, of the Holy Trinity, for the One who sent him to baptize told him that he would see the Spirit descending in the form of a dove upon the One being baptized. Therefore, that which took place was not unexpected, but long awaited and desired.

But can expectation and hope compare with accomplishment and fulfillment? And the descent of the Holy Spirit upon the One being baptized could not bypass the Baptist: he *saw* it — not with corporeal eyes but by illumination with the Holy Spirit. For if the baptismal waters of the Jordan were sanctified for the ages by this descent, can only a meager grace have been bestowed upon the Baptist? No: precisely this was the boundary separating the Old from the New Testament, but also uniting them in the person of the Baptist. Henceforth he is the herald of the Old and New Testament, but one who has already overcome the Old Testament. He is the one about whom it is said: "all the prophets and the law prophesied until John" (Matt. 11:13). Henceforth he is the fully mature and fully formed Forerunner, the Forerunner who has fulfilled his calling, who has done his work on earth and for whom a new ministry was beginning: the preaching in hell. And after the Baptism he completes his mission by attesting — to what? To the fact that "this is the Son of God" (John 1:34).

The Forerunner's testimony is not an isolated fact of his personal life, not a "biographical episode." It is an event in the history of the whole human race. He bears witness before and in the name of the whole human race that the Lord has been received and recognized on earth, that, in revealing itself, the mystery of the Holy Trinity has been perceived, and that the Son of God made man is called by His name.

One should also note that John's testimony fully anticipates Peter's profession (Matt. 16:16), and the other professions of faith that recognized Christ as the Son of God. There thus arises the question as to the relationship between these professions, particularly between those of Peter and John. As regards *content*, the profession of Peter (and others) does not add anything to John's profession, but even appears to repeat it: "Thou art the Christ, the Son of the living God." It is John who proclaims Jesus to be Christ, that is, the Anointed of the Holy Spirit; and John's testimony concerns precisely this anointing, this descent of the Spirit in the form of a dove. It signifies that Jesus is Christ, and that Christ is the Son of God. After John's profession of faith, does not Peter's lose its exclusive significance? No, it does not (although it is neither the first such profession nor the only one, as the Catholic literature usually exaggerates it to be). John's testimony is, after all is said and done, only the Forerunner's profession, representing the first *meeting*. This testimony must yet be lived through, so to speak, realized in experience, manifested to humanity in the persons of the apostles; it must become *post factum*, not *ante factum*. The Forerunner's profession *necessarily* precedes and conditions that of Peter, just as, in general, the coming of the Forerunner precedes and conditions the reception of the Messiah by the people. It is a goal to be attained, a promise to be fulfilled, the summons to a task that must be accomplished. It has a preliminary, anticipatory character. It is the prologue to the Gospel, but this prologue is essential and necessary.

And this inner prologue also becomes an external one as regards the work on earth of the Son of the Father, the Lamb of God. The link and transition between the two are indicated by the evangelist John himself in the same first chapter — unencompassable in content — of his Gospel: "Again the next day after [note the precision with which the Evangelist, an eyewitness and participant in this event, indicates the time of the latter, so memorable for him] John stood, and two of his disciples; and looking upon Jesus as he walked, he saith, Behold the Lamb of God!" (John 1:35-36). This time this is a repetition, in an abbreviated form, of words pronounced the previous day and assumed to have been already heard by the disciples. This repetition is expressly for these two disciples, Andrew and another disciple, not named, but who, according to Gospel interpreters and because of the context and the custom of the Evangelist not to name himself, was certainly John the Theologian himself. Thus, the Baptist repeats to the apostle Andrew, "the first called," and to the future Theologian (the one who was to write: "In the beginning was the Word, and the Word was with God, and the Word was God") the words he had previously spoken about the mystery of the One who is to come, the One he points out to them.

He is therefore the Forerunner of Christ not only in his own person but also in those disciples that he had chosen in advance and prepared for Him. And the disciples listened to their teacher: "And the two disciples heard him speak, and they followed Jesus" (John 1:37). This first decision to follow Christ, which is not mentioned by any other of the Evangelists, was the work of the Forerunner, come to prepare the way for the Lord. This same first chapter of the Gospel of John reveals what happened next: The disciples followed the new Teacher, supplied with the Forerunner's revelation about Him, a revelation that only slowly and with difficulty unfolded in their consciousness, although it contained in advance all that was to be revealed about Him. The Forerunner here is the apostle of apostles, the first apostle. His testimony contains the firstfruits of Christ's Church in the world; it is the beginning of the apostolate. At the same time he manifests here his ministry of Forerunner, offering in sacrifice himself and his disciples, as the friend of the Bridegroom. This second testimony of the Forerunner is also presented in the Gospel of John.

CHAPTER 5

The Friend of the Bridegroom

After the Baptism and his testimony about the Lord, John's work on earth had come to an end; his earthly life was reaching its conclusion. A new mission awaited him, whose mystery the Church suggests to us through iconography and liturgy: the preaching in hell. In the first three Evangelists the story of John's life passes directly from the baptism to imprisonment and martyrdom, as if the rest of his life did not have essential interest. This silence can be taken as a symbol of his life: after the baptism of the Lord, it is only a slow death, the extinction of the predawn star in the rays of the ascending Sun.[1]

Only the Gospel of John, which in this case, as in many others, completes the first three Gospels, gives us some indication of John's life after the Baptism, or rather, about his voluntary extinction, which concludes the Forerunner's spiritual feat (see John 3:23-36). We must first note a capital fact: John, who received knowledge of the mystery of the Messiah, did not follow Him, did not become His disciple, and even did not walk the land to preach His coming. Instead, he limited himself to bearing witness about Him before his disciples and the people in the place where he was baptizing at that time. His role is the same as before, and, as before, he continues to baptize. The only difference is that he changed the place of baptism, crossing from Bethany to Ænon near Salim, "because there was

---

1. St. Ambrose of Milan notes that the birth of John the Forerunner (24 June) coincides with the summer solstice, after which days become shorter and the sun moves farther away from the earth, whereas the birth of the Lord coincides with the winter solstice, after which days become longer and the sun moves closer to the earth. This comparison is often encountered in Church writings (notably in St. Augustine).

much water there" (John 3:23). That is, for a reason that does not have any relation to the preaching about Christ. Why? Because to follow Christ would not have accorded at all with the Forerunner's vocation and work. On the one hand, the mystery of the Incarnation was fully revealed to him at the Theophany; he did not need to be instructed in this mystery, as the apostles did in the course of the Savior's earthly life. The apostles were, as yet, only called *to become witnesses* (see Acts 1:8; 1 John 1:1-3), whereas the Forerunner was already one starting with the Baptism. But to preach the mystery of the Messiah alongside Him Who was the Messiah would, of course, have been inappropriate and even impossible.

John, therefore, did not become the apostle of apostles, or the first apostle. His path as Forerunner required this extinction, this feat of self-renunciation. To him, herald of the Old and New Testaments, it was not given to taste of the sweetness of abiding on earth alongside the Lord. The Forerunner revealed the Lord to the world, but then retreated into the shadows. It is remarkable that he continued to baptize as if nothing had happened. He continued to preach repentance and to confer the baptism of repentance that prepared the way to the encounter with the Messiah, who had already come but had not yet been recognized. This resembles the ceremony of the catechistic initiation, which, in our rite of baptism, precedes the baptism proper. Although the Messiah was already on earth, the preparation for the meeting with Him continued. The baptism of John therefore continued too, although it had never been the central aspect of his work, and now it was even less so. Baptism came to represent the Forerunner's continuing ministry as one of the prophets.

Apparently, a closely knit community was formed of John's disciples, united around its teacher and sometimes marked by human jealousy (see John 3:26). In conformity with the lofty ascetic spirit of its teacher, this community observed a strict discipline of fasting, which made John's disciples resemble the Pharisees: "Then came to him the disciples of John, saying, Why do we and the Pharisees fast oft, but thy disciples fast not?" (Matt. 9:14; also see Mark 2:18; Luke 5:33). In general, his disciples were characterized to some degree by the spirit of Old Testament ritualism. John also gave his disciples a certain rule of prayer (see Luke 11:1). His community had thus acquired a certain stability and even a certain permanence: it outlived John himself (see Acts 18:24-28; 19:1-7), later merging with various sects and gnostic groups.

John did not follow Christ, except in the person of his chosen disciples. He lived out his days, retaining his awareness of himself as the Forerunner, knowing that "He [Christ] must increase, but I must decrease"

(John 3:30). These words express the whole power of the Forerunner's feat, his self-renunciation, his will to kenosis, his limitless but active humility. The whole loftiness of his spiritual feat is manifested in this determination of his to be only the Forerunner, in the activeness of his humility, in his permanent relationship to Christ as the second one behind the First and Unique One.

This is expressed in the third chapter of the Gospel of John, in a new and final testimony, where the Forerunner calls himself the friend of the Bridegroom. The narrative here begins with an episode that is also recounted only in the Fourth Gospel. Here, someone who is clearly an eyewitness, the apostle John himself, reports: "After these things [after the first Passover in Jerusalem and the conversation with Nicodemus] came Jesus and his disciples unto the land of Judæa; and there he tarried with them, and baptized" (John 3:22). In John 4:2 it is clarified that "Jesus himself baptized not, but his disciples." This was baptism with water, which, in the opinion of many interpreters (including Chrysostom), did not differ from the baptism of John. This was not the Christian baptism. The disciples received the commandment concerning the latter only after the Resurrection, and the power to work it only after the Pentecost. It is thus more correct to think that, for Christ's disciples, among whom were disciples of John as well, baptism with water became a means, popularized by the preaching of the Baptist, to solemn repentance and the confession of sins. And in this Christ's disciples merge, as it were, with John's disciples, a merging that is expressed by the Evangelist in John 3:23: "and John also was baptizing."

Also, initially, the preachings of the Forerunner and of Christ were identical: "Repent: for the kingdom of heaven is at hand" (Matt. 3:2; 4:17). This baptism was the baptism of the approach of the kingdom of heaven, not its coming in power. It was not yet baptism "with the Holy Spirit, and with fire" (Matt. 3:11). And, as we have seen, Christ Himself did not baptize. He left this to His disciples, for He Himself baptized humankind only by sending down the Holy Spirit from the Father on the day of the Pentecost. This leads to another question: did Christ baptize anyone[2] and, in particular, did He baptize John? This question is provoked by these words of John: "I have need to be baptized of thee, and comest thou to me?" (Matt. 3:14).

---

2. Cf. S. Vishniakov, *St. John* (Moscow, 1879), pp. 240-243. There is a tradition (which is rather dubious, since it is found in an epistle of St. Evodius, which is not considered authentic) that Christ baptized His Mother, the Forerunner, and three disciples: Peter, James, and John.

There are different interpretations of the possibility implied by these words.³ But one should base one's interpretation of this passage only on firmly established facts. The first such fact is that John, like all people burdened with original sin, *needed* to be redeemed; and in Christ he had the Redeemer. The second is that John's martyrdom is a baptism with blood, but one that took place *before* Golgotha and the Pentecost. This baptism could acquire its full power only in the world beyond the grave, after Christ's descent into hell and after the Pentecost. But here we encounter the question of redemption beyond the grave, about which we have no revelation, although the Church indisputably contains this doctrine. Namely, the Church professes that Christ descended into hell (see 1 Pet. 3:19-20) and led therefrom the souls of the righteous, beginning with Adam and Eve. This is a traditional theme depicted on many icons of Christ's Resurrection.

In fact, we are not inclined to oppose or even to distinguish the baptisms performed by John's disciples and those performed by Jesus' disciples. Rather, we see them as one and the same form of the preaching of repentance. In both cases, the baptism has only a prefigurative significance in relation to the Christian baptism with water and the Holy Spirit. In the general plan of the Gospel of John, the passage in question tends to serve as a frame for John's testimony. That the baptism of Jesus had, so to speak, an episodic character is clear from the Evangelist's remark that the Lord stopped baptizing for the simple reason that He did not wish to provoke prematurely the vengeful wrath of the Judæans: "When therefore the Lord knew how the Pharisees had heard that Jesus made and baptized more disciples than John, (though Jesus himself baptized not, but his disciples,) he left Judæa, and departed again into Galilee" (John 4:1-3). This, evidently, could not have happened if the baptism had acquired a universal Christian significance. But the symbolic and spiritual character of the Gospel of John compels certain (Western) interpreters to seek here too some more profound interpretation. They tend to find here a secret polemic between the disciples of John and those of Jesus, as well as the abolition of the baptism of John and its replacement by that of Christ. However, as we have already said, there is neither abolition nor replacement here: Christ baptized through the intermediary of His disciples *alongside* John, and with the same baptism. Christ did not consider John's baptism outdated and moribund.

---

3. For example, according to the opinion of St. John of Damascus (in *True Exposition of the Orthodox Faith,* book IV, chapter 9): "John was baptized by placing his hands on the Divine head of the Lord and by his own blood."

In fact, the baptism of repentance did not become outdated until the Pentecost. The latter was in fact the baptism with Spirit and fire promised by the Baptist. And the baptism of John was not abolished until Christ's commandment to baptize "in the name of the Father, of the Son, and of the Holy Spirit" (see Matt. 28:19). And this Christian baptism becomes effective only after the Pentecost (cf. Acts 1, as well as the breathing of the Holy Spirit by Christ upon the apostles as recorded in John 20:22). Here the baptism of John is directly *opposed* to the Pentecost and is implicitly abolished by the latter. More precisely, it is transcended and absorbed by the Pentecost: "John . . . baptized with water; but ye shall be baptized with the Holy Spirit not many days hence" (Acts 1:5). After the descent of the Holy Spirit the apostle Peter was asked after his sermon: "Men and brethren, what shall we do?" His response was: "Repent, and be baptized every one of you in the name of Jesus Christ for the remission of sins, and ye shall receive the gift of the Holy Spirit" (Acts 2:37-38). That is, he already expressly institutes baptism in the Name of Christ in the Holy Spirit, and at the same time abolishes and replaces the baptism of John (which, insofar as it survives for a time, is precisely characterized by the absence of the gifts of the Spirit, and even a condition where they are not known).

In contrast, adherents of the aforementioned interpretation support it by comparing baptism to the miraculous transformation of water into wine in Cana of Galilee. Through this miracle, they say, the "element of water," and therefore the whole of the baptism of John, were abolished and deprived of their meaning, as it were. But no one "element of water" exists. Rather, there are the baptismal waters "with the blessing of the Jordan," and there is the Eucharistic water of the "sacred mixture" ("and forthwith came there out blood and water" [John 19:34]).[4] The miracle of Cana of Galilee is a prefiguration of the divine Eucharist. This *first* miracle, around which all the other miracles are centered, is a prefiguration of the redemption and of the redemptive sacrifice. Therefore, it is said about this miracle: "This beginning of miracles did Jesus in Cana of Galilee, and manifested forth his glory; and his disciples believed on him" (John 2:11). Although water is spoken of in this narrative, it has nothing to do with baptism.

It is more justifiable to compare John 3 with John 13, the mysterious passage that describes how Jesus washed His disciples' feet before the Last Supper. Here again we have water, not eucharistic but rather baptismal

---

4. See Bulgakov's essay "The Holy Grail," translated by Boris Jakim in *The Holy Grail and the Eucharist* (Hudson, NY: Lindisfarne Books, 1997), pp. 23-61. — Trans.

water, and precisely that of the baptism of repentance. When Peter resists the washing of his feet, Jesus answers him severely: "If I wash thee not, thou hast no part with me" (John 13:8). But when Peter announces that he is ready to have not only his feet washed but also his hands and his head, Jesus answers: "He that is washed needeth not save to wash his feet, but is clean every whit" (John 13:10).

This also refers to the baptism of repentance, to the preparatory one, for without repentance it is impossible to approach the Kingdom of God. But a supplementary and particular repentance, in the form of the washing of the feet, and only of the feet, is required here for admission to the sacrament of the Body and Blood. At the Last Supper the apostles are, even prior to baptism, admitted to the sacrament of Communion. They have not yet died with Christ, not yet been baptized in His passion, but they become one Body with Him. And the Lord, in washing their feet, operates upon them a purification analogous to baptism, one that is vicarious for this particular need (analogous to confession before communion), as well as an act of humility (see John 13:13-17). For before Christ died, before His side was pierced and blood and water flowed out of it, the Communion offered to His disciples was a kind of miraculous *anticipation* of the event, as well as the end and fulfillment of the signs, the first of which was accomplished at Cana of Galilee. The washing of feet was also an *anticipation* of the baptism that could take place only at the Pentecost after the Lord's salvific Passion, Resurrection, and Ascension.

But this act of the Lord's is, of course, not germane to the question of the relationship between the baptism of Christ and that of John, as posed in the third chapter of the Gospel of John. What is essential in John 13 is the fact that the Lord Himself personally washes the feet of His disciples, whereas in John 3 it was not He but His disciples who baptized. Moreover, the events leading up to the Last Supper took place long after John's death, when the very question of his baptism had ceased to exist (except in the circle of his zealous disciples).

Thus, Jesus' disciples were baptizing, "and John also was baptizing in Ænon near to Salim, because there was much water there: and they came, and were baptized. . . . Then there arose a question between some of John's disciples and the Jews about purifying" (John 3:23, 25). Evidently, the dispute with these unidentified Jews touched on the purifying power of the two baptisms, because in connection with this dispute it is stated further: "And they came unto John, and said unto him, Rabbi [this solemn and respectful form of address shows their desire to bestow a special honor on their teacher, as well as to underscore the importance of the question], he that was with thee beyond Jordan, to whom thou barest witness, behold, the same baptizeth, and all men come to him" (John 3:26). These words show that, even though the disciples of John could not fail to pay attention to the One who was baptized by him and to his testimony about the Lamb of God, they did not understand this testimony with their hearts (in contrast to the two disciples who followed Jesus and led others to Him). It is jealousy and competitiveness that speak in them here; and one clearly senses that the disciples feel that an offense has been done to the honor of the one they call Rabbi in the unique and exclusive sense of this term.

The situation was such that it led the Forerunner to explain himself in a testimony where he diminished himself and preached about Christ. In this third and final testimony the Forerunner finds such ardent and loving words for the One whom his disciples, in their irrational jealousy, thought to be his rival that this speech can truly be called the *hymn* of the Forerunner, his song of love for the Bridegroom. However, this is not a "song of songs" of the bride's love for her Bridegroom, but the hymn of His friend. This is no longer self-diminishing humility but joyously triumphant humility. This is the triumph of the Forerunner.

John first of all teaches his disciples to accept the divine election, to accept one's fate with a humble wisdom: "John answered and said, A man can receive nothing, except it be given him from heaven. Ye yourselves bear me witness, that I said, I am not the Christ, but that I am sent before him" (John 3:27-28). Thus having banished the inappropriate jealousy, John reveals the joy that overfills his Forerunner's heart: "He that hath the bride is the bridegroom: but the friend of the bridegroom, which standeth and heareth him, rejoiceth greatly because of the bridegroom's voice: this my joy therefore is fulfilled" (John 3:29).

"The friend of the bridegroom." This expression evokes, first of all, the familiar, traditional image of the bridegroom's confidant and closest companion, but one who is only a servant, a subaltern. It is required of the friend that he be faithful, for he could prove to be untrustworthy by departing from his subordinate role and proclaiming himself to be the bridegroom. Thus, Eliezer, the servant of Abraham, was entrusted with seeking a wife for Isaac, and he found Rebecca. But this familiar image serves here only as the outer shell for an inner meaning that refers to the most mysterious and moving images of the Old and New Testament. In John's concise words there rises before us the whole mysterious symbolism of the "Song of Songs," of Psalm 45, and of the prophets, as well as of the Epistle to the Ephesians and of Revelation. If in what John says about the Lamb of God we hear an echo of the prophecy of Isaiah 53, what he says about the Bridegroom and the Bride is permeated with the Song of Songs. The Bridegroom is Christ, the Bride is the Church. John is present at this mysterious betrothal; he sees it with the eye of a prophet, and rejoices in it not as a peripheral observer but as a friend, the friend of the Bridegroom. His joy is not for himself; it is for another, for his Friend. Nowhere else does Scripture speak about the friend of the Bridegroom, for John is the unique one.

The Church can be considered as a Bride in the narrow, limited sense of a chosen people, of a Christian community; and it can also signify the universal Church. It can be any Christian soul. And in a special, exceptional sense, it is the personal crown of the Church, the "Unwedded Bride," the Mother of God. But here we again return to the content of the icon *Deisis*: the Bride and the friend stand together before the Bridegroom.

The Old Testament Song of Songs knows only the bridegroom and the bride; it does not know the friend of the bridegroom. It speaks of the joy and bliss of the union of the human with the divine, of the deification of the human essence. It does not speak of the feat and joy of the voluntary kenosis of the human essence, of dying for another, as the precondition of this union. It does not speak of the triumphant joy of humility, which is also the nuptial joy of the Forerunner, the friend of the Bridegroom. The friend found the bride and gives her to the Bridegroom. The Forerunner represents the human essence in its male principle: here this essence is humbled to the point of total self-renunciation. The humility of the Bride, of the female human essence, upon which the Almighty "cast a glance," is united with that of the friend, who goes out to meet the Bridegroom in the name of the whole human race. The Bridegroom receives the love of the *whole* human being, female and male. "This my joy . . . is fulfilled [*hē chara hē emēn*]" (John 3:29). The article imparts an exhaustive determinacy to the concept. That which the Forerunner's soul had desired, that which had filled his entire life, is now before his eyes. And in the presence of this realization, filled with the joy of total self-renunciation in love, he pronounces his Forerunner's profession of faith: "he must increase, but I must decrease" (John 3:30). This is perfect joy.

No man has ever pronounced or can pronounce simpler, more exhaustive, and powerful words of self-renouncing love. Here the Forerunner also makes perfectly clear that he knows that his life is finished, that his work is done, that his goal is attained, and that what remains for him is only a quiet fading in anticipation of an end that is approaching. *The friend of the Bridegroom* . . . That is who the Forerunner of the Lord was. That was his personal vocation, service, and feat. But was it only personal? We observe that feats vary: there are martyrs, desert hermits, holy fools, saintly bishops, saintly women. And we honor each of these feats, but at the same time we do not see in any of them a calling common and obligatory for all, for there are different gifts and ministries. But there *is* a spiritual feat, obligatory for all, without which there is no salvation and which is an element of all forms of saintliness. Thus, every soul that is united with Christ through the Church becomes a bride of Christ, Who is born in her, realizing His eternal divine birth and uniting Himself with her in spiritual marriage, precisely in the name of Christ and the Church. For this reason, the Ever-Virgin too, the Mother of God and the Unwedded Bride, is not only the crown of the Church but also her image, her archetype.

Similarly, the Forerunner, as the friend of the Bridegroom, is the archetype of ecclesialization, taken from the standpoint of human feat. Every soul that comes to Christ must become not only the bride but also the friend of the Bridegroom; that is, it must immolate its human selfhood, its human — and not only human but also Luciferian — self-assertion; it must cast off auto-theism and anthropo-theism, and experience the voluntary death of radical self-giving. Concerning this, the Lord said: "For whosoever will save his life shall lose it: but whosoever will lose his life for my sake, the same shall save it" (Luke 9:24; also Matt. 16:25; Mark 8:35). Also: "Verily, verily, I say unto you, Except a corn of wheat fall into the ground and die, it abideth alone: but if it die, it bringeth forth much fruit. He that loveth his life shall lose it; and he that hateth his life in this world shall keep it unto life eternal" (John 12:24-25). Everyone who comes to Christ must sacrifice his ego, must say about himself: He must increase in me, but I must decrease — I must become a friend of the Bridegroom, who does not desire anything of his own and who does not demand anything for himself: "not I, but Christ liveth in me" (Gal. 2:20).

Spiritual life always consists of two mutually connected and mutually opposed acts: crucifixion and resurrection, human feat and illumination by grace. In order to take part in the marriage feast of the Lamb and become worthy of spiritual marriage, the soul must accomplish this first act by following the path of the preacher of repentance, the friend of the Bridegroom, the Forerunner of Christ.

After testifying about himself, the Forerunner returns to his testimony about the Bridegroom, and his words show once again that he has full knowledge of the mystery of the Incarnation as well as that of the

Holy Trinity: "He that cometh from above is above all: he that is of the earth is earthly, and speaketh of the earth: he that cometh from heaven is above all" (John 3:31). The opposition between the one who is earthly and the one who comes from heaven concerns, evidently, first of all the Baptist in relation to Christ, but also every human being. Christ comes from heaven. "And what he hath seen and heard, that he testifieth; and no man receiveth his testimony. He that hath received his testimony hath set to his seal that God is true. For he whom God hath sent speaketh the words of God" (John 3:32-34).

This expresses the whole opposition between the "world" and God, which, in general, is one of the essential themes of the good news of the fourth Gospel. The phrase, "he whom God hath sent speaketh the words of God," can refer, first of all, to the Son. However, it can also be interpreted as referring to any worshipper of God. (This interpretation is suggested by the Russian synodal translation.) This ambiguity, which, of course, is not accidental, also corresponds to the dual signification of the words that follow: "God giveth not the Spirit by measure" (John 3:34). But having spoken in general of the descent of Christ from heaven, John returns to his testimony about the entire Holy Trinity: "for God giveth not the Spirit by measure." "The Father loveth the Son, and hath given all things into his hand" (John 3:35).

Thus we find here the doctrine that the Holy Spirit is given *not by measure*. This signifies, first of all, that the Spirit sent from the Father rests "immeasurably," fully upon the Son. Second, it signifies that the gifts of the Spirit are distributed not according to a single, *determinate* measure, but without measure, that is, multifariously and multitudinously, from power to power, and from glory to glory. The Forerunner expresses here the law of spiritual growth, and these words represent the fundamental text for pneumatology; they contain the key to the doctrine of the kingdom of grace and the kingdom of glory, the doctrine of the church. This text therefore has a dual meaning and refers both to the Son of God, Who is above all measure in His possession of the gifts of the Holy Spirit, and to creatures, who are always below the full measure and therefore have *eternal* life in growth in the Holy Spirit.

There is no measure for the Son of God in His Divinity; and there is no measure for the sons of God according to grace in their deification: Bottomless is the ocean of divine life and infinite is the immersion into this bottomless abyss.

Revealed here is the interrelationship of the Father and the Son, who is the Father's self-renouncing love. "The Father . . . hath given all things into his hand" (John 3:35) corresponds to the prologue's words "All things were made by him" (John 1:3), and this correspondence concerns not only the supra-eternal aspect of the creation of the world but also the salvation of the world, the Kingdom of God.

Thus, the testimony of John has as its object here not solely Christ but the entire Holy Trinity. His words are a doctrinal interpretation of the event of the Theophany, whose witness he was. All three synoptic Gospels tell the story of this event, and the Gospel of John, as it is wont to do, complements them. In the Gospel of John the Theologian, this is, one can say, the theology of the Theophany.

John's testimony ends with the doctrine of salvation: "He that believeth on the Son hath everlasting life: and he that believeth not the Son shall not see life; but the wrath of God abideth on him" (John 3:36). Here, in a few words, the Baptist expresses the very essence of the preaching of the Gospel concerning eternal life, the message the Lord Himself expounds at the most solemn hour of His earthly preaching, after the Last Supper, in the solemn "high priest's" prayer: "This is life eternal, that they might know thee the only true God, and Jesus Christ, whom thou hast sent" (John 17:3). And after the Resurrection, Jesus again tells His disciples: "He that believeth and is baptized shall be saved; but he that believeth not shall be damned" (Mark 16:16).

These words of the Baptist express *the fullness of the knowledge that he had of Christ.* These words of the Forerunner, when taken together in connection with his preceding testimony about Christ, cannot be characterized as anything else but the *Gospel of the Forerunner.* Prior to the end of his earthly life and his departure to preach in the world beyond the grave, it was given to the Forerunner to explain the Theophany as it was manifested in the descent of the Holy Spirit upon Christ, as well as upon the waters of the Jordan and upon him himself. It was given to him to know the whole mystery of our salvation, at least in its spiritual essence, not in its historical realization (which was yet to come). The Theophany, which was Christ's personal Pentecost according to His human nature, was also a kind of preliminary Pentecost for the Forerunner, for it is not as an Old Testament prophet but as a New Testament evangelist that he speaks these words. No human knowledge has the capacity to know this mystery that is hidden from the angels themselves, especially prior to its full realization. Only the inspiration of the Holy Spirit, the special anointedness of the Forerunner, could bring his consciousness to such a fullness of clarity. That is why he could accomplish the mission that the Holy Church celebrates: "To those in hell he preached the good news of the God who appeared in the flesh, who takes upon Himself the sin of the world, and who bestows His boundless mercy" (troparion of the Forerunner).

The Evangelist does not indicate how long before his death the Baptist gave this testimony. He only mentions, not without establishing an inner relation between the two facts, that "John was not yet cast into prison" (John 3:24).

Thus ends the fourth Gospel's narrative concerning John, but his testimony is confirmed by the One Who was the subject of this testimony. In His speech that follows the healing of the lame man, the Lord speaks about Himself, and, referring to John's testimony about Him, He says (clearly after the death of John): "If I bear witness of myself, my witness is not true [of course, in the eyes of the Pharisees, by reason of their formalism]. There is another that beareth witness of me; and I know that the witness which he witnesseth of me is true. Ye sent unto John, and he bare witness unto the truth. But I receive not testimony from man: but these things I say, that ye might be saved. He was a burning and a shining light: and ye were willing for a season to rejoice in his light. But I have a greater witness that that of John: for the works which the Father hath given me to finish, the same works that I do, bear witness of me, that the Father hath sent me" (John 5:31-36). (Below we will return to this meaning of works, as a witness of Christ.)

The Lord calls his witness John "a burning and a shining light." In order to grasp fully the significance of this image, one must remember that images of light and darkness are found throughout the Gospel of John and have, so to speak, a fundamental significance. Such images appear precisely in the Savior's speech in the same third chapter (3:19-21). In the fourth Gospel it has already been said about John that "he was not that Light, but was sent to bear witness of that Light" (John 1:8). He was a lamp which radiated not its own light and about which it is said that not only did it reflect this Light of another but it itself was burning and therefore shining. It is remarkable that here John is characterized not according to his mission, as the Angel sent to prepare the way for the Lord or as the voice crying in the wilderness, but according to his own essence: he burned with the Light, i.e., God, and shined with God "like a torch radiating Divine light," a coal of the Divine altar.

This brings him close to the angelic world, and by virtue of his ceaseless presence before God and illumination by the Holy Spirit, he is called an angel: "in heaven . . . angels . . . do always behold the face of my Father which is in heaven" (Matt. 18:10). But by his nature he is nevertheless a human being, and, as a human being equal to the angels, uniting in himself the *fullness* of the human essence and the *loftiness and proximity to God* of the angelic essence, he therefore stands higher than the angels (as is made clear by the icons of this subject), as does another human being, the Mother of God, who is "more venerable than the cherubim and incomparably more glorious than the seraphim," as the Church's prayer celebrates Her. Thus, the Lord's testimony about John contains the mystery of the Forerunner's glorification, which is fully revealed by the Church.

The third chapter of the Gospel of John, which contains such important testimony about the Forerunner, has an epilogue, as it were, in John 10:40-42, in the form of a personal remembrance (this testimony of an eyewitness provides a new indication of the historical authenticity of the text). After the Savior's speech following the healing of the blind man, but prior to the raising of Lazarus (chapter 11) and therefore prior to the third Passover, more than two years after the baptism, testimony, and death of John, Jesus "went away again beyond Jordan into the place where John at first baptized; and there he abode" (John 10:40). It was there that Jesus learned of Lazarus's sickness, after which he stayed another two days there (see John 11:6). This place could, naturally, not fail to evoke memories of John and of his testimony in those who were present then. And this detail, so moving in its concreteness, is the final, concluding accord, as it were, of the Fourth Gospel's story of John, of this astonishing symphonic composition. "And many resorted unto him, and said, John did no miracle: but all things that John spake of this man [Jesus] were true" (John 10:41). And clearly, in connection with this posthumous remembrance of John's testimony, "many believed on Him there" (John 10:42). And thus, the seed of his words bore fruit: some seeds sprout at once, while others sprout only after abiding long in the earth without showing signs of life.

These concluding words express what is most significant in the figure of John: in the humility of his ministry he was not a worker of miracles, but a witness of the truth about the Truth. And that constitutes his particular greatness. For there were many workers of miracles before John among the men pleasing to God, but none greater than he was born of women. And he was so great that he did not work a "sign." The work of his life had but one, unique "sign" — he himself, the friend of the Bridegroom, in his humility.

CHAPTER 6

The Forerunner's Agony and the Savior's Testimony about Him

The story of what happened to John after the baptism, that is, the story of his testimony about Christ, figures only in the Gospel of John, in conformity with the task this Gospel sets for itself and its composition. The other Evangelists tell us nothing more about John until his imprisonment and thus the end of his preaching. They thus implicitly confirm that the Baptist's earthly life reached its end with the baptism and that his activity was exhausted by preaching and the baptism of repentance.

The Evangelist Luke mentions John's imprisonment, one of Herod's evil deeds, as a generally known fact, at the same time that he speaks of John's preaching, even before mentioning the Savior's baptism.[1] The Evangelist Matthew also mentions in passing John's imprisonment, taking for granted that it was publicly known (see Matt. 11:2). The Evangelist John does the same. The Evangelist Mark combines the story of the imprisonment with that of the Forerunner's death (see Mark 6:17-19). The duration of the Forerunner's public ministry in the community is not known precisely, but it is probable that it lasted a few months, perhaps half a year.[2]

When the veil of silence about him is lifted slightly, we see him already in prison. And it is during this imprisonment that one of the important events of his life transpires. Two of the Evangelists judged it necessary

---

1. As is known, we can find certain details of this fact in Flavius Josephus (*De Bell. Iud.*, XVIII:5, 2), who calls John "the Baptist."

2. S. Vishniakov, *St. John* (Moscow, 1879), p. 304.

to recount this event, despite the meagerness with which, in general and in particular, they usually describe anything touching upon the Forerunner. This event is the sending of the disciples (with whom the Forerunner could certainly have been in communication even in prison) to the Savior. John's testimony concerned only the Messiah who was coming into the world. But when he was in prison, this coming had already taken place. The miracles worked by the Lord had greatly moved minds and hearts: "And there came a fear on all: and they glorified God, saying, That a great prophet is risen up among us; and, That God hath visited his people. And this rumour of him went forth throughout all Judæa, and throughout all the region round about. And the disciples of John shewed him of all these things" (Luke 7:16-18). Or, more briefly, in Matthew 11:2: "Now when John had heard in prison the works of Christ, he sent two of his disciples."

With what passionate interest the Forerunner must have heard all these rumors, the Forerunner who never had his own life, but who lived in Him about Whom he was now hearing! About this we can only keep pious silence. But the more attentive we must then be to the words that pierced this silence and about which the Gospels found it necessary to tell us. And here is what these words were: "He sent two of his disciples, And said unto him, Art thou he that should come, or do we look for another?" (Matt. 11:2-3). "And John calling unto him two of his disciples sent them to Jesus, saying, Art thou he that should come? or look we for another? When the men were come unto him, they said, John Baptist hath sent us unto thee, saying, Art thou he that should come? or look we for another?" (Luke 7:19-20). There cannot be a more astonishingly unexpected question. How could such a question be asked by one who saw the Spirit descend in the form of a dove in the opened heavens and heard the Father's voice speaking about His beloved Son? The one who bore witness to the Lamb of God and who thus announced the Good News in all its fullness, attesting to eternal life through the Son of God — could he be in doubt now? Could this be the same John? The rationalistic critique radically denies all historical value to what the Gospel of John says on this subject and thus simplifies the problem: John's testimonies are considered to be pious inventions of the unknown author of the fourth Gospel and should not be accepted as actual facts; moreover, the synoptics do not know them. But the entire difficulty remains, even within the limits of the synoptic narratives: with this question the Forerunner erases his own past, as it were, crosses out his whole life and its achievements, by suddenly leaving the question of the Messiah open: "Art thou he that should come? or look we for another?"

The Forerunner's Agony and the Savior's Testimony about Him

We repeat: this is the most tragic question that has ever resounded in the human soul. We must listen to it honestly and sincerely without shutting our ears with all kinds of apologetic considerations. And it is natural that this question has always been a stumbling block in the ecclesiastical literature, both Eastern and Western, both ancient and modern. First of all, attempts have been made to evade the problem by pedagogical considerations, so to speak. According to this interpretation, the question was posed and the answer was needed not for John himself but for his disciples, who did not wish, as we have seen, to free themselves of an inappropriate jealousy with regard to the new Teacher. In other words, this was an object lesson for the disciples. Having a presentiment of his imminent death, the Forerunner wished to teach his disciples a lesson about the promised Messiah. Thus, the question he asked, "Art thou he that should come? or look we for another?" is not a real question but a rhetorical one. Its sole aim is to provoke the Savior's answering discourse.

The opinion that John had posed his question for the sake of his disciples has been widespread since ancient times both in the patristic and in the secular literature.[3] This opinion comes to mind naturally and legitimately. It would even be strange if it did not, since it is, so to speak, suggested by the context of the Gospel narrative. And in a certain sense it can be accepted without difficulty. Indeed, hitherto the Forerunner had considered it his mission to be the Messiah's personal witness, seeing Him and pointing Him out to the people and to his disciples. But now he is deprived of this possibility of seeing and hearing Him; the prison walls separate him from the world; but they do not prevent news of Him from reaching the Forerunner or the Forerunner from communicating with Him through messengers. And here, before departing, the Forerunner wishes, through Jesus Himself, to bear witness about Him, to emplace in Him, as it were, and to fulfill through Him once again, his ministry of Forerunner. Insofar as the sending of the disciples is a continuation of the same testimony about Christ that is related to us in the fourth Gospel, there is no discontinuity, no contradiction here. The Forerunner, even when he is in prison, has no other thought and no other care than to bear witness about the Messiah. And it is precisely in this sense that the question is asked: "Art thou he that should come [i.e., the Messiah]? or look we for another?" The question is asked in such a way that it evokes self-testimony, admits only a direct — affirmative or negative —

---

3. We can find a collection of such testimonies (of St. John Chrysostom, St. Hilary, St. Cyril of Alexandria et al.) in Vishniakov.

answer. And since the negative answer is, of course, excluded, the answer can only be affirmative. And the affirmative answer did follow, though perhaps in a form less explicit than presupposed by the question (about this, see below).

This thesis, within its limits, is thus indisputable. Nevertheless, one can ask if it truly explains the fact of the sending of the disciples by the Forerunner, with the question itself being of negligible value. Does this question contain only an object lesson, or does the very *question* remain a question . . . of the Forerunner? When we attentively examine the scriptural text, we must reject in advance as inappropriate the presupposition that before us something is taking place according to a preconceived plan and agreement: the Forerunner asks, and the Messiah answers. One must also exclude in advance the presupposition that this question has the character of a putting to the test, with an ulterior motive, like the questions posed to Christ by the scribes and the Pharisees in order to trick Him. Christ too sometimes answered a question by asking one of His own, in order to put His questioners to the test, as in the case of the baptism of John (see Matt. 21:23-37; Mark 11:27-33; Luke 20:1-8). But that is not the case here: The question has full force for both the questioner and the answerer. The question is posed to Christ through the intermediary of the disciples, not by the disciples and not for the disciples, but by John himself, who, since he was imprisoned, could ask only in this manner: "When the men were come unto him, they said, John Baptist hath sent us unto thee, saying" (Luke 7:20); and the answer is addressed directly to John without intermediary: "Jesus answered and said unto them, Go and shew John again those things which ye do hear and see" (Matt. 11:4; Luke 7:22). This is a direct conversation between Christ and John through obligatory intermediaries, who, of course, receive instruction for themselves here, though without ceasing to be intermediaries.

There is no doubt that John heard the answer that was addressed to him. What did he hear? Was that terrifying and tragic "or" removed? Was it answered? The Lord did not give a *direct* answer to the question whether He was the Messiah, the One who is to come [*ho erchomenos*] (which was the usual name for the Messiah in the language of the time). He only referred to His messianic works: "The blind receive their sight, and the lame walk, the lepers are cleansed, and the deaf hear, the dead are raised up, and the poor have the gospel preached to them" (Matt. 11:5; cf. Luke 7:22). These words represent only a general description of what was taking place (as we have seen, the Lord considered His works to be a testimony about Himself that was more significant than the testimony of John: see John

5:36). This is also a paraphrase of the messianic prophecy, which the Forerunner, of course, knew very well (Isa. 29:8; 35:5-6; 61:1-3).

But — and this is the most important thing here — these words indubitably demonstrate a desire to evade a direct answer, a disinclination to answer the question. After all, one must remember that John already had knowledge of all of these works. Matthew and Luke clearly point to these works as the reason or occasion for the sending of the disciples: "Now when John had heard in prison the works of Christ, he sent two of his disciples" (Matt. 11:2; in Luke 7:18 the sending is preceded by the fact that "the disciples of John shewed him of all these things"). Thus, it is precisely because John already knew all this that he asked: "Art thou he that should come? or look we for another?" as if he found no certitude in himself. But the Lord, in evading a direct answer, did not give him this certitude.

It is easy to see to what extent a purely pedagogical interpretation of John's sending of the disciples is complicated by the indirect character of the answer. This answer did not essentially yield more than what John's disciples already knew, but this was clearly not decisive for believing in Jesus as the Messiah. For the great prophets too worked miracles, though, to be sure, no one had ever worked miracles such as these. But the difference was not easy to discern for contemporaries, some of whom considered Jesus to be "John the Baptist: some Elias; and others, Jeremias, or one of the prophets" (Matt. 16:14).

Therefore, Jesus answers indirectly, as if with a question. John's question was: Who is he who accomplishes such works? And the answer was: he is the one who accomplishes them. Who is he, then? It was clear that John's question was returned to him; and therefore there was no answer, for an answer was unnecessary. And this absence of an answer, the fact that there was no need for one, is the essential thing here. Not only did the Savior not judge it necessary to give a direct answer, but, in a certain sense, he even rejected the question itself, by adding: "And blessed is he [*makarios*: the singular, not the plural, which would have been the case if these words referred to the two disciples who had been sent, or to all the disciples of John], whosoever shall not be offended in me" (Matt. 11:6; Luke 7:23).

To whom do these words refer, these words that cry out to be compared with the Lord's words to the apostle Thomas: "Blessed are they that have not seen, and yet have believed" (John 20:29)? The proponents of the pedagogical interpretation are compelled to refer these words solely to John's disciples. They, of course, do refer to them as well, but in the same sense as they refer to all who surround Christ and can be "offended in"

Him. But, most specifically, they clearly refer to John himself (to which the singular *makarios* implicitly attests). These words contain an encouraging, affirmative, and, in any case, *personal* answer to John. A secret conversation takes place here with John, and he receives the salvific answer that he needs. This is strange, because the Lord's words sound like a reproach or, rather, like a warning. But they contain not a condemnation but a blessing: Blessed is John because he was not "offended in" Him, despite the test and fiery temptation to which he was subjected. The first half of Christ's answer was addressed to all, for all had seen and could know the prophecies; while the second half is a personal answer to John. The second half should clearly be understood in a positive sense; otherwise, these words would contain a clear condemnation, before his disciples, of the imprisoned Baptist. And the fact that Christ's words have such a sense of blessing is confirmed most of all by the continuation of this speech, also about John, but now addressed to the people: "As they departed, Jesus began to say unto the multitudes concerning John" (Matt. 11:7; cf. Luke 7:24). This speech glorified John as the greatest born of women, one of those in whom "wisdom is justified of her children" (Matt. 11:11, 19; Luke 7:28, 35).

This speech, this preaching about John, occupies the central place in the Gospel narrative about him. And, of course, it could not have been said if John had been "offended in" Him and corrupted thereby. On the contrary, here John is praised for the firmness of his faith, manifested in the temptations and trials through which he had passed.

And so, what happened to John in prison, and what is the significance of the sending of the disciples to Christ? What was the content of the silent conversation between Christ and the Forerunner, which those who were present may not have perceived but which both Christ and the Forerunner understood? Why did John nevertheless send his disciples with the question that contained this "or"?

Here we permit ourselves to present our own hypothesis, without pretending that it is irrefutable. Rather, we consider that, in the case of such mysterious and cryptic questions for which there is no, and can be no, single exhaustive answer, it is permissible to offer one's personal suppositions.

The Gospel text, even if it does not directly contradict it, does not furnish any positive grounds for referring the Forerunner's question only to his disciples, and not to him himself. On the contrary, if it is read in an unprejudiced manner, the text clearly and unambiguously shows that John posed the question through the intermediary of his disciples and the Lord's answer was addressed precisely to John, although through the intermediary of his disciples. Therefore, one cannot evade the question, but must confront it in all its significance: What did the question signify *for John* and how could he ask it in "either/or" form? How could he allow the possibility of either an affirmative or a negative answer? How could the question have arisen in John after the Theophany, after he himself had announced the Glad Tidings, after a saintly life devoted to a *single* thought, a *single* love, a *single* knowledge? How could the friend of the Bridegroom, who had rejoiced in Him with perfect joy (see John 3), suddenly doubt whether this was the Bridegroom? How could he allow that it may be that the Bridegroom has not yet come and that one must await another? Could he have *forgotten* what he had seen and heard at the baptism? Could he have lost the knowledge that he had gained?

It is not suprising that, given the difficulty and incomprehensibility of these questions, one seeks, first of all, to evade them, to explain them in some other way. But we have already rejected this path. Lack of faith then whispers to us the possibility of another path, a broader one: the path of various *psychological* explanations grounded in the Forerunner's temporary or general *weakness*. The Forerunner was supposedly worn down in prison by the burden of the doubts that had seized him concerning certain aspects of the Messiah's coming. He supposedly became impatient awaiting the messianic kingdom, and so on and so forth. These psychological explanations, grounded in the Forerunner's personal weakness, have different variants, whose details are of no interest. But all of them have in common the fact that they denigrate the Forerunner, presuming him to be subject to profound vacillations of faith and mood that are simply incompatible with his lofty ministry and spiritual power. In fact, is it possible to attribute to the Forerunner a spiritual limitation and blindness that could lead to his doubting the Messiah because His figure did not conform to the Jewish messianic yearnings? But where then is his profound knowledge about Christ? Where is his Gospel of Christ, related by the fourth Evangelist (if, of course, one does not, like the rationalistic critics, simply reject this narrative)? This would signify a decline, if not a spiritual fall, which, of course, is impermissible and about which we, of course, have no indication. And given such a decline or fall, could the Lord have spoken about John as He did after the departure of his disciples? Something is not right here. But there is even less justification to see here the influence of the fear of death, which can sometimes be overcome even by those who sacrifice themselves merely for an idea, in the natural order, even without grace. And the narrative of the three Evangelists concerning the Forerunner's righteous death has no indication that this could have been the case. On the contrary, their testimony, together with the consciousness of the Church of all ages and nations, confirms that the martyrdom of the greatest of the righteous took place without fear, in a saintly manner, without the slightest shadow darkening it.

Thus, the psychological interpretation must be abandoned as inappropriate: in the twilight of his ministry, Christ's Forerunner is above the weaknesses that are presupposed here. There are spiritual summits that exclude the possibility of reverse movement or fall; and the Forerunner has, in this respect, arrived at a state equal to that of the angels, that is, a state that excludes any possibility of a fall. Initially, such a possibility was proper to the angelic world as well, as is witnessed by the fall of Lucifer and his angels. But, after him, this temptation was overcome.

No, the Forerunner's question was a sign of the great intensity of his spirit. And it betokened not personal weakness but was a manifestation of the infirmity of the human essence resulting from original sin. This is so normal and legitimate, even in the Forerunner, that its absence would have represented an unnatural and incomprehensible lacuna in the narrative devoted to him. The Gospel narrative of this struggle of the Forerunner attests to his feat; it is a new crowning of the Forerunner.

It is his personal Gethsemane before the Golgotha to come. Nothing in spiritual life is done mechanically, automatically, without combat and personal participation. A human being is never a thing in God's hands, and grace never deprives him of his freedom. From the point of view of the human nature, the Forerunner's work was an unceasing struggle, a feat of faith, will, and hope. This feat is crowned by the grace of the Holy Spirit, by virtue of which he lived in his consciousness of being the Forerunner, the friend of the Bridegroom; and by virtue of which he bore witness about Christ in preaching the Gospel of the Son of God. This preaching was inspired, of course, by the grace of the Holy Spirit, which expanded and deepened his human consciousness. In his ministry as Forerunner, he was constantly in this state of grace, for he was filled with the Holy Spirit from his mother's womb.

In this fullness and integrity, in this unity of the life of grace and human life, it is not given to the creaturely consciousness to see where the human ends and the divine begins, where the boundary is between feat and grace, between human accomplishment and the gift of the Holy Spirit. This boundary exists ontologically: Grace can, by God's will, be taken away from a man, and then the abyss of his human infirmity is revealed in him. In the Old Testament, Job was abandoned in this way. This providential abandonment can be due to sin, but it can also be because "the works of God should be made manifest in him" (John 9:3), as it was in the story of Job, where this was, so to speak, an expression of God's special love, special esteem, for him.

This abandonment by God is a trial and temptation for the human essence, but they are needed for the fullness of feat, for the sake of the freedom of human action, in which the human essence too must participate with all its energies. This trial of abandonment by God is the highest expression of God's love and respect for His creation.

And it is this trial and temptation that we observe in the spiritual state of the imprisoned Forerunner. We are not told whether there were similar temptations in the Forerunner's earlier life, but he could not entirely avoid them; he had to stand firm at the height of his awareness of himself as the Forerunner not only when he was illuminated by divine grace, but also when he was abandoned by God, when his human essence was deprived of grace. The origin of his trial is therefore not subjective and psychological; it is objective and ontological. It consists not in vacillations of his interior spiritual state, not in infirmity, but in a retreat — temporary, of course — of divine grace, in a providential abandonment by God.

The Forerunner's trial therefore can and must be understood not on the basis of human psychology but on the basis of the general laws of *spiritual* life. The key to understanding what was happening with the Forerunner's human soul must be sought in what was experienced by the human essence of the God-Man when He was abandoned by God, in His agony at Gethsemane and in the Passion on the cross. Let us examine this mystery.

About the Son of God, who answered John by a simple reference to His works and to the powers being revealed in Him, the Gospel says that, in Gethsemane, He "began to be sorrowful and very heavy" (Matt. 26:37), "to be sore amazed, and to be very heavy" (Mark 14:33). "And saith unto them, My soul is exceeding sorrowful unto death" (Mark 14:34; cf. Heb. 5:7). "And there appeared an angel unto him from heaven, strengthening him. And being in an agony he prayed more earnestly: and his sweat was as it were great drops of blood falling down to the ground" (Luke 22:43-44). What was the Son of God praying for? What was the cause of His agony? He "prayed that, if it were possible, the hour might pass from him. And he said, Abba, Father, all things are possible unto thee; take away this cup from me: nevertheless not what I will, but what thou wilt" (Mark 14:35-36; also Matt. 26:39; Luke 22:42). And after the arrival of the Greeks, Christ said: "Now is my soul troubled; and what shall I say? Father, save me from this hour; but for this cause came I unto this hour" (John 12:27). And to this must be added the agony on the cross: "And at the ninth hour Jesus cried with a loud voice, saying, Eloi, Eloi, lama sabachthani? which is, being interpreted, My God, my God, why hast thou forsaken me?" (Mark 15:34; also Matt. 27:46).

The Gethsemanic night of God-deprivation and God-abandonment is shrouded in sacred darkness. Nevertheless, this night is revealed to us; it is indelibly chiseled in the Gospel narrative. Our faith teaches us that, in Christ Jesus in one divine hypostasis, two natures, divine and human, are united without separation and without confusion in a theandric unity, so that His human I is also His divine I, and vice versa. However, on the pathways of the accomplishment of redemption on earth, we observe a kind of alternation or differentiation of these self-determinations, which is by no means a separation of the natures (that cannot be!) but a kind of separation in time where now the human nature and now the divine nature is *silent*, without the one separating itself from the other. For example, in the story of the raising of Lazarus, "Jesus wept" (John 11:35) is said about the human nature, whereas "Lazarus, come forth" (John 11:43) is said about the divine nature; and there are many such examples in the Gospel. Not expressible in human word or thought is the mystery of the inseparable life of the one hypostasis in the two unconfusable and inseparable natures. However, the Holy Spirit reveals that the inseparability of the natures does not prevent the silence, as it were, of one nature with respect to the other. And through this silence, first the one and then the other nature of the God-Man is revealed in its proper essence. And in the God-deprivation and God-abandonment of the Son of God, it is precisely His human nature that is revealed, thereby receiving its maximal illumination and sanctification. In effect, according to the authentic words of Christ the Savior, on the cross "God abandoned Him," as if the voice of His proper divine nature had become totally silent and as if the communion with God, the connection between the Son and the Father, had been interrupted.

This is the supreme sacrifice of God's love for the world: for the salvation of the world and together with the world, the Son distances Himself from the Father. Redemption is accomplished with respect to all of human nature, which by feat has overcome in itself the sin of disobedience and the infirmity of lack of faith: In the God-Man, it is not only God who takes human sin upon Himself and redeems it by His love and omnipotence; man too takes upon himself and redeems this sin in the plenitude of his infirm creaturely nature and by the force of his human freedom. Redemption is accomplished by God not upon man as a passive object, but by man himself, who, in this, does not rely on God's omnipotence, for he is *abandoned by God* and left to his human freedom. That is why the abandonment of the Son of God at Gethsemane and on the cross constitutes such an essential and inalienable part of the economy of our salvation: Every soul that submerges its sorrows in the night of Gethsemane finds its very own self, as it were, by this feat and agony, receives an answer to its torments. "Behold the man!" (John 19:5) — this refers not only to the hour when He was brought out by Pilate, but to the entire way of the passion after Gethsemane.[4]

Even though it is free of all sin, the God-abandoned human nature of the God-Man, burdened by the torment of the sinful world and of all humanity, necessarily reveals in itself its creaturely infirmity, which, however, is overcome by feat and healed by union with the divine nature. But this infirmity, just like the freely accepted death, refutes all types of docetism, which, in one direction or another, diminishes the fullness and authenticity of the Incarnation. And the sorrow and agony at Gethsemane represent such a necessary and essential refutation. "Wherefore in all things it behoved him to be made like unto his brethren.... for in that he himself hath suffered being tempted, he is able to succour them that are tempted" (Heb. 2:17-18; cf. Heb. 4:15; 5:2; Phil. 2:7).[5]

To make the comparison complete, it must be remembered that the work of Gethsemane was not the first trial of strength on the path of the God-Man. There was the temptation in the wilderness right after the baptism and the descent of the Holy Spirit, when, in the fullness of His divine and human powers, the God-Man, prior to the beginning of His ministry,

---

4. A special accent on the significance of the Gethsemane agony in the Savior's redemptive feat is what marks Metropolitan Antonii's theory of redemption, as expounded in his "Catechism" and on the pages of *Bogoslovsky Vestnik* [the *Theological Messenger*, a major Russian theological journal of the early twentieth century — Trans.]. The Gethsemane agony can, of course, neither be separated from nor opposed to the Golgotha agony; on the contrary, the two form an indivisible whole in the work of our redemption. That which was freely accepted and inwardly suffered through in Gethsemane ("thy will be done!") finds its fulfillment and realization on Golgotha. And just as Gethsemane would be incomplete without Golgotha, so Golgotha would be impossible without Gethsemane. Their relationship is one of thought and deed, word and fulfillment.

5. Also pertinent here is Heb. 5:7-8: "Who in the days of his flesh, when he had offered up prayers and supplications with strong crying and tears unto him that was able to save him from death, and was heard in that he feared; though he were a Son, yet learned he obedience by the things which he suffered."

"was... led up of the Spirit into the wilderness to be tempted of the devil" (Matt. 4:1; cf. Mark 1:12-13; Luke 4:1-2). But here the temptation was directed not at his human but at his divine nature ("If thou be the Son of God" [Matt. 4:3]). This was predominantly a temptation to disobedience and pride (although its occasion was the weakness of the flesh due to hunger). In this form, this temptation demonstrated the blindness of Satan, who did not yet know Whom he was tempting. Satan was still only attempting to fathom the mystery of His being. The Son of God was inaccessible to such temptation. Without any struggle or effort whatsoever (as the Gospel's silence about these things testifies eloquently), He repulsed the temptation and said: "Get thee hence, Satan" (Matt. 4:10). "Then the devil leaveth him, and, behold, angels came and ministered unto him" (Matt. 4:11). But "when the devil had ended all the temptation, he departed from him for a season" (Luke 4:13), until a favorable moment, which was, according to the generally accepted interpretation, the temptation at Gethsemane. Was this a personal manifestation of the power of evil and a new effort of its direct personal action? About this the Gospel says nothing, and therefore any suppositions on this subject are inappropriate.

It appears that the enemy of the human race did not risk here a personal temptation but waited for the weakness of the human nature, corrupted by him in Adam and burdening with all its weight the Sole Sinless One, to arrive at such a point of enervation that he could, after that, do his work of temptation. If in the first temptation he acted openly and was shamefully vanquished, then here it remained for him to wait and to observe what was going to happen. And if to the first temptation the Son of God was led directly by the Spirit, this new temptation was only tolerated. The Son of God found Himself in an agony of sorrow, in a state of abandonment by God, and the tempter could expect that the infirmity of the nature and the force of the sorrow unto death would pass into weakness and prostration. Infirmity is not yet weakness and prostration; it can be overcome and defeated. And it was defeated once and for all in the Gethsemane agony. And we are present at this agony and feat.

"Abba, Father, all things are possible unto thee; take away this cup from me: nevertheless not what I will, but what thou wilt" (Mark 14:36). "Now is my soul troubled; and what shall I say? Father, save me from this hour: but for this cause came I unto this hour" (John 12:27). What do these words mean? What does this prayer to "Abba, Father," "with strong crying and tears" (Heb. 5:7), mean? This is the voice of natural human infirmity in the state of abandonment by God. Although His *personal* human nature, free of all sin, abided in its original integrity and purity, it too — owing to its unity with all of humankind — was burdened by natural infirmity, which now, in this providential abandonment by God, manifested itself and made itself heard. This is indeed the voice of the human nature: "save me from this hour"; "let this cup pass from me." This is not the direct voice of the God-Man Himself, for His own voice covers this voice of the infirmity of human nature: "not what I will, but what thou wilt." This voice is not His, but it is in Him and speaks through Him. His filial obedience is accomplished by a victorious struggle; it implies the triumph of "yes" over "no"; that is, it represents victory over infirmity, the feat of salvation and redemption.

The temptation was overcome precisely where the God-Man's human nature was accessible to it, that is, in the infirmity inherent to the human race. This duality of "yes" and "no," overcome in "yes," is the redemptive feat, the victory over the flesh. At the same time, it attests to the authenticity of the incarnation, of the in-humanization, the entire human nature having been assumed, including its infirmity. And this infirmity is overcome in the God-Man, not only by virtue of His divinity but also by His humanity. Even though the latter remains inseparable from the divine nature, it attains, as it were, independent self-determination in the abandonment by God at Gethsemane and on Golgotha. That is why this agony, this abandonment, is so salvific for us, so necessary for the salvation of the world. God so loved the world that He abandoned His beloved Son, and the Son was patient of this abandonment, bearing witness of it with His cry.

The God-Man's abandonment by God is an essential part of the salvation and redemption of the human race. But it also represents the model for personal salvation, since the Lord manifested, in His human nature, the perfect man and the perfect path of salvation. And on the path of every human being too there is a time of agony when he is abandoned to his own human powers and perceives the ultimate depths of his infirmity; but at the same time, with his own powers, he gives his life to God. Here, of course, he can withstand or not withstand the trial by fire, in which fall and ascent are equally possible. But without it the measure of the feat cannot be fulfilled, so "that the trial of your faith, being much more precious than of gold that perisheth, though it be tried with fire, might be found unto praise and honour and glory at the appearing of Jesus Christ" (1 Pet. 1:7). That is why, whether in life or in death, man must approach the sacred enclosure of the Garden of Gethsemane, and gain in it his own self.

The Friend of the Bridegroom

These considerations can explain John's sending of his disciples and his question. The Forerunner, who had so clearly foreseen Christ's path and work as pre-accomplished in himself, was, in his life and fate, its living anticipation. And he could not fail to coparticipate in the Gethsemane agony and the abandonment by God, although only in anticipation; he could not fail to experience it *as the Forerunner.* In prison, on the eve of his martyrdom, clearly aware of its inevitability and fully prepared for it, of course, the Forerunner experiences the abandonment of man by God, his own night of Gethsemane. The light of grace that from his very birth was the source of his faith and knowledge fades for him. His garments of grace are removed from him, and he is reduced to his human powers alone.

However great these powers may have been in the greatest of those born of women, and these powers had been nurtured and strengthened by the feat of his entire life, even they turned out to be insufficient, for no human powers are sufficient, by themselves, to fathom the mystery that even the angels do not know. That which he saw and professed under the influence of the Holy Spirit, in prophetic inspiration; that which he saw and heard when his hand touched the head of the One being baptized — all this, although it remained in his human memory, lost, as it were, its power and the force of its persuasiveness as immediate evidence. Our memory is a highly unreliable and insufficient means for bringing to life for us the power of revelations and spiritual gifts we have once known. Otherwise, how could falls be possible? Abstract knowledge and remembrance alone are insufficient to retain the living power of divine gifts and revelations. It even happens that these gifts and revelations do not lend themselves to human expression, and vanish like smoke when an attempt is made to express them.

The ordinary perplexities thus lose all their power: How could the Forerunner question what had been revealed to him with such incontrovertible certainty, and what he himself had attested to? All this was given to him in the illumination by the Holy Spirit, but all of it could lose its power if the illumination ceased. And he was then abandoned to his human powers alone; he had to find his path as the Forerunner relying solely on these powers; he had to seek *humanly* the Messiah, whom he had already known by grace. Of course, the very possibility of such a providential abandonment, of such a trial of the Forerunner's human powers in his ministry, already indicates the great height that had become accessible to him at the end of his path, at the hour when he was to depart into the next world in order to preach in it. This fiery trial of faith represents the crowning and glorification of the Forerunner, indicated by the Savior Himself in His words after the departure of the apostles, words that thus become perfectly comprehensible.

If, in His abandonment by God, the Savior, the Sole Sinless One, experienced the whole infirmity of the human condition, then, in the Forerunner, who is subject by nature to original sin, this infirmity becomes a trial of his faith, *the temptation of the Forerunner as the Forerunner*. The loftiest ministries are subject to the temptations that are proper to them, and they are subject to them at the most critical and decisive moments of their course. In such temptation, a human being is left to his own resources by the divine will.

In this respect the Forerunner's agony can be compared, above all, with the agony of the Mother of God during the passion on the cross, when "the lance pierced Her soul." The Gospel does not disclose anything of this agony; it limits itself to mentioning the station of the Mother of God at the foot of the cross (and this only in the Fourth Gospel). But the Church describes Her agony in different ways in its hymns, in its numerous canons and "theotokions of the cross." It describes the sobs, the lamentation, the doubt, the maternal torment, the co-crucifixion, Her own abandonment by God (cf. especially the "Lamentation of the Mother of God" in the canon of Good Friday, as well as the matins of Holy Saturday).

The station of the Mother of God at the cross is fully analogous to the torment on the cross. And the Holy Church teaches us that, at this time, the Mother of God too was left to Her human nature and its creaturely infirmity, which She was to overcome by the feat of Her faith. In Her station at the cross, She too experienced agony and the trial of Her faith, and therefore She too participated in the Gethsemanic feat of obedience: "not as I will, but as thou wilt" (Matt. 26:39). And it is clear that the Mother of God's greatness and glory could not have attained their fullness without this great trial, this great struggle against temptation, from which the Son Himself was not exempt and from which He could not exempt His Mother. Christ's Forerunner could not directly participate in this feat, for he had to leave this world before these events. But he too, in his own way, had to perform this feat of faith, to undergo the trial of his awareness of himself as the Forerunner. If not for this culminating temptation his mission would not have been fulfilled; the fullness of his sacrifice would not have been consummated.

What did John's agony, his trial, consist in? It consisted in the fact that, for him, *it stopped being a self-evident truth* that Jesus is Christ, *ho erchomenos*. This truth, which previously had not admitted any question or doubt, suddenly became for him an open question, as it were. It was as if the Forerunner had returned to those times when he was baptizing on the Jordan, and, although he was awaiting One stronger than he, "he did not yet know Him." It was as if everything that had taken place since the Baptism was taken away from him, stopped existing; and he was left to his human assumptions and judgments about what had taken place. Is this He or not He?

Such thoughts could have had different causes. They could have been clothed in different hypotheses concerning the motives behind his sending of the disciples: If He is the Messiah, why is He delaying? Why is He not revealing Himself to the world? Why does He abandon him, John, on the eve of his death, in prison, without offering clear, external, human proof that He is the Messiah (for the inner proof and certitude had been vouchsafed him long ago)? Or, why, hitherto, has the testimony about Him come only from others, first of all from John himself, whereas He personally has not provided any testimony about Himself? Is it not necessary to oblige Him, by a direct question, to proclaim Himself the Messiah, to manifest His glory?

One can make yet another supposition on this subject: in what concerned Christ, John had returned to a state of uncertainty that one can call properly human. He had been suddenly deprived of his former knowledge, which he had received by the grace of the Holy Spirit and which by no means can be replaced by any abstract, theoretical remembrance. It was once again incumbent upon him to seek and to find the Messiah, this time by his human powers, but also with his creaturely infirmity, without doubting Him. It was given to him to assume the *human feat* of the Forerunner through the trial of his faith, through the temptation of the Forerunner. The world has not been given knowledge of this trial of the imprisoned John, but a ray of light penetrating this darkness, namely the narrative of the sending of the disciples, attests sufficiently to this agony that crowns him with a new grandeur.

And John came out the victor from the trial. He overcame the temptation, as is confirmed by the Gospel narrative.

John was abandoned to the human infirmity of being deprived of knowledge that had once been granted to him. The either/or question that this infirmity poses is posed precisely in terms of deprivation of knowledge, or ignorance. It is the voice of infirmity that is heard in the Forerunner's question: "Art thou he that should come, or do we look for another?" (Matt. 11:2-3). But this voice of ignorance and infirmity is not a voice of doubt or unbelief, just as the prayer, "let this cup pass from me"

(Matt. 26:39), does not signify the refusal to drink from this cup or the unwillingness to do the Father's will. This voice is silenced the instant it sounds. As soon as the question is uttered, it is annulled by the answer that is already known. The infirmity is manifested not to vanquish but to be vanquished: in manifesting itself, it does not gain power but becomes impotent.

Nevertheless, two possibilities remain with regard to this manifestation of infirmity: (1) the questioning can be silenced by a feat of faith or (2) doubt and perplexity can arise and faith can fail. Neither possibility is formally excluded with reference to the question the Forerunner conveys through his disciples. Is this a question to which he already has the answer, acquired through a feat of faith ("no" being overcome in him by "yes"); or is it an expression of ignorance, perplexity, doubt? (Similarly, the Gethsemane cry of the human nature, "let this cup pass from me," taken out of context, can be interpreted either as fear and anguish in the face of suffering or as the readiness to accept this suffering that is felt in all its violence: "let Thy will be done.")

Here we find precisely a "no" answered and defeated by "yes." The very "yes" would be incomplete and inauthentic if it did not include the defeated "no." The affirmation would not be an affirmation if it were not a victorious answer to the question posed. And faith itself would not be living faith were it always to remain a passive knowledge and not presuppose struggle. John's sending of the disciples sheds light on this feat of faith, attests to it. If not for this, one could get the wrong idea that John's awareness about himself as the Forerunner, his knowledge of the Messiah, was solely a free gift of grace, given to him without effort. Of course, in its fullness, it could only be such a gift of grace. But it was not given to him for free, but was acquired by effort, feat, struggle. And his sending of the disciples is the sole evidence we have of this in the Gospel.

We repeat: viewed formally, the question expresses either struggle and the feat of faith, or doubt and retreat from faith. But, in actuality, it expresses only the first; and it was precisely in this sense that it was interpreted and answered by the Savior. In the course of the mysterious dialogue that unfolds here between the Savior and the Forerunner, the latter offers his now-fading voice to the One Who is to come. And, of course, the answer given is not the one that would be demanded by doubt and that would silence the latter; it does not contain the "yes" that would be needed by a vacillating and doubting consciousness. And, in general, there is even no answer at all, for Christ's words only describe what the Forerunner already knew. But this signifies that no answer, in the real sense, was required. The answer given is not an answer but rather a greeting from the One Who comes to the one who departs.

Even if it could have had a certain significance as a confirmation and indication for the people surrounding John, as well as for his disciples, this form of answer would have been completely insufficient for John if he had in fact fallen into doubt. But, in actuality, the Forerunner needed not an answer but only a salutation to confirm that he had been heard. For his question was not really a question; it was a testimony to his faith and to its triumph through struggle. In saying "or," he did not leave any place for doubt. In short, by asking his question, the Forerunner attested to his faith no longer by the language of triumphant inspiration but by human effort that overcomes the agony of the human nature.

And this indeed is how the question was received and heard by the Lord, who with reference to it, said: "Blessed is he, whosoever shall not be offended in me" (Matt. 11:6). The Savior answered by blessing the firmness of John's faith, which was not "offended" in Him at the hour of the agonizing trial in the face of an implacable destiny, of an ineluctable death. The Forerunner goes to his death having recognized the One who is coming in the One who has come, but without seeing His glory. But he was not "offended" in this either. Thus, the question was the *farewell salutation* addressed to Christ by the Forerunner when he was departing this life. It was an act of faith affirmed in agony; a testimony to his faithfulness, as manifested in trials.

This ultimate farewell before his death, which at the same time was a profession of faith, could not have been conveyed by the disciples in the form of a triumphant testimony of the kind that had been proclaimed by the Forerunner himself. Such a testimony does not tolerate intermediaries, cannot be transmitted by a third party. This time the Forerunner's testimony in the form of a question became the testimony of the Messiah about Himself, a direct occasion for the latter. That is why it was expressed in the form of a question, which for the Forerunner had only a single, definitive answer: "yes." In this sense, the Forerunner's question could be viewed as rhetorical, although it was formulated as an actual question. By the intermediary of his disciples John could testify only by appealing to the One being testified about to testify. John's testimony here is the *content* of the question, not its form. The question therefore represents the glorification of the Forerunner and of his faith. And the Forerunner received this glorification from the lips of the Lord Himself. True, he himself did not hear it, for he himself did not have need of it: to find no ease or consolation in his agony corresponded to the fullness of

The Forerunner's Agony and the Savior's Testimony about Him

his feat. Nor did his disciples hear it, for they too, evidently, did not need it. Only after the departure of the disciples did the Lord address the people with praise of the Forerunner. And His words contain not only praise but also the doctrine of the Forerunner expounded by the Lord Himself.

CHAPTER 7

The Savior's Discourse about John the Forerunner

After having dismissed John's disciples, the Lord addressed the people with a discourse, a eulogy, so to speak, in praise of John. To no one else does the Lord accord such attention, and His praise indicates, more than anything else, how He had received and interpreted John's sending of the disciples. At the same time, these words of the Bridegroom about His friend contain the whole doctrine of John the Forerunner stated by the Truth Himself.

The Savior's words are reported in Matthew 11:7-19 and Luke 7:24-35 with certain differences, as we shall see. The Savior addresses the people, many of whom knew John, for they went out to him in the wilderness: "What went ye out into the wilderness to see? A reed shaken with the wind?" (Matt. 11:7) A dry reed shaken by the wind was the most ordinary kind of object, and it was not to see it, and not for mere gawking or empty curiosity, that the people went out into the wilderness. But at the same time the image of a supple reed implies, by contrast, tacit praise of the Forerunner's firmness and faithfulness, just attested to by his sending of the disciples. At the same time, this rejects the impression that some might have had that the Forerunner had had doubts, that his faith in the Messiah had been shaken.

Thus, it was not ordinary and petty interests that drew people from the usual places of their habitation into the wilderness. "But what went ye out for to see? A man clothed in soft raiment? behold, they that wear soft clothing are in king's houses" (Matt. 11:8). It was not the spectacle of human vanity and luxury, nor that of false grandeur that seeks to exhibit itself in king's houses, that drew the people into the wilderness, for the latter is not a place for such exhibitions. Here, the Lord implicitly praises the Forerunner's severe asceticism, as well as his total independence from the powerful of this world, who live in king's houses.

Not idleness and not illusory goods drew the people into the wilderness. They went there to see and to hear the one who was becoming famous as a prophet. "But what went ye out for to see?" — the Lord asks a third time, and gives the answer Himself: "A prophet? yea, I say unto you, and more than a prophet. For this is he, of whom it is written [Mal. 3:1], Behold, I send my messenger [angel in the Russian Bible] before thy face, which shall prepare thy way before thee" (Matt. 11:9-10).

The Lord attests here that John is indeed His Forerunner, who at the same time is accomplishing the prophetic ministry. But his mission is more than a prophetic one, for prophets announced what was to come, whereas the future announced by John is already the present, which he sees and knows at the moment that he announces it. And, in this sense, he is the intermediary between the Old and New Testaments. The prophecy about the Forerunner, applied to him by all the Evangelists and by him himself, is also applied to him by the Savior.

Once again, one cannot fail to see in this a tacit way of banishing the doubt that could have arisen in some after the Forerunner's sending of his disciples: by His solemn testimony the Lord confirms, as it were, John's unshakeable faithfulness precisely as the Forerunner. The Lord confirms him in his dignity. This means, of course, that the Forerunner's question does not in any way shake or violate his fidelity to his mission. Together with this, the Lord indirectly testifies about Himself as the One for Whom the angel sent by God is preparing the way, that is, as the Messiah. Therefore, John's wish is fulfilled: once again, and now for the final time, he testifies about the Messiah whose Forerunner he is. And he testifies precisely as he desires: by the words of the Messiah Himself.

This is the real answer to John's question, which contained two inseparable parts: is Jesus *ho erchomenos,* the One who is to come, i.e., the Messiah? And is John himself, therefore, His Forerunner? For John's question referred equally to the Messiah and to himself. And when the Lord testifies about John, he simultaneously testifies about Himself. The Lord thus responds to John's wish that He testify about Himself, and He does this, of course, before whom this was necessary, before the people who witnessed His miracles and listened to His preaching. John himself did not need this testimony, for he believed and did not tremble like a reed shaken by the wind. Nor was John thinking about his disciples, as some interpreters of these Gospel passages claim. Otherwise, it would be necessary to suppose that the Lord did not fulfill John's wish. But there is not the slightest reason to think this.

The general meaning of the narrative is, then, as follows: in prison, John heard of the miracles, that is, of the messianic works, of the Messiah; and, as a faithful witness, he desired that, alongside these works, there also be proclaimed the testimony of a witness about the One who had accomplished them, as the Messiah. But now being unable to proclaim this testimony himself, he, by the sending of the disciples, asks and obliges, as it were, Christ Himself to pronounce this testimony and to attest that His works are His own as the Messiah. Thus, the answer to John's disciples about the messianic works and the discourse to the people about the Forerunner are fused into a single whole, precisely into the testimony that John wished to provoke. The Lord heard his wish and satisfied it — not in the direct form, however, of testimony about Himself, but in the indirect form of testimony about the Forerunner. But, as we have explained, this testimony of Christ's was also testimony about Himself, and it could not have been received otherwise by His listeners. The Lord avoided direct testimony about Himself at this time — in order not to provoke the premature intervention of the Pharisees and thus prematurely precipitate the inevitable denouement. Having fulfilled John's wish and having responded to the people by testifying about John, the Lord speaks about him exclusively and explains to His listeners who he is, the one who is called to be the Lord's Forerunner.

Who is John — not as the Forerunner of the One Who is to come, but in and of himself, as a human being? It is this question that the Lord answers, and He does so with the express power of conviction that He uses on particularly solemn and important occasions: "Verily I say unto you, Among them that are born of women [*en gennētois gunaikōn* (masculine gender)] there hath not risen a greater [*meizōn*] than John the Baptist" (Matt. 11:11). (Also see Luke 7:28: "Among those that are born of women there is not a greater prophet than John the Baptist.") That is the solemn and authoritative judgment of the Truth Himself: all other human greatness is inferior to John's; he is the greatest among human beings. One must grasp with mind and heart the whole meaning and importance of these words of the Word; one must consider all of their numerous aspects, for they contain the key to Christian anthropology.

But one must first precisely delimit the meaning of these words. In the Greek, the phrase "among them that are born of women" is in the masculine and refers, therefore, to persons of the male gender. This, of course, does not mean that John's superiority fails to extend to the female gender, since a general primacy is ascribed to him in both the Old and New Testament. (The Church celebrates the Forerunner simply as "the most venerable of those born.") But, in particular, this superiority does not have to extend, and actually does not extend, to Mary, the Mother of God, born of a woman, more venerable than the cherubim and incomparably more glorious than the seraphim. On the other hand, the Forerunner's superiority to male persons born of a woman does not, of course, extend to the One Who was born not of "women, *gunaikōn*," but of the Virgin, that is, to the Son of God. Nevertheless, with reference to the human race in its entirety, John is the first and the greatest; he is the measure of true greatness.[1]

But what kind of greatness is this? People speak of different kinds of greatness: of great scientists, leaders, rulers, teachers, and so on. The term "great man" is usually applied to both Plato and Napoleon, to both Goethe and Alexander of Macedonia, to both Pushkin and Suvorov,[2] to both Shakespeare and Peter the Great, and so on. Clearly, the person considered great is gifted in one way or another. This giftedness usually corresponds to the general spiritual quality of the individual considered great,

---

1. There nevertheless remains a certain lack of clarity as far as the Mother of God is concerned — not with regard to Her glorified state as the Queen of heaven, where Her immeasurable and incomparable greatness is totally obvious, but with regard to Her state before the Annunciation and the beginning of Her divine maternity as a result of the descent of the Holy Spirit. Are the Forerunner and Mary not two pure and personally sinless sprouts on the tree of the human race, having different fates and predestinations but an equal power of virginity and spiritual integrity? Evidence *against* this is the fact that the glorification of the Mother of God does not extend to the Forerunner. But evidence *for* it is the fact that the Church unites the Mother of God and the Forerunner in the presence of Christ, in the *Deisis*. In any case, we must take into account the fact that the Lord's words leave this question unresolved; and this uncertainty is not accidental of course. Perhaps it is just not appropriate to measure and compare the human greatness and the personal feats of the Mother of God and the Forerunner. Nevertheless, we are led to such a comparison by the Lord's words, which compare the Forerunner with *all* human beings (and of course not just with all males). The fact that there is no greatness among human beings that exceeds the Forerunner's does not exclude a greatness that is equal or similar to his; and such a greatness can be attributed only to the Mother of God in Her *human* greatness. Perhaps for this greatness there is only one measure: self-renunciation and personal victory over sin. This is then the common measure of the "Servant of the Lord," upon whose humility the Lord cast His glance, and of the "friend of the Bridegroom." In this case the theme of the *Deisis* appears in a new aspect. But we do not have the audacity to express a definite opinion about it.

2. Alexander Suvorov (1729-1800) was Russia's greatest general and military hero of the eighteenth century. — Trans.

but in and of itself it is not evidence of greatness of spirit, of absence of sin, of saintliness, of spiritual integrity. Saints, i.e., bearers of genuine *spiritual* greatness, rarely belong among the "great men" of history; and it seems inappropriate to call St. Seraphim of Sarov great (unless we use the phrase "great saint") in the same way we call the poet Pushkin great. The greatness of Zacharias's son, attested to by the Son of God, is not, of course, a worldly greatness, consisting of those mixed, ambiguous achievements that are the works of men. It is the greatness of purity, saintliness, innocence, spiritual integrity.

Great in the eyes of God is the one who more than anyone else has approached the true greatness of man, the Image of God implanted in him; the one in whom this Image is least obscured by sin. The whole human race was created in the greatness of God's Image and is called to the greatness of God's likeness, but, taken as a whole, it has lapsed from this greatness, having fallen into original sin. But a personal liberation, if not from sin, then at least from sins, remains possible, as well as a personal sinlessness even in the case of original sin. It is this kind of greatness that the Lord attributes to John the Forerunner. It attests to John's purity, to his immaculateness, to his personal victory over sins *(paraptōmata)*, but not over sin *(hamartēma)*. All other criteria for evaluating greatness are relative, conventional, and, in the end, erroneous. John is the greatest of mortals because he is the more pure and saintly among them, aside from the Most Pure and Most Immaculate Virgin. And as the first among all the saints, St. John the Forerunner is commemorated before all the saints at the Holy Proskomide: at the eucharistic liturgy, for the preparation of the oblations, the portion designated with his name is the first to be extracted from the nine parts of the prosphora that represents the saints, but after that of the Mother of God.

This once again confirms the previously stated idea that the Forerunner's feat and path have a universal meaning; and in this sense he is exemplary for the whole human race, and the soul that desires to advance toward God cannot fail to follow in his footsteps. The Forerunner's supreme and authentic greatness represents the *norm* of human life, insofar as the latter follows the right path. His greatness consists in giving himself voluntarily to his Friend, in sacrificially renouncing himself, in consecrating himself to God, in surrendering himself to God with all his being and all his energies. This is opposed to all anthropotheism and autotheism, to luciferian self-assertion, to "ye shall be as gods" (Gen. 3:5). This is the path of sacrificial humility and of the immolation of the human ego.

But it would be erroneous to understand this self-immolation as a repudiation and suppression of all human creativity, as a spiritual laziness that buries the talents given to one, without giving them a chance to multiply. But a man's greatness does not at all depend on this gift, on the "ten talents" that God gives and that He can take away. It depends wholly and exclusively on to whom or to what this gift will be consecrated and how it will be used. And in *this* sense, all human beings are equally called to spiritual greatness; and it is we ourselves who make ourselves great or small. People erroneously assess greatness according to gifts, and they take pride in their gifts, whereas giftedness has the significance only of a means, of a particular form of the sacrificial service of God, equally accessible to all men, by and in all things that they possess. The Forerunner is great by this generally human greatness; and all human beings are called to this service in the formation of their personal lives, in the labor of self-creation, possible to all: "Not unto us, O Lord, not unto us, but unto thy name give glory" (Ps. 115:1).

The Lord's declaration that the Forerunner is the greatest of those born of women is, however, immediately followed by an antithetical declaration: "Notwithstanding, he that is least [*ho de mikroteros*] in the kingdom of heaven is greater [*meizōn*] than he" (Matt. 11:11). What does this antithetical declaration signify? In his "Homily on Matthew" (36-37), Chrysostom gives an interpretation, accepted by a number of Eastern and Western exegetes, that can be called allegorical. "He that is least" is interpreted as referring to the Lord Himself, Who was considered, by the people surrounding him, to be obscure and unimportant. It is difficult to accept such an interpretation: it does not much accord with the whole of the Lord's testimony about the Forerunner, from which, as we have indicated, the Messiah's testimony about Himself follows directly. It would be surprising if, after this solemn declaration about himself, the Messiah would deliberately hide behind the imprecision of the expression "least."

But even if we accept this interpretation as a possibility on the basis of the authority of the theologians who have advanced it, it by no means excludes or contradicts another interpretation, a more generally accepted one and one that was formulated long ago. This interpretation compares *human* achievement and the grace of the kingdom of heaven (of God): even what is humanly loftiest cannot compare with and become what is full of grace. The gracious gift of the Holy Spirit that is conferred in the Church is a new, supernatural life; it is deification. Man cannot deify himself by his own powers, although he can and must strive toward deification, toward the meeting of the divine and the human.

The Friend of the Bridegroom

To this one objects that the reign of grace and its gifts has not yet begun. But the Lord's words do not only apply to a precise moment of time; they have a general significance. Moreover, with regard to inner accomplishment, this reign ("the kingdom of heaven is at hand") began when John, and then Christ, started preaching. As we recall, both began their preaching with the same words: "Repent ye: for the kingdom of heaven is at hand." It "is at hand" with the Incarnation, since it is fulfilled only with the Redemption and the Pentecost. It is here precisely that the human nature situated outside of the deification that is accomplished through the Incarnation is distinguished from the human nature deified as a result of the Incarnation, of course in those who have assimilated its fruits. In other words, those who have the "power to become the sons of God," who are born of God, are distinguished from those born of blood, of the will of the flesh, of the will of man (see John 1:12-13). An insuperable limit is established here for anthropotheism, man's unlawful desire to be God. It is precisely in this sense that the Savior further clarifies His thought (only in Matthew; in Luke [16:16] this is in the context of another speech): "From the days of John the Baptist until now the kingdom of heaven suffereth violence, and the violent take it by force. For all the prophets and the law prophesied until John" (Matt. 11:12-13). John the Baptist figures here as the limit beyond which the possibility of taking the Kingdom of God by feats of struggle, by violence, is revealed for the "violent." He is the limit beyond which the prophetic power and the insight contained in the law and the prophets cannot go. Why is John the Baptist (and not even the Mother of God) this limit? Because of his personal feat and his ministry.

In the first case, John fulfilled the *law* to the extent that it can be fulfilled by a human being. Although Paul says that "by the deeds of the law there shall no flesh be justified in his sight: for by the law is the knowledge of sin" (Rom. 3:20), nevertheless, this impossibility of justification does not at all signify impossibility of fulfillment. The law was given not only to make us conscious of sin but also to be fulfilled with a view to salvation as the norm of Old Testament piety, as Psalm 119 so eloquently testifies. The peak of the Old Testament saintliness was attained in the Forerunner. Although this saintliness was not deprived of grace and was not merely natural, that was how it appeared in comparison with the New Testament holiness: "For the law was given by Moses, but grace and truth came by Jesus Christ" (John 1:17). John the Forerunner is the fulfillment of the Old Testament, and it is precisely he (and not the Virgin Mary) who is designated as such, for the law is directly related to the masculine principle (which is why genealogies, notably that of Christ the Savior, are given according to the male branch). Since he fulfilled the law to the extent this is possible for a human being, the greatest of those born of women is the mediator between the Old and New Testaments, stands at the boundary between them, for he sees the *fulfillment* of the prophecy. "For all the prophets and the law prophesied until John" (Matt. 11:13) about Christ's Incarnation, but John saw the fulfillment of the prophecy (which is why the Church celebrates him both as a prophet and as an apostle, as the "mediator between the old and the new grace"). In this sense, the "prophets" find their conclusion and fulfillment in him.

But also, in a special sense, the ministry of John the Baptist (as the Lord calls him, not by chance of course, in His discourse: *Ioannou tou Baptistou*, the article signifying not only a baptist in general but also the Baptist of the Lord) represents the boundary between the Old and New Testaments. His ministry completes the Incarnation, fulfills the law and the prophets, precisely through the baptism of the Lord and the descent of the Holy Spirit upon the God-Man's human nature. After His baptism, Jesus truly became the Messiah, Christ, and could now directly apply to Himself Isaiah's prophecy: "The Spirit of the Lord is upon me, because he hath anointed me" (Luke 4:18). The Kingdom of grace is thus revealed, which "came by Jesus Christ" (John 1:17), and which can be taken by force by the violent and will last to the end of this age, until the revelation of the kingdom of glory in the Lord's second and dread coming. It is, of course, in this general sense that one must understand the expression "until now [*heōs arti*]" (Matt. 11:12). Related to this, of course, is John's preaching about repentance as preparation for the Kingdom of God: "Repent ye: for the kingdom of heaven is at hand" (Matt. 3:2); that is, Jesus has come into the world and has been anointed by the Holy Spirit.

Thus, continuing His discourse on John, the Lord also speaks, although indirectly, about Himself, for John's significance is defined only in relation to Christ. And with this the Lord again fulfills the Forerunner's final wish — He bears witness about Himself, though only indirectly. The Lord confirms the particularly significant and also mysterious character of His discourse, requiring the closest attention, by adding a phrase that He usually employs in cases of similar importance: "He that hath ears to hear, let him hear" (Matt. 11:15).

However, prior to this conclusion the Lord expresses a new idea concerning John (which one finds only in Matthew): "And if ye will receive it, this is Elias, which was for to come" (Matt. 11:14). In their most general sense, these words signify, as we have just indicated, the Lord's continuing testimony both about Himself and about the Forerunner: according to the prophecy of Malachi 4:5, Elias was viewed as a forerunner of the day of the Lord, which is also the day of the Messiah. Thus, the Lord here confirms John's role as the Forerunner of the Messiah; and He thus bears witness about Himself as the Messiah, Whose Forerunner John is. This text is thus woven into the general fabric of this discourse, which is messianic in substance though indirect in form. However, another theme is introduced here, which requires examination: the likening of Elias to John. But we shall examine this below, so as not to interrupt our study of the Lord's discourse.

Matthew 11:15 ends the first half of the Lord's discourse, which is devoted to His testimony about the Forerunner and, in connection with him, about Himself as well. The second half is entirely devoted to the people's attitude toward the Forerunner and, once again, toward the Messiah. Here, Christ gives Himself the Old Testament messianic name from Daniel's prophecy (7:13-14): the Son of man. This part of the speech, in the fuller exposition in Luke (7:29), contains severe reproaches. After denouncing the Pharisees, the Lord attests to the greatness of John as the first of those born of women: "And all the people that heard him, and the publicans, justified God, being baptized with the baptism of John. But the Pharisees and lawyers rejected the counsel of God against themselves, being not baptized of him" (Luke 7:29-30). Here, the Lord says directly that the baptism of John was according to God's will but that, in the end, it was rejected by the Pharisees and lawyers. At first they went out to hear John (cf. Matt. 3:7), but then they turned against him and did not accept baptism from him. Thus, there was a division on the subject of the Baptist.

Addressing the people, the Lord uses various comparisons to denounce the people's instability and willfulness in the face of God's great prophet: "But whereunto shall I liken this generation? It is like unto children sitting in the markets, and calling unto their fellows, And saying, We have piped unto you, and ye have not danced; we have mourned unto you, and ye have not lamented" (Matt. 11:16-17; cf. Luke 7:31-32). This comparison shows capricious children playing at various games (weddings or funerals) and quarreling amongst themselves because some of them do not wish to fully participate in the games of the others. This puerile capriciousness, difficult to satisfy, is compared to that of the people: "For John came neither eating nor drinking, and they say, He hath a devil. The Son of man came eating and drinking, and they say, Behold a man gluttonous, and a winebibber, a friend of publicans and sinners" (Matt. 11:18-19; cf. Luke 7:33-34). The two forms of righteousness, severe and tolerant, equally displease the people. They find reasons to criticize and reject both forms,

The Savior's Discourse about John the Forerunner

so that their hearts remain unopened. With these bitter words the Lord concludes His speech, affirming that His preaching was ignored as much as that of the Forerunner. This is followed by a denunciation of the scribes and the Pharisees, with tears of compassion for the people who remain blind. And then the final judgment: "Behold, your house is left unto you desolate" (Matt. 23:38; Luke 13:35).

This part of the Lord's discourse on John is complemented by other Gospel passages. Thus, speaking with the high priests and the elders of the people, the Lord once again tells them: "John came unto you in the way of righteousness, and ye believed him not: but the publicans and the harlots believed him: and ye, when ye had seen it, repented not afterward, that ye might believe him" (Matt. 21:32). Also, the synoptic Gospels contain a parallel between John and his disciples and Jesus and His disciples on the subject of fasting: "The disciples of John and of the Pharisees used to fast: and they come and say unto him, Why do the disciples of John and of the Pharisees fast, but thy disciples fast not? And Jesus said unto them, Can the children of the bridechamber fast, while the bridegroom is with them? as long as they have the bridegroom with them, they cannot fast. But the days will come, when the bridegroom shall be taken away from them, and then shall they fast in those days" (Mark 2:18-20; cf. Matt. 9:14-15; Luke 5:33-35).

The Lord, in all three synoptic Gospels, continues this discourse with the parables of the new cloth on an old garment and of the new wine and the old bottles. Clearly, there was a difference between the severe, legalistic, implacable Old Testament fasting of the preacher of repentance and the spirit of freedom, joyous and unconstrained, around the Bridegroom. Such is the relation between the forty days of the Great Fast and the fifty days of the Pentecost period; between Holy Week and Easter. The two condition each other, each having its laws, its spirit, its specificity. Being the living fulfillment of the law, John was associated de facto with the legalism of the Pharisees. But the Pharisees did not recognize him, for he fulfilled the law in order to surpass it, whereas they did not wish to know that such a possibility existed.

With this reproach to the people the Lord concluded His glorification of the Forerunner and His farewell to him. But His discourse ends (in both Matthew 11:19 and Luke 7:35) with an unexpected and mysterious passage: "but wisdom [*hē sophia*] is justified of her children" (i.e., works, with Luke having "all her children"). What does this surprising passage about Sophia signify and why is it applied to the Forerunner? The answer will be given in the final chapter of our book. Here we will only note that the expression *hē Sophia* (with the article) of course implies the specific concept of the Wisdom of God, in contradistinction to wisdom as a personal quality, which can also be found in certain Gospel passages, sometimes without the article. This term implies, of course, the entire Old Testament doctrine of Sophia, the Wisdom of God, as it is expounded in the Proverbs of Solomon, the Wisdom of Solomon, and the Wisdom of Jesus, Son of Sirach.[3] The exegesis of this passage must necessarily take into account this Old Testament context.

---

3. Besides the passage noted, the only other case of the ontological signification of the term Sophia in the Gospel occurs in Luke 11:49: "Therefore also said the wisdom of God [*hē sophia tou Theou*]" (in a more particular sense, the wisdom of God refers to the Word of God). It is worth mentioning that this text, like Luke 7:35, presents the words of the Lord Himself, whereas in all cases where the term *Sophia* refers to a property or force, it is used (except in Luke 21:15) by the people or by the Evangelist himself. [. . .]

CHAPTER 8

John and Elias

In His discourse about the Forerunner, the Lord said: "If ye will receive it, this is Elias, which was for to come" (Matt. 11:14). (This is according to the prophecy in Mal. 4:5-6: "Behold, I will send you Elijah the prophet before the coming of the great and dreadful day of the Lord: And he shall turn the heart of the fathers to the children, and the heart of the children to their fathers.") Jesus thus pronounces the name Elias together with the name John, as if it were a name common to them. In a certain sense, John is also Elias, though Elias is not John. The Forerunner somehow contains Elias, but transcending him and without coinciding with him.

As we know, even before John's birth, the angel told Zacharias that John "shall go before him [the Lord] in the spirit and power of Elias" (Luke 1:17). And the name Elias is applied to John not only by the scribes and Pharisees (see John 1:21) but even by the Lord Himself. The doctrine (so firmly rooted in later Kaballistic mysticism) of the reincarnation of souls, specifically of the righteous, was professed by the Pharisees, and through them it spread among the common people as a kind of superstition. Traces of this doctrine can be found in the Gospel as well. Herod's superstitious fear of the Forerunner was expressed, first of all, in the following supposition: "King Herod heard of him [Jesus]; (for his name was spread abroad:) and he said, That John the Baptist was risen from the dead, and therefore mighty works do shew forth themselves in him" (Mark 6:14; cf. Matt. 14:1-2; Luke 9:7-9). However much this supposition might have gone against the evidence, it was also widespread among the people, who allowed that Jesus was Elias, or Jeremiah, or one of the prophets (see Matt. 16:14; Mark 6:15; 8:28; Luke 9:19). This expressed a perplexity and confusion that used superstition to defend itself against faith. This also shows how easily people assimilated the idea that Elias could be repeated, so to speak, in Jesus.

Besides His discourse to the people, the Savior also had a conversation about this with three chosen disciples after the Transfiguration, at which they had seen Elias and Moses speaking with the Lord about His passion. After the conversation on the way to Caesarea Philippi and after the Transfiguration on the mountain, the disciples understood that Jesus was the promised Messiah; and they knew from Malachi's prophecy that His coming was prepared by the prophet Elias. That is why His disciples asked Him: "Why then say the scribes that Elias must first come? And Jesus answered and said unto them, Elias truly shall first come, and restore all things. But I say unto you, that Elias is come already, and they knew him not, but have done unto him whatsoever they listed. Likewise shall also the Son of man suffer of them. Then the disciples understood that he spake unto them of John the Baptist" (Matt. 17:10-13; cf. Mark 9:11-13).

Thus, the Lord clearly and repeatedly refers to John as Elias. Does this signify their personal identification? Aside from more general considerations, the Forerunner's own response to those sent by the priests and Levites sufficiently clearly opposes such an identification: "What then? Art thou Elias? And he saith, I am not" (John 1:21). One must remember that the Evangelist John was aware of the synoptics' account of Christ's testimony that John was Elias. John is not Elias, but nevertheless, "if ye will receive it, this is Elias" (Matt. 11:14). This has to do, first of all, with the similarity of the ministries of the Forerunner and Elias: John announces Christ's first coming, whereas Elias announces the second, but the Jews did not distinguish the two. In the troparion of his feast, the Church celebrates the glorious Elias as "an angel in the flesh, the foundation of the prophets, the forerunner of Christ's second coming." Chrysostom (in "On Matthew," Homily 57) interprets this in the sense of the similarity of their ministries; and the majority of exegetes follow him on this point.

The Lord's words imply, however, more than a simple convergence of the ministries. They indicate a certain mystery that is not revealed to us: that of a personal relation between Elias and John. To attempt to fathom this mystery is inappropriate, but to ignore it is unjustified. We must, of course, reject the crude interpretation that is given by the adherents of metempsychosis. Apart from this crude, non-Christian theory, there can exist other, still unknown, relationships of kinship or descent. The link between Elias and John, established by the Savior with such certainty, compels us, in any case, to look more attentively at the similarities and differences between the two prophets.

John and Elias

Elias and John are both preachers of the true faith and repentance, and thus denouncers of false beliefs, with the difference that Elias is portrayed with Old Testament severity and dread (cf. the narrative of the slaughter of the prophets of Baal in 1 Kings 18:40; and the massacre of the "fifty" in 2 Kings 1). There is an outward similarity in the austerity of the lives and ascetic aspects of the two prophets; and this similarity, of course, struck the popular imagination: Elias is described as a "hairy man, and girt with a girdle of leather about his loins" (2 Kings 1:8); while "John had his raiment of camel's hair, and a leathern girdle about his loins" (Matt. 3:4). Elias, like John, received his most important revelation in the wilderness, where, after the murmur of a light breeze, God's glory was manifested to him. Elias was a great miracle-worker; in this he differed from the Forerunner, who did not work miracles. Despite the Old Testament character of Elias's spiritual aspect, there was something so partaking of the character of the New Testament in him that, together with Moses, he appeared before the Lord on the mountain of the Transfiguration. By this vision of the Lord's face on earth (in His glory), Elias resembles the Forerunner. And the Church celebrates Elias: "Christ showed you to be a guardian of mysteries, a cultivator of purity, and a witness on Tabor of the divine fruit of virginity, of the Incarnation of God" (office of the prophet Elias, canon, ode 8, tr. 3).

One must think that it is because of this New Testament quality of the Old Testament prophet that he is considered the second Forerunner: the prophetic ministry is assigned to him in both the Old and the New Testament, which, of course, leads to a further resemblance with John, "the mediator between the Old and the New Testament." Elias, taken up into heaven like Enoch, did not partake of death. And according to Revelation, both will appear on earth in the last times for the final admonition (Rev. 11:3-6), when they will be killed by the Antichrist (Rev. 11:7) to general jubilation, "because these two prophets tormented them that dwelt on the earth" (Rev. 11:10). They will partake of death, having paid their tribute to the common human lot; but then they will rise from the dead and ascend, once again, "to heaven in a cloud" while "their enemies beh[o]ld them" (Rev. 11:12). Here Elias is associated with Enoch; but in the Lord's discourses, in the prophecy of Malachi, and in the tradition of the Church, he is distinguished as the express forerunner of Christ's second coming, even as the first Forerunner prepares the first coming. Thus, both are preachers of implacable repentance.

But the ministry of the Forerunner, since he is the first among those born of women, clearly has precedence over that of Elias and that of

The Friend of the Bridegroom

Enoch. He is not only the forerunner but also the *witness* of Christ and the *friend* of the bridegroom, as well as a preacher in hell. Therefore, he is Elias only "if ye will receive it" (Matt. 11:14), that is, only in a certain limited sense; and precisely the superiority of John's ministry to that of Elias hinders their complete personal identification.

One could also say that the ministry of Elias as a forerunner is only one of the aspects of the life and work of one who is celebrated by the Church as "a preacher of Christ and His baptist, as an angel, apostle, martyr, prophet, forerunner, bearer of the flame, close friend, seal of the prophets, most pure of mortals, mediator between the old and the new grace." But however great may be the one who is "an angel in the flesh, the foundation of the prophets," he is neither an eyewitness of the Word, nor the friend of the Bridegroom, nor an apostle.

The Savior speaks of John as being Elias when he testifies about Himself in His testimony about the Forerunner, both in His discourse on John and in His conversation after the Transfiguration. On both occasions, He is asked if He is the Messiah, and *consequently* if all the other conditions correspond to those required for the messianic coming, in particular the generally expected coming of Elias. The Lord's answer to the first and more important question is in the affirmative, confirming that the other conditions have also been fulfilled, in particular the preparation for His coming through Elias, although this time it was realized in a wholly other manner and hidden from men: it is John who in *one* of his ministries is manifested in the capacity of Elias. Therefore, in the identification of Elias and John, the logical accent lies on the identity not of the personal but of the messianic aspect. Nevertheless, there remains a certain undeciphered mystery in this resemblance between Elias and John.

CHAPTER 9

The Honorable Death of the Forerunner

"He must increase, but I must decrease" (John 3:30), the Forerunner said about himself. By meeting the Lord, baptizing Him, and bearing witness about Him, the Forerunner had accomplished his earthly work; his earthly life was inwardly concluded. He was now called to a new ministry — the preaching of the coming of Christ to those in hell. He is "sent in advance to those in hell as Christ's proclaimer" (office of 29 January, sticheron). Along with this, the Forerunner needed, above the glory already given to him, to receive the martyr's crown. On his feast day, the Church sings: "How should we call you, prophet? Angel, apostle, or martyr? Angel because you lived as though without flesh. Apostle because you taught the Gentiles. Martyr because you were decapitated for Christ."

The murder of the Forerunner is one of the most heinous misdeeds and most terrible crimes known by the world, which is drowning in crimes. But this crime exposes the whole impotence of evil, for the greatest triumph of good is accomplished precisely in this crime. Is there a greater triumph for the Forerunner than the fact that torment unto death could not bend him? Was his voice stilled? Was the tongue silenced that, according to tradition, was pierced with a needle by Herodias in her satanical rage? Can there be a greater triumph of truth than the acceptance of suffering and death for its sake?

The Forerunner's martyrdom was needed for the fullness of his glorification on the path of his new mission. By no means was a long life with a natural end necessary and possible for him. For the Forerunner's mission on earth had a temporary and even fleeting character. His activity alongside Christ, his preaching of repentance, would have gradually lost much of its meaning; and after the Lord's death and resurrection it would have

The Friend of the Bridegroom

been completely meaningless. A minor star must fade when the sun rises. Could the Forerunner outlive his Lord? Could the friend of the Bridegroom remain on earth *after* the Bridegroom had gone? It is sufficient to pose this question to see that the only answer must be in the negative.

True, one might wonder why the Mother of God, the Bride of God, greatly outlived Her Son, the Bridegroom of the Church. Why could this not have been the case with the Forerunner? It is because their situations were different, due to their different ministries. After Christ's birth, the Mother of God recedes into the shadow of Her humility. She is present at and contemplates Her Son's earthly path, but She remains outside it, as if not participating in it. However, after the Pentecost, She becomes the Church's active center, the Church's incarnation and head, while realizing Her own path to dormition and heavenly glorification. In contrast, the Forerunner's ministry is integrated into Christ's ministry and His redemptive work, which extends beyond this world. Although the Forerunner's ministry occupies a definite place in the world, it is not exhausted by this place but continues beyond the world. For this reason, the Forerunner's glorious life had to move rapidly toward its sunset. The Forerunner *could not* outlive the Lord on earth. That is the inner necessity that marked the Forerunner's ministry.

On the other hand, could the greatest servant of good and the greatest witness of truth among men have lived in the world without attracting an implacable hatred? Could the prince of this world and his numberless servants have let his ministry go unpunished and unhindered? Could they have failed to confer upon John the glory and supreme triumph of martyrdom and of the confession of the faith? Speaking more concretely, could the Forerunner, by his preaching and fearless words of truth, have failed to attract an enmity that, sooner or later, would have a fatal outcome? Toward the end of his relatively brief ministry (all told, about a year and a half), he found himself surrounded by enemies, whose number did not cease to increase. These enemies included lawyers and Pharisees, who did "not believe him" (Mark 11:31; cf. Matt. 21:25; Luke 20:5), but who "rejected the counsel of God against themselves, being not baptized of him" (Luke 7:30) and "knew him not, but have done unto him whatsover they listed" (Matt. 17:12). They included the powerful of this world and their servile entourage. They included the vicious of this world, whose incorruptible denouncer John was. Given all these threatening possibilities, the means the world would have used to take revenge on its denouncer would have, in a certain sense, been a matter of chance. As it turned out, "the disciple of the much-malicious devil" in this case was Salome, together with her mother and the crazy Herod, whose illicit, incestuous marriage had been condemned by John. This evil deed may have been a random one in the sense that it was only *one* of various means the prince of this world could have used to take revenge upon the greatest of the prophets, but it was not random in its particulars.

The first thing one notices is that the Forerunner's death was caused not by the ecclesiastical but by the civil authorities; he perished not because of religious but because of personal and political motives, despite the fact that his preaching contained nothing political or personal. Here, one cannot fail to notice the difference between John's condemnation and Christ's: Although, outwardly, it was politically motivated (the accusation that he was a political pretender: "the King of the Jews"), Christ's condemnation was, in its essence, religiously motivated, the responsible parties being the religious leaders of the people, the scribes and the high priests.

The latter looked askance at the Forerunner too. They were troubled by his preaching: in general, they did "not believe him," and in particular they did not, of course, believe what he proclaimed about the Messiah. They sent missions to him to try to tempt and compromise him, but there was no decisive confrontation with him, since he was precisely the Forerunner. On the one hand, in his Old Testament nature that was subordinate to the law, he did not differ from them. That is why, on the subject of fasting, Christ was asked: "Why do the disciples of John and of the Pharisees fast, but thy disciples fast not?" (Mark 2:18; cf. Matt. 9:14; Luke 5:33). On the other hand, once pronounced, his testimony about the Messiah was not repeated; for after the appearance of the Messiah, the Forerunner receded into deep shadow, to "decrease" before the One who was increasing; the latter was already preaching about Himself and attracting upon Himself the full force of hatred. Therefore, concerning the question of the Messiah, the confrontation with the Pharisees could not go beyond a certain point, precisely because he was only the Forerunner.

But it should be mentioned that the confrontation with Herod and his wife was incited by that denunciation of mores that generally characterized the prophets (cf. Nathan's opposition to David and Elijah's opposition to Ahab and Jezebel; cf. also Amos and Jonah, Isaiah, Jeremiah). And, in and of itself, this confrontation contains nothing specifically New Testament-like in nature. It is noteworthy that, in His preaching, the Lord Himself did not engage in personal denunciations; and even His discourse against the scribes and Pharisees in Matthew 23 attacks not personal sins but a mind-set, and does not mention any names. It is as if the Lord did not attach any significance to such denunciations in His preaching, for His sole purpose was to proclaim the teaching of the doctrine of the Kingdom of God and the teaching of Himself.

One should not forget that Jesus, like John, was a contemporary of this same Herod, about whom He pronounced the most severe judgment that he ever applied to anyone: "tell that fox" (Luke 13:32). Herod himself even wished to see Jesus, so that he was "exceeding glad" when he saw Jesus at the trial, for "he hoped to have seen some miracle done by him" (Luke 23:8). And even after receiving news of John's death, the Lord silently went away into the wilderness, without condescending to say a single word about the perpetrators of this heinous deed. In general, the Lord seemed not to notice, or did not consider deserving His attention, the specific evil deeds of men in power (cf., for example, Luke 13:1-3, with reference to Pilate).

In the Forerunner's death there is an element proper to the fate of an Old Testament prophet. He died not because of his teaching but because of his condemnation of evildoers, whereas the Lord was hated and crucified exclusively because of His teaching, and primarily because of what he professed about Himself. "Herod had laid hold on John, and bound him, and put him in prison for Herodias' sake, his brother Philip's wife [and for all the evils which Herod had done: Luke 3:19]. For John said unto him, It is not lawful for thee to have her. And when he would have put him to death, he feared the multitude, because they counted him as a prophet" (Matt. 14:3-5). Also: "Herodias had a quarrel against him, and would have killed him; but she could not: For Herod feared John, knowing that he was a just man and an holy, and observed him; and when he heard him, he did many things, and heard him gladly" (Mark 6:19-20).

In the story of John's death, it is noteworthy that he was the direct victim of *female* rage and vindictiveness; for even Herod, despite an enmity provoked by John's condemnations, involuntarily reveres and respects John (as the Evangelist Mark attests). This feature is remarkable and cries out to be compared to the case of the Lord. It is a highly significant fact of evangelical history that, in the Gospels, there is not a single instance of hatred or even hostility in a woman's soul against the Lord. On the contrary, the Lord was always surrounded by devoted and loving women, who followed Him from their homes and served Him; and these were His future bearers of myrrh, who remained faithful to Him even after His death on the cross. Among these loving women are Martha and Mary, whom Jesus loved (see John 11). There were also sinful women, whom He forgave: they anointed His feet with myrrh and wiped them with their hair. There were also somewhat accidental but highly significant encounters, such as with the Syrophenician woman, "the woman diseased with an issue of blood," and the Samaritan woman. On the way of the cross, among the people who accompanied Him, there were many women who "bewailed and lamented him" (Luke 23:27); and the Lord addressed them with words of compassionate love. Also, the first appearance of the Resurrected Christ, as described in the Gospel, was to a woman, Mary Magdalene; and hers was the first name he uttered after His resurrection. These are not accidental facts, of course; they permit one to conclude that it was not natural for a woman's spirit to resist the summoning Lord. This observation is confirmed in various ways in the history of the Church, but this is not the place to speak of this.

Compared with this fact, it becomes even more astonishing that John the Forerunner, around whom, evidently, there were no women at all (their presence could hardly conform with the circumstances of baptism), became a victim of female rage and vindictiveness. True, this appears to be a chance coincidence of circumstances: by condemning Herod, the Forerunner also touched Herodias. That in fact is how the Evangelist portrays it: as a result of his condemnation of Herodias, she became enraged and "would have him killed" (Mark 6:19). Much less clear are the motives of her daughter, who directly executed her mother's evil intent. Having pleased Herod by her dance at the feast and having received from him the insane promise that he would fulfill any desire she might have, Salome asked for John the Forerunner's head on a platter. According to Matthew (14:8), this monstrous desire, which would make anyone shudder and which is especially unnatural for a woman, especially one so young, was suggested to her by her mother. Likewise, in Mark we find: "And she went forth, and said unto her mother, What shall I ask? And she said, The head of John the Baptist. And she came in straightway with haste unto the king, and asked, saying, I will that thou give me by and by in a charger the head of John the Baptist" (Mark 6:24-25).

The daughter was worthy of the mother. In church hymns she is called a "disgusting dancer," an "illicit female," a "disciple of the much-malicious devil," an "unclean whore." The obedience and readiness with which the daughter listened to her mother allows us to speculate that she too was consumed with an evil and unsated passion, which was transformed into a monstrous concupiscence of hatred. The image of a girl bearing in her hands her reward, the head on a platter of the greatest of those born of women, has something satanical in it. And here, of course, we see not only obedience to the mother, but also solidarity with her. Obedience is possible only as regards what is good; as regards what is evil, we have not obedience but criminal participation. The daughter willingly and easily obeyed the mother's monstrous instruction, went "with haste" to the king to demand the Baptist's head on a platter. This is sufficient evidence that the girl was consumed with the same evil passion for the Forerunner as the mother. There is no reason to think that this was solely rage for her mother's sake, rather than for the sake of her own lust.

In any case, female depravity and malice were united here, and rose against the Baptist in the figure of an "unclean whore" carrying on a platter the head of the Forerunner, an "angel" most venerable. Outwardly, it might appear that this angel in the flesh, this prophet, ascetic bearer of perfect purity and chastity, could have no connection at all with these unclean women, receptacles of debauchery and playthings of sensuality. But vice is attracted to saintliness and sin to purity. Between them a decisive combat inevitably arises; here it ends outwardly with a repulsive paroxysm of malice before a head lying on a platter. Inwardly, however, it ends with the triumph of good.

Original sin entered the world through a woman. Satan poisoned our first mother, Eve, by his unclean breath and made her an instrument of sensuality and debauchery: cruel lust, the fire of sex, entered the human esssence and determined the form of its being, from conception ("Behold, I was shapen in iniquity; and in sin did my mother conceive me": Ps. 51:5) to inevitable death. The first combat for purity was fought in a woman, and corruption was victorious. But this victory was not definitive, for in woman herself a new battle between purity and corruption began. And this time purity triumphed: the old Eve was restored by the new Eve, the Ever-Virgin, from whom, conceived without seed, was born Christ the Lord, absolutely free of original sin. No concupiscence can affect him, for He abides *beyond* the fallen human esssence that is perverted by sin and cast into sex. Therefore, even the temptation by Satan in the wilderness, which, no doubt, included *all* imaginable possibilities, did *not* include the temptations of lust.

That is why there could never be any element of passion in personal relationships between the female esssence and the Lord; only the primordial strings of the chastity of the female spirit could sound there. Neither conflict nor concupiscence could exist here; original sin and passions were silent here.[1] They were silent near the Ever-Virgin too, for, although

---

1. "The body of the God-Man was exceptionally harmonious and beautiful: 'Thou art fairer than the children of men,' His forefather, the holy prophet David, praised Him

She was born a natural human being and subject to the infirmity due to original sin, She, in Her ever-virginity, was delivered from the corrupted female essence by the divine nativity and the descent of the Holy Spirit Therefore, She was free of the temptation of the first Eve and could not be subject to it.

The case of the Forerunner was somewhat different. Although he was the greatest of those born of women, his feat was a human one accomplished in human esssence burdened with original sin. The greatest of those born of women accomplishes the greatest victory over sin: he attains the highest degree of personal sinlessness in his life that is equal to that of the angels. But it was precisely this supreme degree of sinlessness that attracted the most violent attack of sinful sensuality and malice. Both women, mother and daughter, exercised an art of seduction that was irresistible to those around them. Representing a kind of personal incarnation of Eve's fall and of poisoning by the satanic seed, they were prepared to be carriers of female seduction. But having no effect here, the latter was transformed into satanic rage against the one who was inaccessible to its power; the same passion was manifested in both lust and vengeful malice. The fury of the two women was indirect evidence of the Forerunner's inaccessible loftiness and chastity.

In a confused manner they hated in the Forerunner the conqueror of sins who was nevertheless subject to original sin, a virgin by spiritual feat but not by nature — in other words, not yet an *ever-virgin*, whom temptation could not touch. But the satanical envy did not see far enough; it did not fully fathom the mystery of the Forerunner (just as Satan could not fully fathom the mystery of the Incarnation, which is why, during the temptation in the wilderness, he kept asking: "If thou be the Son of God" [Matt. 4:3], without knowing that with certitude).

Before the baptism of the Lord, John was merely a virgin, but during and after the baptism, having received something from the Spirit that descended upon Christ in the form of a dove, he set out on the path of ever-virginity as the Baptist. Here, his path converged with that of the Ever-Virgin Mary, who became the Mother of God in the Annunciation, al-

---

prophetically (Ps. 45:2). But the God-Man's bodily beauty did not produce in women those emotions that masculine beauty is wont to produce in them. On the contrary, Christ's body healed all passions, both of the soul and of the body. The property that permeated it, this was the property that it communicated. It abundantly bestowed Divine grace upon all who looked at it, upon all who touched it, both men and women" (Bishop Ignatii Brianchianinov, *Works*, vol. IV: *Exposition of the Orthodox Church's Doctrine of the Mother of God*, p. 400).

though She attained the fullness of this state only after the descent of the Holy Spirit at the Pentecost. By baptizing, the Baptist himself was baptized, was cobaptized by the Holy Spirit, who descended upon the Baptized One and sanctified the waters of the Jordan, in which both stood. John's wish, "I have need to be baptized of thee" (Matt. 3:14), was then fulfilled, for the Baptist, whose hand touched the head of the Baptized One, was not a mere spectator, who only saw but did not receive anything.

Baptized in the Baptism, John too was anointed by the Holy Spirit, by the grace of baptism, which crowned his feat and allowed him to participate in ever-virginity. Only by virtue of this participation could he have a place near Christ, alongside the Ever-Virgin. Only this could make the *Deisis* possible. Just as the Mother of God could not have become the Mother of God, could not have come so close to the Lord, so at one with Him, if She were not purified in advance for that purpose by the Holy Spirit, so the Forerunner could not have touched with baptizing hand the Lord's head if the Holy Spirit had not descended upon him.

But this descent of grace upon him, this cobaptism with the Lord, is not yet the perfect and definitive baptism. The latter is possible only in the Savior's redemptive death, not before or outside it (there can be no exceptional "privileges" here). This was therefore only a *pre*-baptism for John. He approached ever-virginity, but was not yet liberated from original sin, which liberation could only be accomplished by the Savior's redemptive death.

By being the Baptist, John received a certain preliminary gift of anointment toward ever-virginity, but he was much farther away from it than the Ever-Virgin Mary, who fully received it at the Pentecost. A "disciple of the much-malicious devil" could, in her blindness, be deceived by this, in a certain sense, transitional state, and direct her passion, a mixture of lust and hatred, at a being who by no means is a suitable object for it. Having seduced, through Eve, the first Adam, Satan turns out to be impotent in his instruments as far as Adam's descendant is concerned. And the hatred of Herodias and that of her daughter represents a vengeful impotence of sin that does not have power over the Baptist. It is Satan's vengeance through his baser instruments. But the good laughs at this vengeance. Thanks to this vengeance, the Baptist was sent on his ministry in the world beyond the grave. As the Church hymn says: "Christ's proclaimer is sent in advance to those in hell, in order to prepare life there, in order to preach to those who are in the shadows."

The manner of the Forerunner's death is not accidental: The decapitation by a sword is full of mysterious meaning and significance. The

Church particularly loves and venerates the "decapitation." The Church kisses the icon of the venerable head separated from the body and lying on a platter; and she sometimes portrays the Forerunner as holding his own head in his hands. The Lord explained His own death by crucifixion in the following way: "And I, if I be lifted up from the earth, will draw all men unto me. This he said, signifying what death he should die" (John 12:32-33). The instrument of the Lord's death was repeatedly predicted and prefigured in Scripture. Crucifixion was one of the common methods of execution employed then in the Roman Empire, a representative of which was Herod.

However, the Forerunner did not precede his Lord by being crucified, but was executed by decapitation. The latter, like most of the forms of martyrdom, is, first of all, a baptism by blood, which is shed copiously here. Furthermore, it is a division of the body: the head, the seat of thought and word, is separated from the rest of the body, which contains the organs that govern the sensuous and sensual life. Was not this separation, this liberation of spirit from flesh, accomplished by the Forerunner himself in the course of his entire saintly life that was like that of an angel? And is this not expressed by the icon that represents him as holding his own head in his hands? Angels are often represented on icons by a head and wings, but without a body. This decapitation constitutes the Forerunner's silent answer to those powers of sin and evil that, in the person of the criminal mother and daughter, wished to possess him through the infirmity of the fleshly nature: The Forerunner was not subject to the latter. And the Forerunner's head continues its life, as it were, without the rest of the body. The Church celebrates with a profound devotion "the decapitation of the Forerunner," uniting on this occasion the contrition of a strict fast with an ecclesial festivity (as on the day of the Exaltation of the Holy Cross). The Church also celebrates the two "acquisitions" of his venerable head.

"His disciples came, and took up the body, and buried it, and went and told Jesus" (Matt. 14:12). The Forerunner's star had set. "When Jesus heard of it, he departed thence, by ship into a desert place apart" (Matt. 14:13). The Lord received the news in silence. He alone knew the mystery of the Forerunner. He knew that what had happened was inevitable, just as He knew the inevitability of His own passion and death, for which it would soon be necessary to prepare His disciples. What was left for Him to say about the Forerunner that He had not yet said? Should he praise his ministry? But He had already praised it in the farewell discourse about him. Should He mourn his martyrdom? But was it not for this hour that the witness of the Truth had come, the lamp that shone and burned? Or finally, should He speak about the pitiful instruments of satanical malice, who were unworthy of His words?

What was more magnificent and eloquent than this silence? The Lord departed to a desert place alone. Why? To pray. The Gospel does not explicitly say this, but it is whispered, as it were, by this silence. Moreover, this same fourteenth chapter of Matthew says of Him after this seclusion: "And Jesus went forth, and saw a great multitude" (Matt. 14:14); "and when he had sent the multitudes away, he went into a mountain apart to pray: and when the evening was come, he was there alone" (Matt. 14:23).

The Holy Church pronounced her judgment upon this event: "The insane Herod has you decapitated without pity, exposing the baseness of his nature. But Christ made of you, most blessed one, as baptist, the head of the Church" (little vespers, sticheron). The Forerunner becomes the head of the Church. This must, of course, be understood correctly. The Forerunner cannot be considered the head of the earthly and heavenly Church. That is Christ. He is not the head of the Church even in the sense that the Ever-Virgin is such a head, as the personal incarnation of the Church in Her relation to Christ. Finally, he is not the head of the Church in the sense that — correctly or incorrectly — the apostle Peter or the pontiffs are considered heads in relation to the militant Church. The Forerunner is here called the head of the Church in the sense that he is *first* in the Church, the greatest of those born of women. That is his grandeur and primacy; and that is what we must now discuss on the basis of what the Church teaches about him.

CHAPTER 10

The Glorification of the Forerunner

The Forerunner's ministry in the world beyond the grave is limited in time, for it continues only until Christ's arrival, that is, until His descent into hell and preaching there, which corresponds to the foundation of the Church in the world beyond the grave. With this, the Forerunner's ministry as such ends, and a new mission begins for him, which is a sacred mystery. The Church gives us a glimpse of this mystery, partly by means of hymns, but especially by means of iconography.

Here, as in certain other questions, we must refer to iconographic theology, as a branch of liturgical theology.[1] Orthodox iconography provides a basis for the study of what can be called the *glorification* of the Forerunner. It contains *visions* of the Forerunner, a seeing of God's mysteries. These icons are of two types: First, there are those that relate to events of his earthly life, the chief of which is, of course, the Baptism of the Lord, but which also include his birth and his decapitation. These can be called *sacred-historical* icons. Second, there are a number of representations that are not historical but *dogmatic-symbolic* in character. In such icons, he holds a cross (we find this mainly in Western iconography), a cup, in which reposes the Divine Infant, the "Lamb of the world," or his own head. He is sometimes depicted with wings or a crown; or standing before Christ together with the Mother of God (the *Deisis*). There are icons where he stands before a fiery angel, i.e., Sophia, the Wisdom of God; or before

---

1. Unfortunately there exists no monograph on the iconography of the Forerunner. Neither the chronology nor the history of this iconography has been traced. Because of a lack of information, I have no possibility of filling this lacuna and so am compelled to limit myself to interpreting the symbolism.

Christ at the Last Judgment. We also find him on the iconostasis, in the "order" where he frames the image of the Savior together with the Mother of God and among the angels, forming the "spiritual heaven."

All of these representations of the Forerunner have a common feature: they separate him from the rest of humankind, putting him above humankind, as it were, together with the Mother of God; or outside it, as an Angel. We will now try to pinpoint the dogmatic meaning of these images.

The large, broad wings are the most widespread iconic attribute of the Forerunner, encountered when he is portrayed alone as well as when he is portrayed in the *Deisis* or with Sophia. The wings indicate, first of all, his angel-like life, owing to which the church hymn calls him an "angel": "O prophet, what should we call you: angel, apostle, or martyr? Angel, for you lived incorporeal . . ." (sticheron of 29 January, of Patriarch German). "Come, people, praise the prophet and the martyr, and the Baptist of the Lord, for he is an angel in the flesh. . . . to those in hell he announced the glad tidings of the resurrection of the dead . . ." (ibid.).

It is noteworthy that at the Feast of the Decapitation a sticheron of the Dormition is sung. This is an allusion, as it were, to a correlation between the Dormition of the Mother of God and the death of the Forerunner, in conformity with the theme of the *Deisis*.

We can cite a number of other liturgical texts that mention John's relationship with the angelic world: "He lives together with the angels" (7 January, ode 3). "The angelic hosts are in astonishment before you" (29 January, sticheron). "Baptist and angel who spares all" (ibid.). "The Word of God wishing to be born of a virgin, an angel issued from elderly loins" (24 June, sticheron of Anatolii). "Limit of the prophets and beginning of the apostles, earthly angel and heavenly man" (sticheron to "Glory," of Andrew of Crete). And so on.

Note also what the Church says about Elias (office of 20 July): "We have known you as an angel on earth, O divine prophet, and in heaven as a man of God" (canon 2, ode 9, tr. 2). "You lived on earth as if you were in the flesh, and now we exalt you to heaven, so that you may rejoice with the angelic orders" (ibid., tr. 3). "You resemble an angel, marvelous Elias, God-bearer" (ode 6, tr. 1).

Corresponding to this is the phrase about the angel in the prophecy of Malachi 3, although the term used can also be understood in the more general sense of a messenger. However, this explanation is insufficient. Certain saints are said to have lived an angelic life, but they are not portrayed with wings. It is noteworthy that the Church directly celebrates only the prophet Elias as an "angel in the flesh." Is this not another indication of the mysterious resemblance, approaching identification, between the Forerunner and the prophet Elias? Do we not have a mysterious indication here that the close approach between the angelic and human worlds realized in the Forerunner had already begun in Elias? If we cannot answer these questions, at least we can pose them.

Therefore, one must see in the attribute of the wings more than a symbolic or allegorical significance. They must be accepted as real. One must also take into account the whole significance of the fact that, in His discourse to the people about the Baptist, the Lord Himself applies Malachi's prophecy to him: "For this is he, of whom it is written, Behold, I send my messenger [angel] before thy face" (Matt. 11:10; cf. Luke 7:27).[2]

The Forerunner is a heaven-dweller, who, like the angels, the "second lights," stands before the Unfading Light. But he differs from them in that he is a human being and, moreover, the greatest of human beings. Ontologically, though not hierarchically, man is superior to the angels. Only to man, the crown of creation, His regal creature, did God give *dominion* over the world, whereas He created the angels only to serve the world as the messengers of His will.[3] And the Lord assumed the human, not the angelic, nature. Union in one being of the human nature (in its supreme manifestation) and the equi-angelic nature makes its bearer capable of rising equally above both worlds by virtue of this union: The Forerunner is, as it were, a humanized angel or an angelic man, a living and personal communion of the two worlds.

His nature represents a mystery that cannot be fully fathomed in this age. But it has been manifested and partially unveiled. Was this union of the angelic and human worlds accomplished at his birth, or is it a consequence of his heavenly glorification? There is no answer. But one can consider it established that the boundary between these two worlds was abolished at the moment of the Incarnation, and this abolition was one of the consequences of the Incarnation. These worlds were united in the person of the Forerunner, who thereby became not only a being who, as an angel, surpassed man, but also a being who, as a man, surpassed an-

---

2. The words of Malachi's prophecy are usually inscribed on the scroll held by John on icons where he is also represented with wings like an angel (e.g., on the seventeenth-century fresco of the Yaroslavl Church of John the Baptist). The Church thus implicitly gives a literal interpretation of this prophecy, to the effect that the Forerunner is an angel not only by his ministry but also by his essence.

3. "Who maketh his angels spirits; his ministers a flaming fire" (Ps. 104:4).

gelic being. Therefore, his presence before God is loftier and closer than that of any other created being, whether angelic or human; and he approaches the place where only the Mother of God, "more venerable than the cherubim and *incomparably* more glorious than the seraphim," abides. No one but the Mother of God stands closer to the Lord than the Forerunner.

But the two have radically different relations with the angelic world. The Mother of God is *incomparably* more glorious and higher than the angelic world, from its highest orders, the cherubim and seraphim, to, of course, its lowest orders. Her essential superiority to the angels results from Her closeness to the God to whom She gave birth. Her superiority to the angelic world is, ontologically, the superiority of the One born of Her, of the One Whom the angels serve (see Matt. 4:11). She is praised by the angels as the Queen of heaven, as "higher than the angels and archangels; more pure than any other creature; a great wonder to the angels." Here we have the direct ontological superiority to the angelic nature of the Divine nature, in which the Mother of God participates in the highest and ultimate measure (or rather, without measure) by the grace of the descent upon Her of the Holy Spirit and by virtue of Her divine maternity.

But the Forerunner is not *incomparably* (in the ontological sense) superior to the angelic nature as such. However, since he is not only a man and not only an angel, but an angel-man, the saintly Forerunner turns out — by virtue of this duality and complexity of his nature — to be superior to all angels and all human beings (and not only as the "greatest of those born of women" but also as an angel-man). And precisely when he stands before Christ, no one is closer to Him than the Forerunner except the Mother of God; and together with Her he stands before Christ as God's loftiest creature.

The boundary, as well as the relationship, between the angelic and human worlds is mysterious. There is no doubt, however, that these two worlds are interdependent, are linked, somehow exist one for the other and one together with the other (which finds expression in the very name "angel," messenger). But *prior to the Forerunner,* this relationship was external in some sense; there was a chasm between the angelic and human worlds. But in the person of the Forerunner (as in the person of Elias) this distance was overcome by an inner unification of the two natures, by a kind of humanization of the angel, by an ontological union, with the autonomous being of the two natures preserved.

This was an event in both worlds. In John, the angelic world is drawn into the work of the Incarnation and in-humanization of God not only in the sense of service but also for and according to itself. In fact, is the Incarnation not an event in all the creaturely worlds? In particular, its effects must be manifested in the angelic world too: the human nature has really received in Christ the dignity with which it was potentially endowed at the beginning. This dignity must place man at the center of creation and define him *anew*, inwardly, in relation to the angelic world.

But how did this happen and in what did it find expression? The Lord did not directly assume the angelic nature, for it does not conform with His nature. But the angelic world too experienced an indirect co-assumption and co-inclusion in the Incarnation. Because of this, the angelic world was not deprived of the benefits of the Incarnation and of human glorification, which is the glorification of all creatures and thus of the angels as well. This is accomplished through the Mother of God, the Queen of heaven and earth, of the whole creaturely world, more venerable than the cherubim and incomparably more glorious than the seraphim. But apart from and alongside this, there is a certain direct convergence between the angelic and human worlds, not, of course, in the person of the Redeemer Himself, the Angel of the Great Council, but through the angel of this Angel; not through the Bridegroom, but through the friend of the Bridegroom. The Mother of God unites the Logos with the human nature. But in the Baptist the human and angelic natures are united by virtue of the Incarnation, which, expanding, necessarily draws all creatures into itself, including the angelic world. Such is the new aspect that consists of the Forerunner's participation in the Incarnation, not only as the Baptist through the baptism of Christ, but also as an angel, through the unification in him of the human and angelic natures.

What does this union of natures consist in? We do not have an answer to this question. Unfathomability is of course a distinguishing feature of divine mysteries. The union of the human and divine natures in one hypostasis is unfathomable. However, the dogma of Chalcedon clearly marks out the boundaries: one hypostasis, Divine, the Second Person of the Holy Trinity; and two natures, divine and human, united without separation and without confusion. But what does the union of the angelic and human natures in the one person of the Forerunner mean? And is the hypostasis angelic or human? Or is it both angelic and human? Is the Forerunner an incarnate angel from his very birth? But in that case how would such an incarnation be possible? Or does his angelic being result from the purification and sanctification of his human nature, which raises him to the angelic nature? But how is it possible to pass from one nature to the other? Or, finally, does he live simultaneously in both worlds, angelic and human? But how would this simultaneity be possible? All we can do is pose these questions on the basis of the *Church's* direct testimony, but, limited to our human powers, we are unable to answer them. Nevertheless, we tend to think that the Forerunner's angelic being is directly related to his participation in the work of the Incarnation.

On the night of His birth, the Savior received the angels' praise. In the person of the Forerunner, He was greeted and confessed not only by the human but also by the angelic world. In other words, the Forerunner's work was significant for both worlds, human as well as angelic. But how a man could have become an angel without ceasing to be a man is a mystery to which the Church clearly and solemnly bears witness but which it does not elucidate further. Only one thing is certain: a man, by virtue of the ontological fullness of his being, can become an angel; but an angel, however high his elevation, cannot assume the human nature, for it is alien to the angelic nature. However, an angel can take on a temporary human *appearance*, a reflection of man's being, if God chooses to send him as a messenger to human beings.

The general idea that the Forerunner has an angelic dignity (and not merely an equi-angelic nature) is directly confirmed by the place that he occupies in the order of the iconostasis. In the second row of the iconostasis, above the feasts (if this row is missing, then in the first row), the Savior is placed at the center, with the Mother of God and the Forerunner to each side. One angel, or two, follows on each side, followed by icons of *human* saints, those of the apostles. The idea expressed here is crystal clear: the central part represents the heavenly, or angelic, world, which is followed by the human world. And in this heaven, in the angelic surround, closer to the Lord than the angels, but in their midst, there stand not only the Mother of God but also the Forerunner. He is therefore missing from the human saints and is closer than the angels themselves to the Lord's Throne. This entry into the heavenly world from the earthly world is sometimes iconographically expressed by rendering both the Mother of God and the Forerunner with wings. In the present case, this expresses not so much the fact that they both belong to the angelic world, but the fact that they both participate (although in different senses) in the heavenly world. Such is the Forerunner's hierarchical place.

This idea is indirectly confirmed by an iconographic feature that we examined previously: the depiction of the Forerunner holding his own head (in a cup or on a plate). We see this on icons of the decapitation where the head forms the second plane of the icon, as it were: before and after the decapitation. We sometimes see this on icons of the martyrdom of other saints as well; but we also see analogous features on icons that do not depict decapitation. For example, on an icon in the Church of John the Baptist in Yaroslavl, he is depicted with wings, holding in his right hand a cup with his head and a scroll with the text of Malachi's prophecy (Mal. 3:1): "Behold, I will send my angel, and he shall prepare the way before me." The central figure is framed on all four sides by scenes from the Forerunner's life, including the baptism of the Lord. His decapitation can also be understood, as we explained above, as a symbol of emancipation from the fleshly, concupiscent nature and of his communion with angelic life. The representation of the head apart from the rest of the body can have the same significance. These icons represent him in both of his natures: angelic and human.

As an angel, the Forerunner is often represented holding a cup in which the Divine Infant is sacrificed: "Behold the Lamb of God, which taketh away the sin of the world" (John 1:29). An allegorical interpretation is the first that comes to mind for this icon: it can be considered as an illustration to the well-known Gospel story about the Forerunner's testimony. However, such an explanation is not sufficient, though it is acceptable and even indisputable as far as it goes. This important icon fills us with fear and trembling; it clearly represents the vision of a mystery.

One must also note that the Forerunner, together with Christ Himself and the Mother of God, is always represented on the holy chalice. This indicates his special nearness to and participation in the Divine Eucharist. There is no sacred-historical basis for such a nearness in the Gospels, if we do not count John 1:29. It is significant, however, that the Forerunner's words are fully incorporated into a ritual of the Divine Liturgy, the *proskomide*: "Sacrificed is the Lamb of God, which taketh away the sin of the world, for the life and salvation of the world." John the Forerunner was not present at and did not participate in the Last Supper, for at this time he was already in the world beyond the grave (by the way, in his earthly life he partook neither of bread nor of wine, the two species of the Divine Eucharist: "John the Baptist came neither eating bread nor drinking wine" [Luke 7:33]). Nevertheless, the Church expressly attests his presence at the Divine Eucharist, together with the Mother of God. She, too, was not present at the Last Supper; She was present only at the prefiguring miracle at the marriage in Cana of Galilee. Nevertheless, in Her own manner She does directly participate in the Divine Eucharist: to Her Son, She gave the Body and Blood, of which the faithful partake. In a certain sense, the Divine Eucharist is also Her body and blood. That is why the giving of thanks that follows communion is addressed not only to Christ,

God, but also to Her: "We give thanks to you, who made us worthy, we who are unworthy, of partaking of the most pure body and most sacred blood of your Son" (fifth prayer of the giving of thanks). And it is the portion extracted in honor of Her memory that the priest deposits first on the plate, saying: "By Her prayers, Lord, accept this sacrifice at Your heavenly altar." The Mother of God prays for this; She co-celebrates the liturgy. Also, after the sanctification of the sacred gifts, the first prayer is solemnly addressed to the Mother of God, Who is mysteriously co-present at the Body and Blood of Her Son.

The nearest co-presence after Hers is the Forerunner's. Both during the *proskomide* and after the sanctification of the sacred gifts, he is named before any of the other saints, right after the Mother of God; it is also in his name that the first portion of the third prosphora is extracted.

Summarizing and synthesizing all these particulars, we inevitably arrive at the conclusion that the Holy Church attributes to the Forerunner a special place, the first, at the Divine Eucharist. It is to this ministry that the icon of the Forerunner with the cup refers. As a Levite and the son of a priest, the Forerunner was an Old Testament priest, although he never exercised this right in the temple of Jerusalem, saving it until his new ordination, through his decapitation, in the New Testament. He participates in the Eucharist not only as the Baptist but *also as an angel,* for heavenly angelic powers "serve invisibly with us." His dual nature, angelic and human, gives him the first, exclusive place after the Mother of God. The one who stood before Christ at His earthly Theophany is eternally present in this eternal mystery of His glorified body, which is accomplished at the holy altar: the friend of the Bridegroom participates in the wedding feast of the Lamb.

In this connection we must examine another iconographic attribute of the Forerunner: a cross, which he usually holds in his left hand, but sometimes in his right. In an icon of the Moscow school of the sixteenth century (in the Likhachev collection), a winged Forerunner holds a chalice with the Infant-Lamb in his right hand and a cross in his left, which imparts a eucharistic significance to the symbolism here. On another sixteenth-century icon, of the Moscow Cathedral of the Annunciation, the Forerunner holds a cross in his left hand, while the fingers of his right are pressed together to form a sacerdotal benediction, symbolizing his priesthood, his "mediation between the old and the new grace."

It is noteworthy that the Gospel narratives do not contain any foundation, even a verbal one, for this symbol of the cross in the Forerunner's hand. It has appeared spontaneously, as it were, on his icons and is perceived as something that belongs there. This can only be explained by the fact that the friend of the Bridegroom penetrated the depths of the mystery of the Cross, of Christ's redemptive sacrifice, and descended into hell as the herald of this redemption, as the Lord's apostle and evangelist.

Finally, on certain icons of the *Deisis* and especially of Sophia, the Wisdom of God, both the Forerunner and the Mother of God are represented in royal crowns, of the same type on all of these icons. This is a highly significant attribute. The crown is a symbol of glory, as well as of glorification. It figures on certain icons of the Mother and Child, as well as on icons of Christ, the Pantocrator. A similar crown, of royalty and glorification, is proper to the Forerunner (it differs, of course, from those of martyrs and those of certain kings, such as David). The theme of the crowning of the Mother of God *(le couronnement de la Vierge)* is fairly common in Western iconography. It is not foreign to Orthodoxy either: for example, on the icon called "It Is Worthy," the crown is held by angels; and above it the figure of God the Father is giving His blessing. On certain icons of Sophia, the Wisdom of God, the same sort of crown is worn not only by the Mother of God and the Forerunner but also by a flaming angel who sits on a throne. This crowning, which the Mother of God and the Forerunner have in common, indicates the special and exclusive glorification of the latter in some sense *alongside* the Mother of God. This by no means removes the difference between them, but indicates a certain similarity in their situation and state.

This brings us to the very essence of the doctrine of the *Deisis*. Here, on the one hand, one must accept in all its *dogmatic* significance the fact that the Church reveals through the icon. No preestablished forms are prescribed for the tradition of the Church: the Holy Spirit that lives in her "bloweth where it listeth." In this respect, as sources of the sacred tradition, the canons, the patristic writings, the liturgical texts, and the icons are of equal value. All this — not in isolation but in its living and organic totality — expresses the truth of the Church.

Thus, according to the testimony of the *Deisis,* the Forerunner and the Mother of God stand closer to Christ than the saints and even the angels. This is made clear from their position in the "order" of the iconostasis. There is no barrier between Christ and those who stand in close proximity to Him in the *Deisis*. This is also true for the icon of the Last Judgment. Here too, the Forerunner and the Mother of God stand in the closest proximity to Christ, this icon being a particular case of the *Deisis,* as it were. This nearness of theirs to Christ attests to the superior sanctification that they have received, the highest possible. They are representatives of the *whole* Church, earthly and heavenly, visible and invisible. They are at her head, embodying her holiness in themselves. But this similarity of their positions does not in any way negate the difference between them.

Let us begin with this difference. The Mother of God is the Glory of the World, God's perfectly deified creature. In this respect, She is the creaturely manifestation of Sophia, the Wisdom of God. This state does not admit any increase in its grace or any change in its destiny. In particular, the Mother of God is subject neither to the universal judgment nor to the universal resurrection. At the Judgment, She is present only as Intercessor; and the Judgment will touch Her only in virtue of Her love for humankind, Her compassion for the sinners that are judged. Nor does the universal resurrection apply to Her, since She has already been resurrected in Her body and abides in it in the heavens. Her body has a glorified nature, similar to that of Christ after the resurrection. As Mother and as Queen, She is bound by ties of love to this world and humankind. But She Herself does not belong to the world and humankind; She has surpassed them by Her dormition, resurrection, and assumption. She is not in this world; and the latter is not capable of preserving that tie with Her that it preserves even with the greatest saints: "The Mother of God who prays without ceasing . . . the grave and mortification could not hold Her" (Feast of the Assumption, sticheron).

All this can be expressed in the following dogmatic formula: The Mother of God did not leave her *relics* in this world. And just as in the Savior's sepulchre the apostles saw "the linen clothes lie, And the napkin, that was about his head, not lying with the linen clothes, but wrapped together in a place by itself" (John 20:6-7), so in the Mother of God's grave too, when it was opened for the apostle Thomas, only the burial clothes were found. The Queen of heaven abides in the heavens in Her glorified body.

In complete contrast, the Forerunner has his sacred relics on earth. Attesting to this is not only the negative fact of the absence of any grounds in Church tradition for believing in his resurrection, but also, and much more importantly, the positive testimony of the Church, which celebrates the "acquisition" of his head and venerates his precious remains. This fact of the existence of his remains is of extreme importance.

Relics are the sacred remains, full of grace, of the bodies of saints. Saints have attained such a spiritual mastery over their own bodies and have sanctified them to such a degree over the course of their earthly lives that this connection continues even after death. Saints continue to live, as it were, in their remains, or, more precisely, are present in them by grace.

This anticipates the resurrection of the body, the "first resurrection," the beginning of the body's glorification, although the latter is visible only to the eyes of faith, and refers only to the spiritual body, not to the natural body. Depending on God's will, the natural body can remain incorruptible, or it can be subject to the general laws of nature — which is why physical incorruptibility is not a necessary attribute of "repose in relics," to use the expression of St. Seraphim of Sarov. "Repose in relics" is the beginning of the glorification and resurrection of the body, but only the beginning. Saints too, like all people, await the universal resurrection. Although their afterlife state consists in blessed presence before God and the contemplation of His face, this state is not yet perfect. They are separated from their bodies, although this separation is not final and definitive. They have yet to live through an event on which the fulfillment of their being depends: the universal resurrection. This is the reason they have not transcended this world, have not definitively entered into the heavenly world, in which they participate incompletely in their incomplete being, deprived of a body. Thus, this state is essentially a preliminary one, transitional and dual.

The *absence* of relics of the Savior and the Mother of God and the impossibility of their existence attest to their total and definitive glorification, to the authentic revelation of God's Glory in the Creator and in the supreme creation. Conversely, the presence of John the Forerunner's sacred relics keeps him in this world in a sense and prevents his glorification from being total. Although the first of those born of women remains first, he remains on earth among those born of women. And in his presence before God, the Forerunner, like all saints, remains deprived of his flesh, in contrast to the Mother of God, who abides in the fullness of her glorified human nature with Her body of resurrection.

But this ontological implenitude appears to contradict the supreme degree of sanctification in virtue of which the Forerunner finds himself, together with the Mother of God, in immediate proximity to Christ the Savior. The fact of their presence *together* before Christ would be incomprehensible if one of these two human creatures, the Mother of God, were in a state of fullness of being, while the other, John, was considered to be in a divided state and one that was therefore defective in this sense.

This is a problem that does not have a *direct* solution, although it is possible to propose theological hypotheses, to compare and speculate. In the Forerunner the human nature is united with the angelic nature. Being incomplete because of his humanity, his angelic nature, as free from flesh, does not need the latter for its total sanctification and glorification. The destinies of the angelic world are generally unfathomable to us, although it is considered established in the Orthodox dogmatics that angels, who "behold the face of my Father which is in heaven" (Matt. 18:10), and among whom is Gabriel who stands "in the presence of God" (Luke 1:19), have attained immutability in the good. At the Last Judgment they are present only as messengers and agents of the divine will, who surround the Son of God: "And he shall send his angels with a great sound of a trumpet, and they shall gather together his elect" (Matt. 24:31; also Mark 13:27; cf. Matt. 13:39-49).

The angels are only present at the Judgment; they themselves are not judged. True, this appears to be contradicted by the apostle Paul's mysterious words: "Do ye not know that the saints shall judge the world? . . . Know ye not that we shall judge angels?" (1 Cor. 6:2-3). These words signify that the angels have a certain co-responsibility for the destinies of the world, of human beings, and of the Church; and this co-responsibility will be established with the participation of the "saints." But Paul does not say that the angels will be subject to the Last Judgment in the same way as human beings. Michael and his angels, who prevailed in heaven and cast out the dragon, who "overcame him by the blood of the Lamb, and by the word of their testimony; and they loved not their lives unto the death" (Rev. 12:11), are, of course, already affirmed in the good. Their nature remains incorruptible and whole. They are not subject to the ontological catastrophe that resurrection and judgment are for all of humankind. Thus, we can allow that the angelic orders know a state of glorification in virtue of their nature, although we do not know if this goes for all the angels and to the same degree for all of them. And this corresponds precisely to their proximity to God's throne, which they surround, praising Him. Their relation to God, as well as this proximity, is in some sense absolute. It results from the supreme perfection which their nature has attained and which makes possible the sanctification of their nature.

Insofar as the Forerunner is also an angel, he also possesses this supreme perfection of nature. He will not be subject to the Judgment, but will only be present at it as an angel. The universal resurrection applies to him too as the greatest of those born of women, as the mediator between the Old and New Testaments, who stands at the boundary between the human and angelic worlds and unites them in himself. This will be the fulfillment of his *human* nature, as well as that of the whole human race, but it has only a subordinate significance for the totality of his angelic-human nature.

The fact that he is both an angel and a man makes him not subject to death, as it were, even prior to the universal resurrection. Thus, he already belongs to the other world, together with the Mother of God, but to a different degree. He leaves on earth his precious head (which the Holy Church venerates on 25 February and 25 May) and his sacred relics. The fullness of his glorification therefore refers only to his spirit which is liberated from the flesh, that is, to his angelic nature. In his corporeal nature, the Forerunner does not have the cosmic significance that is proper to the Mother of God, as the Mother of the Logos, by whom all things were made (John 3:1). John's power and knowledge reside in the spiritual domain, where he overcomes the human nature and becomes an inhabitant of heaven. His decapitation, liberating him from his body, is, for him, not only an external but also an inner fact of deliverance from the body, as it were. In John's person, both humankind and the angelic order are present before Christ.

During his earthly mission, John came closer to the Holy Trinity than any other human being: "By hearing the Father's voice, by seeing with his eyes the divine Spirit, John the Forerunner, having placed on thee, O Christ, his hand . . . he is a God-bearer" (office of 25 February, ode 8, tr. 3). There was never a moment in his life when he was not sanctified by the grace of the Holy Spirit: he received this grace even in his mother's womb. And this was done according to the laws of the spiritual world: "whosoever hath, to him shall be given . . . but whosoever hath not, from him shall be taken away even that he hath" (Matt. 13:12; 25:29; Mark 4:25; Luke 8:18; 19:26). Spiritual gifts are multiplied by one another, and the human gifts of the greatest of those born of women are multiplied by the angelic gifts that, unfathomably for us, he possesses. He is present before the Holy Trinity as an angel and as the Forerunner, closer to Christ than any other human being.

The *Deisis*, showing the presence of the Forerunner and of the Mother of God before Christ, fully reveals the mystery of the Incarnation. It is the icon of the Incarnation, for the latter was accomplished through the Mother of God, who gave Christ Her flesh, which became for Him a living temple, as well as through the Forerunner, who baptized Christ, thus accomplishing His anointment through the descent of the Holy Spirit on His human nature (cf. 1 Tim. 3:16). Both the Most Pure Mother of God and the Forerunner manifest in themselves the fullness of the Theophany, not only of Christ but of the entire Holy Trinity, for the Father's love reposes upon the Son in the Holy Spirit.

Linked together, the Most Pure Mother of God and the Forerunner personify the whole Church, heavenly and earthly, of angels and of human beings. The Mother of God, in whom all creatures rejoice, both the angelic choir and the human race, stands at the head of all creation, forming an indissoluble inner union with Her Son, the world-creating and world-governing Word. She represents the Church as the Mother of God and the Bride of God. But we know that motherhood and bridehood do not exhaust the Church's life and power, for the Church is also the heavenly friendship in which the human soul finds, in Christ, its friend. And, in the name of all creation, this friend of the Bridegroom is the Forerunner, who therefore represents a necessary aspect of the Church. Preparing the way before Christ, he leads humankind to Christ by his earthly ministry; and by his angelic ministry he also leads the angelic choir to Christ. For even the angels, who surround the throne of the divine majesty and praise God, are not personally present before God in the same manner as the Forerunner and the Mother of God. And it is only by approaching the two of them and uniting themselves to them that the angels, according to the celestial hierarchy, approach Christ. They cannot withstand His immediate proximity.

In this sense, the Forerunner is *first among those who are present before Christ*, first in the whole creaturely world, angelic and human — not as the maternal principle, which contains and unites all things in itself, but as the personal principle that wills itself and gives itself, as the first representative of the entire Church in prayer before her heavenly High Priest. The Forerunner can be called the *Angel of the Church,* and in this sense he is "her head" (according to a liturgical hymn that is already familiar to us), her first representative. He is the *Guardian Angel* of the whole human race, even now with his prayer preparing the way to Christ for the human race. The Mother of God is the God-bearing Church, while the Forerunner is the Church that is obedient to God. Alongside Him, Christ has both the Mother-Bride and the friend.

The presence of the Mother of God and of the Forerunner before God expresses the Church's relation to Christ as well as to the Holy Spirit. As the Mother of Christ and as His Forerunner and friend, the Virgin Mary and John manifest the mystery of the Son's in-humanization. As the temple of the Holy Spirit that dwells in Mary according to the archangel's annunciation and as the Baptist, who at the baptism saw the descent of the Holy Spirit and received it upon his Baptist's nature, the Ever-Virgin and the Forerunner represent the Church as the *receptacle* of the Holy Spirit. And the revelation of the Son and of the Holy Spirit is the revelation of the Father, who manifests Himself in both of these hypostases. That is why the icon of the *Deisis,* which shows the Mother of God and the Forerunner present before Christ, is a representation of the mystery of the

Theophany, a manifestation of the Most Holy Trinity, which lives in the Church by virtue of the Incarnation.

We do not know when or where the icon of the *Deisis* appeared, but the fact is that it was very widespread in the Church.[4] It clearly has an enormous dogmatic significance for what can be called a unified Mariology and Johannology. "Deisis" means prayer. On this icon the Savior is represented in royal or high-priestly garments, in His power and glory, sitting on a throne and with the Mother of God and the Forerunner standing before Him with hands raised in prayer. What are they praying for? Not for the forgiveness of their sins, for they do not have any. Nor, in general, for themselves. Those who are in a glorified state have nothing to ask for, for they have everything. It only remains for them to praise and to give thanks, like the angels. Therefore, they pray not for themselves but for the world and for the human race. In standing before the throne of God and showing great audacity in their prayer, they are first in the Church, the greatest representatives of the human race.

In her prayers and hymns the Church bears witness to the fact that the Mother of God prays to Her Son for all humanity. Among testimonies of this sort let us note the Feast of the Protection of the Mother of God as well as the existence of various miraculous icons of the Mother of God. The Holy Church also confesses that the saints, of whom the Forerunner is the first, pray to the Lord for the sinful world.

But the *Deisis* implies something even more significant. Here it is a question not of a prayer among the prayers of other saints and with them, but of a certain primacy of presence, a leading of the entire Church in prayer. And this concerns the presence not only of the Mother of God and not only of the Forerunner but of the two *together*. This is not only a presence together in prayer but a *union* in Christ and through Christ in the fullness of the *whole* prayer of the Church. It is a kind of high-priesthood in the Church, a presence before Christ's throne in prayer, a liturgy celebrated in the name of the whole Church.

---

4. "The *Deisis* is an icon depicting Jesus Christ in royal or episcopal habit, with the Mother of God on His right and John the Forerunner on His left (sometimes it comprises three separate icons with the same sacred representations). It is usually placed in the third row of the iconostasis, above the icon *The Last Supper*. One supposes that the name *Deisis* originated in the fact that, below this icon, the prayer ended with the Greek word *Deisis* (prayer), and those who did not know Greek took this to be the name of the icon. This name could also have come from the fact that the Mother of God and the Forerunner are represented in prayer before the Lord" (*The Orthodox Theological Encyclopedia*, vol. 4, pp. 975-6).

The *Deisis* expresses the fullness of the love of the Church for God and for man. It is the *praying Church* that is present before God and surrounds Him with the assemblies of angels, apostles, and saints. It is the Church's prayer for the Church. The *Deisis* is the unification of the heavenly and the earthly, of the angelic and the human, in Christ's Divine Humanity, in the Church that is His Body. It is a veil of intercession spread over the world. It is the glorified humanity, praying to Christ for the humanity that is not glorified. It is the audacity of the Spirit, crying in our hearts, "Abba Father," and teaching us to pray with unutterable words. It is the two — or three, if one counts the Son of man Himself, sitting on the throne — gathered in His Name; and He Himself is in their midst. All-powerful and all-ecclesial is the prayer of the Most Pure Mother of God, but even more all-powerful, for more all-ecclesial, is the *Deisis*. The Church is not only a multiple unity but also a unitary multiplicity; and for the fullness of all-ecclesiality, two or three are needed, in the image of the Most Holy Trinity: unity in trinity and trinity in unity.

The *Deisis* is the intercession and prayer of the Mother of God and the Forerunner for the human race in its *earthly* life: they pray for and with all people who, by their sins, do not shut themselves off from the action of this prayer. This is the veil of intercession spread over the world and the assistance of grace to human infirmity. It is the Church's unceasing prayer for her children. But there is also a special form of the *Deisis* which the Church attests: it refers not to the course of earthly life but to its final hour, beyond time. This is *the prayer at the Last Judgment* for the pardoning of sinners. On icons of the Last Judgment (as on icons of the conventional *Deisis*) the Mother of God is present in prayer before Christ together with the Forerunner. Above the rest of humankind, which is subject to the Last Judgment, and closer than all the angelic armies that are present there, the Mother of God and the Forerunner are present before Christ, praying for mercy and pardon. In their person it is the already glorified Church that prays for the Church that is passing through the final separation that divides time from eternity, the kingdom of grace from the kingdom of glory.

We have written elsewhere about the participation of the Mother of God at the Last Judgment.[5] Mercy is united with justice. The Comforter heals the wounds inflicted by the punitive sword of the Word of God. The Son of Man's action is united with that of the Mother of Man: "Mercy and truth meet, justice and the world embrace." The Forerunner's participa-

---

5. See *The Burning Bush: On the Orthodox Veneration of the Mother of God* (Paris, 1927).

tion in this prayer, attesting to his elevated place and his nearness to God's throne, merges with the work of mercy of the Mother of God. Together with Her, he is the Church, in which lives the Holy Spirit, interceding before the Father and the judging Word with ineffable sighs. And although the judgment is the Son's, its final accomplishment is the work of the entire Holy Trinity, including the Holy Spirit, who, after the dread sundering, restores the world and heals its wounds.

Why does the Forerunner occupy this position of intercessor alongside the Mother of God? For even the angels gaze with fear and trembling upon what takes place here and are only obedient agents; whereas, by his prayer of intercession, the Forerunner opposes the condemnation, as it were; he desires to soften the decree of the righteous judge and to replace it with mercy. The Forerunner occupies this position because he is not only an angel but also a human being. And it is as a *human being* that he, like the Mother of God, intercedes for forgiveness. For the judgment is entirely the Son of God's, because He is also the Son of man: "And [the Father] hath given him authority to execute judgment also, because he is the Son of man" (John 5:27). Therefore, it is precisely His voice that will be heard on the last day by all who are in their graves (John 5:28). And His verdict is one of impartial and perfect justice: "I can of mine own self do nothing: as I hear, I judge: and my judgment is just; because I seek not mine own will, but the will of the Father which hath sent me" (John 5:30).

When the Son of man walked on the earth, He pardoned sinners. He attested to the superiority of mercy over justice. He said that the last will receive as much as the first, that the prodigal son will be given more than the prudent son, that heaven has a greater joy in one repentant sinner than in ninety-nine righteous men. But at the Last Judgment sinners will receive not merciful indulgence but merciless justice. Here, Christ seems to renounce the mercy for the sake of which He came to save those who were lost. But mercy itself is not thereby abolished: It is accomplished by the Holy Spirit, who lives in the Church. And this work of the Church is realized by the Mother of God and the Forerunner. Since they are both human beings, they know creaturely, human infirmity and sorrow, and beseech not justice but mercy.

Here, another comparison comes to mind. We know that the Lord promised to the apostles that they would play a certain part in the Judgment: "Verily I say unto you, That ye which have followed me, in the regeneration when the Son of man shall sit in the throne of his glory, ye also shall sit upon twelve thrones, judging the twelve tribes of Israel" (Matt. 19:28; Luke 22:30). This promise is mysterious: what do these twelve tribes signify? Is this simply a division of the nation of Israel, or is it a division of the whole of the spiritual Israel? Does the apostolic judgment represent only the human role in Christ's tribunal, or are the apostles entrusted here with the total and definitive judgment?

Icons of the Last Judgment usually portray the apostle judges sitting on thrones surrounding Christ, but they are, of course, apart from the Mother of God and the Forerunner. The Last Judgment takes place in the presence of all the nations, when all hidden acts will be revealed. The whole Church, with the holy apostles presiding, will be present at the Last Judgment and participate in it in some manner, convinced of its justice. The apostles will therefore not pronounce some particular judgment, but will proclaim God's manifest justice for the whole world, and this justice is also human justice ("because He is the Son of man"). It was for this very same reason that the apostle Paul told the Corinthians and, of course, the whole Christian world: "Do ye not know that the saints shall judge the world? and if the world shall be judged by you, are ye unworthy to judge the smallest matters?" (1 Cor. 6:2). This indicates, of course, the general participation of the Church, of all her members, in the revelation and thus the judgment of the works that are connected with her destiny and, through her, with the destiny of the entire world. The Church is judged by the Church herself, headed by Christ. And the world, in its essence, is not other than the Church in the process of becoming: the destiny of the world is the destiny of the Church. It is not difficult to understand why and how the Church in her faithful, in the "saints," participates in Christ's Last Judgment, together with the holy angels (see Matt. 24:31; 13:41, 49). Their failure to participate in the Last Judgment would be much more difficult to understand.

But the remarkable thing is that the apostles judge, whereas the Mother of God and the Forerunner do not judge, but only preside in their presence before Christ. The apostles serve Christ on the paths of His justice, whereas the Mother of God and the Forerunner oppose justice, as it were, on the path of mercy. It is as if these two paths, that of Christ and that of the Holy Spirit, are separated and opposed to one another for the salvation of the world. The apostles remain in and together with this judged world; they are not separated from it, whereas the Mother of God and the Forerunner are elevated above the world and the human race.

One must conclude from this that the Forerunner is not subject to the Last Judgment that weighs over humanity, that he remains outside it. This seems evident with regard to the Mother of God, who abides in the heavens at the right hand of Her Son. But it is less evident with regard to the Forerunner. The Mother of God abides in the heavens in Her glorified body, whereas the Forerunner abides there *bodilessly* at the side of the Lord. He participates in the universal resurrection with all the other human beings, but he is not judged, for, by virtue of his position, he is above the judgment. This does not contradict what the Church says about the universal judgment, based on the apostolic testimony: "we must all appear before the judgment seat of Christ" (2 Cor. 5:10; cf. Matt. 25:32; Acts 10:42; 2 Tim. 4:1). Not only does the Church explicitly and indisputably exclude the Mother of God from this Judgment; but, according to the evidence of iconography, she also excludes the glorified Forerunner. (Does his glorification not refer precisely to the moment of the Lord's descent into hell, where He was received and proclaimed by the Forerunner? On this subject we can only speculate, of course.)

In general, Scripture contains two points of view, antinomically conjugate, concerning the Last Judgment. On the one hand, the Judgment will be universal; it will not admit any exceptions. On the other hand, we have the Lord's words: "Verily, verily, I say unto you, He that heareth my word, and believeth on him that sent me, hath everlasting life, and shall not come into condemnation; but is passed from death unto life" (John 5:24). These words evidently refer, first of all, to the saints, whom the Church knows and venerates, for they are full of audacity before the Lord. For them there is resurrection and then judgment in the sense of a definitive separation of the wheat from the weeds, of good from evil, even in themselves, for not even saints are free from sin. But for them there is no judgment in the sense of a definitive verdict, for the latter will already have been given at the so-called preliminary judgment after death, attested to by the Church in her glorification of them as saints and agreeable to God. This corresponds to the general meaning of a mysterious passage in Revelation: "Blessed and holy is he that hath part in the first resurrection: on such the second death hath no power, but they shall be priests of God and of Christ, and shall reign with him a thousand years" (Rev. 20:6). This text is usually interpreted to mean that the first resurrection applies to the saints who live in the Church. This gives them an exceptional status with regard to the Last Judgment, for the question of their final destiny has already been decided. Thus, although the judgment is universal, its meaning and applicability will differ depending upon the person concerned: for some it will be eternal condemnation; for others it will be the exiting from an indeterminate, undecided state in one direction or another; finally, for God's elect it will consist in receiving the crowns that have already been prepared for them. This will be their glorification.

Thus, despite the universality of the judgment, the situations of the righteous differ with respect to it, although for all of them it signifies their definitive glorification. The Forerunner's position here is singular, unique of its kind. He does not appear at the judgment, for he already abides in God's glory. Nevertheless, by reason of his human nature, he will assume, together with the whole human race, the glorified resurrected flesh; he will be present as an angel-man, participating in the glory of the world. How can that transformation of his human essence which is due to resurrection be harmonized with his glorified state and his presence before Christ's throne? How can his exemption from judgment be harmonized with his participation in the resurrection? This is a new mystery for the human mind; but we must confine ourselves here to a mere mention of this mystery. This transformation does not, evidently, change anything in the degree of the Forerunner's glorification. This is the mystery of the union of man and angel in the Forerunner, to which the Church attests.

The righteous who participate in the first resurrection are resurrected not in the flesh, but in the spirit: "And I saw thrones, and they sat upon them, and judgment was given unto them: and I saw the souls of them that were beheaded for the witness of Jesus, and for the word of God ... they lived and reigned with Christ a thousand years. But the rest of the dead lived not again" (Rev. 20:4-5).

Revelation says explicitly that only the souls of the beheaded, not their bodies, come back to life in the first resurrection. In this resurrection the first place belongs to the first among those born of women and the first among the beheaded, John the Forerunner.

This represents a general and fundamental answer to the question of the Forerunner's glorification prior to the universal resurrection, which Revelation calls the *second* resurrection, with the flesh. The bodilessness that characterizes the first resurrection does not prevent its participants from being worthy of reigning with Christ in a state of glorification: "They shall be priests of God and of Christ, and shall reign with him a thousand years" (Rev. 20:6).

This first resurrection, which is of *souls only*, is, for those worthy of it, a kind of *life* ("they lived"), although in separation from the body. This must be affirmed even more forcefully with reference to the one who is both a man and an angel, and who is therefore more free from the flesh than any other man. His first resurrection can, in general, be his total and definitive glorification, to which neither the second resurrection nor the restoration of the flesh can add anything. For the flesh is a kind of garment, which is taken off or put on without disrupting the ontological makeup of his nature. The resurrection of the flesh concerns him not so much for his own sake as for the sake of the entire human race, of which he is a member corporeally. Nothing can be taken away from or added to his fullness, for, in the *Deisis,* he is elevated to a height of glory that approaches that of the Mother of God.

The Lord said about the Forerunner that, although he is the greatest of those born of women, the least in the Kingdom of God is greater than he. This distinction concerns not the human essence itself but its state. Christ's Church contains a fullness, superiority, and abundance of gifts before which pales all grandeur outside or prior to the Church, prior to grace. But this does not exclude a further question which the Gospel implies, without directly asking: What place in the Kingdom of God is in fact reserved for the greatest of those born of women, if and when he enters there? This question is posed and answered by the Church — in the *Deisis.* And the answer is simple and clear: the *first place.* To the Forerunner belongs the *first place* before Christ's throne, or (what is the same thing) in the Kingdom of God, just after or together with the Mother of God. The first among all males born of women remains first also in the Kingdom of God. Such is the Forerunner's heavenly glorification.

* * *

The Forerunner's glorification has an aspect we have not yet considered: the sophiological one. "Wisdom is justified [*edikaiōthē*] of her works."[6] These words of the Lord's on the subject of the Forerunner are reported, as we know, by two Evangelists in versions with different shades of meaning. Matthew 11:19 has "wisdom is justified of her works"; this refers, so to speak, to an objective, impersonal result of the works of wisdom ("The Lord by wisdom hath founded the earth" [Prov. 3:19]). By contrast, Luke 7:35 has "wisdom is justified of all her *children,*" that is, by the persons in which she is embodied. Luke speaks of many children, of an indefinite multitude, but also of a totality: of *all (pantōn).* But this is said with regard to one child, the first of those born of women. This child represents and embodies Wisdom, who is justified by her works, i.e., is revealed, actualized, glorified by her children. In addition, the word "all" here signifies not only all the children taken in their totality, but also each taken indi-

---

6. Here the King James translation has been modified to conform with the Russian Bible. — Trans.

vidually, insofar as each one is justified by the works of Sophia, insofar as each one participates in her, to the measure of his sophianicity.

Exegesis of the text, "wisdom is justified of all her children," must therefore take into account two aspects: the relation of Wisdom to all her children, and her relation to John the Forerunner in particular. The first aspect is evidently connected with the doctrine of the relation of Wisdom to humanity in general, as we find it, first of all, in the Old Testament, especially in the Proverbs of Solomon, the Wisdom of Solomon, and the Wisdom of Jesus, Son of Sirach. The second aspect, a special theme of Forerunner studies, can be formulated in the following question: Why are these words spoken by the Lord precisely on the subject of the Forerunner?

We have treated the first problem more extensively in a special excursus.[7] The general idea of the biblical doctrine of Divine Wisdom is that man, who bears the Image of God, participates in Divine Wisdom, and not only in a general sense, like all creatures, but in a particular sense as well, as her express manifestation: "And my delights [those of Wisdom] were with the sons of men" (Prov. 8:31).

The fundamental anthropological principle of the Christian teaching postulates a certain *conformity* of man to God, enabling the inhumanization of the Logos, the incarnation of the new Adam, the heavenly man, in the old Adam, the earthly man. This ontological foundation of the world cannot be abolished by any creaturely being (not even by the "prince of this world," who has stolen the world for a time). The world exists, even in sin, in virtue of its sophianicity; and this being or life of the world is a wonderful gift of God, by which Wisdom has already been justified by her works in the most general cosmological sense.

The world was created as "good" (Genesis 1) by Divine Wisdom, in a certain absolute manner. No creature, neither Satan nor any human being, can shake the foundations of the world's being; the force of evil and theomachy is powerless to destroy God's creation. Even though they are sinful, God does not destroy the world or humanity. This world is "reserved unto fire" (2 Pet. 3:7) on the day of the Lord, "in which the heavens shall pass away with a great noise, and the elements shall melt with fervent heat, the earth also and the works that are therein shall be burned up" (2 Pet. 3:10). "Nevertheless we, according to his promise, look for new heavens and a new earth, wherein dwelleth righteousness" (2 Pet. 3:13).

---

7. See the excursus "The Old Testament Doctrine of the Wisdom of God" in *The Burning Bush*.

Thus, the world faces fiery transfiguration, not destruction. Also, resurrection, not annihilation, awaits all human beings; "for God made not death: neither hath he pleasure in the destruction of the living. For he created all things, that they might have their being: and the generations of the world were healthful; and there is no poison of destruction in them, nor the kingdom of death upon the earth" (Wisdom of Solomon 1:13-14). "God created man to be immortal, and made him to be an image of his own eternity" (Wisdom of Solomon 2:23). The fact that the condemned are sentenced to eternal torments, not to death (for the "second death" [see Rev. 20:14] is not an annihilation), attests to the indestructibility of creation, upon which has been bestowed the honor of being formed in the image of God, which is its supra-eternal and absolute foundation.

Thus, the world and man have been created by God with such ontological perfection that they can never fall apart in their foundations and return to their precreaturely nonbeing and nothingness. And in this sense, "Wisdom is justified of her works." The Son of God Himself attests to this: by His incarnation He has given an eternal power to the being of the world and to man, for His divine life is indissolubly united with them. Wisdom is justified in creation by the Incarnation; and in this sense the words pronounced by the Lord refer to Him Himself (Matt. 11:19).

These words conclude the Lord's discourse on John, where He responds to the messengers sent by the latter. With these words the Lord returns to the question: "Art thou he that should come, or do we look for another?" (Matt. 11:3). Interrupting His discourse, He expresses a new thought — now not about John but about Himself. It is for this reason that these words are appended to the speech by an unexpected and hard-to-understand *kai*[8] (Matt. 11:19), which so perplexes exegetes. This word marks the addition of a new, concluding thought. Thus, the general plan of the speech is such: first the Lord responds to the Forerunner's disciples about Himself; then, addressing the people, He speaks both about Himself and about John; then He speaks about John alone; and finally, He again speaks about Himself. This is the meaning we find if we read Matthew 11:19 in accordance with the currently accepted text: "And Wisdom is justified of her works [*apo tōn ergōn autēs*]."

But Wisdom is justified not only by her works but also by her children. It is the human race that constitutes her children, for her "delights were with the sons of men" (Prov. 8:31). It is given to man to possess not

---

8. The original Greek has *kai* (and), not "but" (the King James translation). — Trans.

only God's image but also His likeness. He is not only born a child of Wisdom; Wisdom also fills him with the power of spiritual integrity and virginity of the soul by the purification of sins (in the Office of Sophia, she is called "the soul of virgins"). Therefore, the Most Pure, Most Immaculate Ever-Virgin is the temple of Wisdom. And the Lord's Forerunner too, because he is the first of those born of a woman and has attained the highest degree of spiritual integrity and virginity, comes closer to God's Wisdom than any other human being. He is her first child after the Mother of God. He is the "head" of the human race and its representative, as it were — not only as the Forerunner who meets the Lord but also as a chosen child of Wisdom, by whom she is justified.

We find the same idea in the version of Luke 7:35: "Wisdom is justified of *all* her children." This verse applies to the *whole* human race, of which John the Forerunner is first. Therefore, although these words, pronounced at the end of the discourse about the Forerunner, directly concern him, he is taken here not as an isolated individual, but as the pinnacle and representative of the whole human race. These words, concluding the Lord's discourse about the Forerunner, are a summing up as it were of what was said before; and in this sense the word *kai* acquires the significance of "thus." But the sense of these words in Luke does not oppose the version of Matthew, where there is a veiled reference to the Incarnation. The latter became possible only when the human race was ready to meet and receive God. It was realized by God's will, thanks to His Divine condescension, but only when the human nature was ready for it.

The justification of Wisdom in the Incarnation is accomplished through the union of God's Wisdom, of the Son of God who has descended from heaven and become incarnate, with God's Wisdom in man in the persons of the Mother of God and the Forerunner. The two of them together participate in the work of the Incarnation. And through them and in them, "all the children of wisdom," the entire Church, in which the Wisdom of God lives and acts, participate in it. We return here to that twofold meaning which, as we have seen, can be found at the beginning of the Savior's discourse about the Forerunner: in speaking to the people about the Forerunner, He was speaking about Himself as well, whose Forerunner John is. In affirming here that wisdom is justified by all her children, and first of all by the Forerunner, the Savior also speaks about the One whom the Forerunner meets, i.e., about Himself. The work of the friend of the Bridegroom is inseparable from the Bridegroom Himself; and this testimony about the Forerunner is thereby a testimony about the Messiah Himself.

Thus, all interpretations of this difficult but exceptionally important text suggest that John the Forerunner finds himself particularly close to the Wisdom of God, is illuminated and glorified by her. This general idea is directly confirmed by the iconography of the Church: On icons of Sophia of the Novgorod school, the Forerunner is invariably depicted together with the Mother of God, who are present at the sides of a fiery Angel, who sits on a throne and represents Wisdom herself.[9] This invariable presence of the Forerunner on the Novgorod icons is a fact of dogmatic significance, which can be interpreted in two ways: first, according to the Forerunner's relation to Sophia, the Wisdom of God, and his place on her icon; and second, according to his relation to the Mother of God given their conjoint presence before Sophia.

In this sense this icon has a general significance both for sophiology and for the doctrine of the Mother of God and of the Forerunner. First of all, this once again confirms the exceptional relation between the Forerunner and Sophia, which is indicated also in the Lord's discourse about him. It confirms his particular closeness to Sophia, where all distance and mediation have been removed, as it were. The Forerunner is human sophianicity, Wisdom in man. In virtue of his spiritual integrity and virginity, the image of creaturely Wisdom becomes so clear in the Forerunner that, according to the idea of this theological composition, he himself is a kind of icon of her. He is part of a representation that symbolizes both her eternal essence and her creaturely revelation, her "justification" by her children.

This sophiological meaning is reinforced by the fact that, on certain (but not all) sophianic icons, the Forerunner, like the Mother of God, is represented as wearing a crown, as a sign of his glorification (we find this, in particular, on the altar apse of the Moscow Cathedral of the Dormition). To be sure, here we encounter anew the question of the specific foundations of sophianicity in man, the applied question of sophiological anthropology, namely: Does sophianicity in a human being depend on his specific gifts and talents? As we have seen, in the Forerunner we have, as it were, a deliberate ascetic absence of such gifts, miracles, and signs: the preacher of repentance applied all his spiritual energy to this repentance, to active spiritual integrity and virginity (for this reason he is usually depicted on sophianic icons as holding a scroll with the inscription: "Repent

---

9. The *Deisis* can also be viewed as a type of sophianic icon, where the place of the fiery Angel, above whom Christ is represented in the Novgorod icon, is taken by the Lord Himself, God's power and wisdom, framed by the Forerunner and the Mother of God.

ye"). He possesses a *single* gift, which encompasses *all* gifts: the power of repentance, the power of movement from the world toward God. And this power of repentance is grounded in the Incarnation, in which the image of Wisdom shone forth in men thanks to the Incarnation of the Logos and the descent of the Holy Spirit. Together with the Mother of God, the Forerunner here too represents the Church, which lives and moves by virtue of Sophia, the Wisdom of God.

As regards the relation between the Forerunner and the Mother of God on sophianic icons, one must first note the perfect similarity of their stations before the fiery throne of the Wisdom of God. The Mother of God is, in Her own person, the creaturely Wisdom of God, her living temple, as the Ever-Virgin and Glory of the world. In the name of the human race, of "all her children," these two chosen ones represent the Divine Wisdom in the human nature, in conformity with their participation in the Incarnation. They manifest the *human* aspect of the Incarnation. Wisdom is revealed in the fullness of the human being, and thus in its male and its female essence. The Forerunner and the Mother of God are at the head of "all of Wisdom's children."

But this common station of the Mother of God and of the Forerunner in relation to the Wisdom of God does not remove the *distinction* between them, even though both are glorified and crowned. First of all, let us not forget that, besides the Novgorod Sophia, there is also the Kiev Sophia, the Sophia of the Theotokos, where the Mother of God, surrounded by saints (patriarchs and prophets), is depicted without the Forerunner. But there is, evidently, no sophianic icon which portrays only the Forerunner, without the Mother of God. The Office of St. Sophia, celebrated on the day of the Dormition and composed of christological, mariological, and sophiological themes, does not contain any mention of the Forerunner. Nor do the various offices of the Forerunner contain any sophiological themes. (This can be partly explained by the fact that most of these offices are of an ancient Byzantine origin, whereas the iconography and the offices of Sophia on the feast days of the Mother of God are primarily a fruit of Russian inspiration.)

The Mother of God is venerated as the Queen of heaven, the summit of creation, who abides in the heavens at the right hand of Her Son. The Church has never confessed anything comparable with regard to the Forerunner. We not only pray to the Mother of God, at the same time as to all the saints, that She intercede for us before Her Son. We also implore Her: Most Holy Mother of God, save us! Of course, nothing comparable is conceivable in relation to the Forerunner. Thus, the co-presence of the

Mother of God and the Forerunner on icons of Sophia, of the *Deisis,* and of the Last Judgment does not, of course, abolish or diminish the depth of this difference. This difference is an essential one not only with regard to the degree of their sanctification and glorification but also with regard to their very essence. The Theotokos and the Baptist, the Mother-Bride of God and the friend of the Bridegroom, differ from each other, and this difference is permanent and eternal.

But in addition to attempting to understand this self-evident difference, our pious contemplation must also attempt to understand the special and mysterious closeness of the Mother of God and the Forerunner, which the Church attests. This closeness is revealed by an attentive examination of various elements of Church tradition: Scripture, liturgical offices, iconography, patristic writings. Such an examination and comparison will reveal to the eyes of the spirit this mysterious and startlingly important fact of the *Deisis,* before which all speech ceases: the fact of the presence of the Forerunner, alongside the Mother of God, before the throne of the Lord. Fully cognizant of the feebleness of his talents, the author has attempted to disclose this fact and to set it before the consciousness of the Church, in all its scope if possible. May the author be forgiven his audacity by the prayers of the saintly Forerunner and Baptist of the Lord.

"You were a prophet of Christ and an apostle, an angel and the forerunner, the baptist of the divine incarnation, a priest and martyr, a faithful preacher to those in hell, a model for virgins, and a fruit of the desert" (office of 24 February, canon, ode 9, tr. 2).

EXCURSUS 1

On the Interrelationship of the Angelic and Human Worlds

Because he was a human being, the Forerunner of course always remained a human being. A human being can never, and in no manner, stop being a human being; he can never be un-humanized. If John were not a human being, he could not have become the Forerunner and the Baptist, or the friend of the Bridegroom, for this is possible only for a human being. Nevertheless, this human being became an angel, was raised to the angelic order. The angelic image was incorporated in him (and this was realized not in the sense of a mere resemblance but in some essential way).

Clearly, this participation in the angelic order should not be understood as the abolition, or even as a diminution, of the human nature. The latter cannot be abolished or diminished, for it was assumed by the Lord Jesus Christ, the true God and perfect human being, the God-Man. The human nature cannot be enriched further, for it contains everything. Man was created by God to have "dominion" over creation. Therefore, the addition of the angelic image to man signifies not a change of the human nature but an emancipation of the latter from the lusts and passions of the flesh, as it was said about antediluvian man: "He also is flesh" (Gen. 6:3). It is in this sense that the Church hymn says of the Forerunner that he was "an angel because he lived as one without flesh." But this expression does not signify incorporeality in the sense of de-incarnation, which is impossible for human beings and would signify their diminution. Rather, it signifies maximal emancipation from fleshly sensuality, whatever its manifestation might be. It signifies self-renunciation.

On Orthodox icons, the Forerunner is usually portrayed as a severe ascetic, with body emaciated by fasting, but preserving a great beauty of the human form. This form is beautiful both by the splendor of its saintliness and by the beauty of a body purged of sin by ascesis. These features are preserved even when he is portrayed as an angel, with wings. In this sense, the angelic aspect in a human being signifies *freedom* from the flesh, from sinful passion, from the lusts of sensuality. It is perfect passionlessness.

The Lord invokes this angel-like passionlessness, which will be proper to the future age, in His response to the Sadducees: "In the resurrection they neither marry, nor are given in marriage, but are as the angels of God in heaven" (Matt. 22:30). This is even more expressive in Luke 20:34-36: "The children of this world would marry, and are given in marriage: But they which shall be accounted worthy to obtain that world, and the resurrection from the dead, neither marry, nor are given in marriage: Neither can they die any more: for they are equal unto the angels; and are the children of God, being the children of the resurrection." The angels who remained in their habitations and guarded themselves in God's love possess a perfect passionlessness which human beings do not possess. But this is proper to the angelic nature. As *fleshless* spirits, angels are free of fleshly temptations, for they are free of the flesh. For human beings, such freedom is the greatest of achievements, the conquest of their passionate nature; whereas, for angels, it expresses their very nature, in virtue of their fleshlessness.

To be sure, angels too possess the freedom of self-determination, and the creatureliness of their nature contains the possibility of their fall. Satan with his armies underwent just such a fall. This fall corrupting their nature, Satan's angels discovered in themselves the possibility of all sorts of lust — but only in the spiritual domain. Their spiritual lust can be satisfied only through other beings who possess flesh, i.e., through human beings, who are corrupted by them. The fleshly sins of human beings serve to nourish and to give pleasure to demons. And this fall is, of course, immeasurably deeper than human sin, for it is not justified by the presence of flesh. This fall results in the imparting of flesh and concupiscent passion to fleshless spirits, in something unnatural. In contrast, to overcome the lusts of the passionate corporeal nature, to approximate angels, is something *super*-natural for human beings with regard to their fleshly nature. This approximation to angels is attained through spiritual feats, and it will be given fully in the age to come, as a creative gift of God's grace, as an accomplished salvation. But this approximation to angels, manifested first in the Forerunner, makes the man-angel superior to the angels, since he is not fleshless but an angel in human flesh, an angel-man.

The approximation to angels is achieved through spiritual combat. Every Christian life must pass through this self-crucifixion of the flesh with its passions and lusts, through this ascesis. The latter is necessitated by the struggle between the Divine law and the law of sin in our bodies (see Rom. 7:21-24; Gal. 5:17, 24). The struggle against the flesh for the spirit is also the struggle for the body — not the fleshly body but the spiritual body.

This combat can assume two different forms: direct and indirect. The first consists in suppressing all that can be suppressed of the body without destroying it, and thus without total or partial suicide (e.g., castration). The second consists in a system of equivalences, or antagonistic forces, in the case of which the sinfulness of the flesh is attenuated and redeemed by spiritual struggle and suffering. Such, for example, is conjugal life, in which a certain encouragement of the flesh is justified, redeemed, and overcome by the ascesis of family life, with its cares and suffering. Such, also, is economic and governmental activity, where the impulses of passion and egotism are purified in an ascesis of self-restraint and self-control. Such, in general, is life in the world, which, in this sense, can and must be an ascetic creative activity or an active asceticism. Without ceaseless ascetic struggle, without a certain monastic circumcision of the heart, life in the world becomes a mere appeasement of the flesh, a paganism.

Holy baptism delivers us from the burden of original sin, which is redeemed by the Lord, and gives us the possibility of a new life. But the power of the consequences of original sin — a perverse tendency to evil and the lust of the flesh — remains in us: it is defeated but untamed, and must be overcome by us personally. The ascetic struggle against the lusts of the flesh develops precisely on the basis of the liberation from original sin by baptism. The Old Testament humanity did not know this struggle, and, in its simplicity, it retained a certain ignorance of sin compared with the New Testament humanity. Christianity bestowed upon man possibilities of spiritual life that he did not possess in the Old Testament, and that is why he judges himself and his life with a judgment that was inaccessible to the Old Testament humanity.

The norms of Christian life are therefore much more ascetic and demanding than those under the law. The path of direct struggle against the flesh, of renunciation, is the monastic path. The Church calls this path *the putting on of the angelic habit.* This is the path of liberation from one's concupiscent nature by direct struggle against it, the goal being to arrive at a state without passion. Such a state is proper to angels and natural for them, whereas, for human beings, it is supernatural.

This is the path of self-crucifixion and self-mortification, but not of suicide, the path of liberation from the flesh but not from the body. And in this sense it is a struggle for the body (which makes possible the glorification of holy relics). Its goal is not de-incarnation and bodilessness, but passionlessness and a glorified state of the body in the age to come. This is, of course, the *supreme* path, "narrow," uncompromising, straight. It is the path of departure from the world, not from God's cosmos, but from that sinful world about which it is said: "Love not the world, neither the things that are in the world . . . the lust of the flesh, and the lust of the eyes, and the pride of life" (1 John 2:15-16). Monastic vows associated with the putting on of the angelic habit (the vows of virginity, poverty, and obedience) therefore speak of renunciation as the path to a perfectly passionless state.

This is the path of the Forerunner, who followed it to the end and thus demonstrated that it is possible. And in so following it to the end he "surpassed the limits of nature" (office of 29 August, canon 1, ode 1, tr. 2). The Forerunner is the true founder of monasticism, of the putting on of the angelic habit, for he himself was an angel and therefore attained a perfectly passionless state. The Archangel Gabriel proclaims this aspect of the Forerunner's feat to the priest Zacharias: "He shall be great in the sight of the Lord, and shall drink neither wine nor strong drink" (Luke 1:15). But it should be clearly understood that this is the path only of the "friend of the Bridegroom," not of the Bridegroom Himself. The Lord repeatedly insisted on this difference. When, for example, He was asked, "Why do the disciples of John fast . . . but thine eat and drink?" He answered: "Can ye make the children of the bridechamber fast, while the bridegroom is with them?" (Luke 5:33-34; also Matt. 9:14-15; Mark 2:18-19).

In general, the idea of the "imitation of Christ," of walking "in His footsteps," of imitating how He might behave in one circumstance or another, is a fallacious and seductive idea. The Lord summoned us to learn from Him, to be meek and humble in heart, to bear our cross after Him, always to have His image in our hearts, to assimilate His "mind" (Phil. 2:5). But He did not invite us to *imitate* Him, mentally placing ourselves in His place and Him in ours. He is the perfect Man, the only true Man — "Ecce homo!"

It is precisely because of this perfection that He is close to and accessible to everyone without regard to social position, sex, or nationality (see Rom. 1:14; Gal. 3:28; Col. 3:11). In Him, all people must seek and find themselves, their own eternal, heavenly countenance ("until Christ be formed in you" [Gal. 4:19]). But this never takes place through external, uncreative imitation. Christ is with us and within us. We are similar to the people who surrounded Him; and we find ourselves in them, and our circumstances and relationships in their circumstances and relationships. This is possible for us, but it is not possible for us to put ourselves in His place. This general governing idea, which needs to be developed and applied in asceticism, is the reason why, despite the unity of the image of Christ inscribed in each of us, there are multiple ways of salvation and multiple countenances of saved saints. This is why this is always a creative path, on which one receives one's *own* cross and follows Him.

The complete detachment from lust, the path of passionlessness, cannot be applied to Christ Himself. This is not His path but only the path that leads to Him, because, conceived without seed from the Holy Spirit and the Virgin Mary, He had not the "flesh of sin" but only its "likeness." His flesh could suffer for the sins of the world unto death on the cross, but it itself was free of all sin and possessed perfect passionlessness, for all sinful lust was alien to it.

That is why the path of detachment, of the putting on of the angelic habit, is totally inapplicable here. Monasticism is alien to the Lord, for He is superior to it. "The sole sinless One," He does not need to liberate Himself from lust. Free of the sinful burden of sex, He does not need to struggle against it. His ascetic life, the fact that He was homeless, expressed His freedom from all earthly dependence ("The foxes have holes, and the birds of the air have nests; but the Son of man hath not where to lay his head" [Matt. 8:20; Luke 9:58]). But this did not constitute a means of detachment, for He did not require it.

That is why His disciples "pluck the ears of corn" on the Sabbath (Matt. 12:1), citing the example of David, who partook of the breads of the proposition and violated the law in his freedom. Christ freely appears at a marriage feast and a meal ("The Son of man came eating and drinking" [Matt. 11:19]); that is, He shows Himself to be free of the prohibitions that are natural and appropriate for the pious zealots of the law and of Nazarite vows. It would have been unnatural and impossible for John the Forerunner to recline with Him at the marriage feast, and he did not accompany Him there, remaining instead in his wilderness. This is, of course, a negative but a sufficiently eloquent fact.

This acquires a special significance in the light of the fact that the Mother of God was present at the marriage feast in Cana of Galilee, and that it was precisely She who was the first to direct a question/request to

Him: "They have no wine" (John 2:3). For Her path too is not the path that "seeks the angelic habit"; She has no need to liberate Herself from the flesh to arrive at the state without passion. It would be more correct to say that She had already followed this path to its end when She stayed at the temple (which is why She is venerated as the Mother of nuns, as the Mother Superior of Mount Athos). After the Annunciation, for the sake of Her Son, She achieves perfect passionlessness, becomes the Ever-Virgin, and therefore no longer needs, *for Herself,* the renunciation of the concupiscent nature. She follows the path of sacrificial self-renunciation in the footsteps of Her Son, but this is not for Her own sake, but for others, for the salvation of the human race. In contrast, in his earthly life, John does not attain such freedom and fullness of ever-virginity, which is bestowed upon him only at his righteous end and in the glorification that follows it. Thus, he is the true founder of the monastic ascesis, of the putting on of the angelic habit.

Thus, the putting on of the angelic habit has only relative, or conditional, value: it is only a path. The Lord Himself and the Mother of God did not need to follow this path. They are sinless, passionless human beings who possess perfect humanity and do not need to renounce their humanity to arrive at the state without passion. In other words, monasticism, the putting on of the angelic habit, is only a means, not a goal. For man the true goal is to become not an angel but a passionless human being, in all the ontological fullness and richness of his nature. To achieve the angelic state is not to disincarnate oneself but to become passionless.

And as a path and means, monasticism is neither universal nor obligatory. It is not for all people, only for some. It is the most sacrificial path, only for the few chosen ones. Gifts differ and ministries differ: Near Christ, besides the Forerunner, were the apostles, whom He sent not into the wilderness but into the Judean cities. Their vocation was one of severe asceticism, but not that of the putting on of the "angelic habit." "Dominion" (Gen. 1:28) and therefore creative activity are proper to the human nature. By contrast, the bearers of the angelic nature are properly "angels," messengers of God's will, obedient agents, who do not have a basis in their nature for *their own* desire, which becomes in them a luciferian revolt against God. To a human being it is given and proper to love the human being in himself, his humanity, which God loved to the point of assuming it, of Himself becoming human; whereas to the angelic nature it is proper to be transparent for God, to be not in itself but in God. Therefore, for a human being to put on the angelic habit is only a means for him to save and affirm in himself his true human nature. A human being must not and cannot affirm himself *only* in himself, without God, as a human god ("ye shall be as gods" — the satanic temptation). But at the same time he cannot displace the center of his being out of himself once it has been sanctified by the Incarnation: He must have his being both in himself and in God. That is the practical meaning of the dogma of the union of the two natures and the two wills in the one person of the Lord Jesus Christ, the dogma of the deification of human beings.

In the Forerunner the putting on of the angelic habit was accomplished fully. That is why it is said of him not that he "resembles an angel" (as it is said of the prophet Elias), but simply that he is an angel, or an "earthly angel and a heavenly man." This attests that the Forerunner had arrived at a state of total detachment from his human passion, a state of liberation from lust, from the flesh. The Holy Church explains it thus: "The word of the prophet Isaiah has now been fulfilled by the birth of John, the greatest of the prophets. For it is said that I have sent my angel before thy face to prepare thy path before thee. This warrior of the heavenly king has come. He truly makes straight the ways for our God. This is because he is a man by nature, but an angel by his life; for he has certainly attained purity and spiritual integrity; and having them by nature, he realized them above nature" (office of 24 June, sticheron to Glory, of the nun Cassia).

The Forerunner fully ("certainly") loved purity and spiritual integrity, possessing them not only by nature but also above nature, being an angel by his life, while retaining his human nature in an angelic form, that is, passionlessly. This is such an overcoming of sin, such a liberation from human passion, that there spontaneously arises the question of the power of original sin, to which he was subject as a consequence of his fleshly birth. This sin cannot be overcome by the powers of human holiness alone; neither the Forerunner nor even the Most Pure Mother of God are exempt from it. Only the One who was free of fleshly conception, the Sole Sinless One, is free of original sin.

There is, first of all, liberation from original *sin*, or redemption. The latter consists in the total annihilation of this sin and in the resulting glorification and salvation of the body of resurrection. Second, there is liberation from *sins*, which represent particular consequences of the general sickness of humanity and which are accompanied by the exercise of will. This is the place of spiritual struggle, the place where the path of salvation for man begins through the exercise of his personal freedom. And since they are incapable of liberating themselves from sin or redeeming it, human beings can and must liberate themselves from sins; they must cooperate in their salvation by actualizing the gracious gift of redemption that is given to them.

Related to this is the "putting on of the angelic habit" in the struggle against passions. What is impossible for man is possible for God. But that which is possible for man, God does not do without him and apart from him. God proposes to man "the way of righteousness" that John followed (Matt. 21:32). This way of *human* righteousness was followed to the end by the greatest of those born of women. By itself, this path can never lead to liberation from original sin, that is, to self-salvation, but it can make one "great in the sight of the Lord" (Luke 1:15).

By calling the Forerunner an angel, the Church attests that he attained such personal sinlessness. Although his nature is subject to original sin, this sin, which dwells in his nature, does not have dominion over his will. This sin is tamed, reduced to a mere potentiality, by virtue of human freedom, reinforced by Divine grace. The Forerunner is an angel in the sense that he is the greatest of those born of women, the greatest of human beings. He had attained the highest human holiness that can be attained in the struggle against sin: he had attained a perfect resemblance to the angels, a perfectly passionless state.

But this also marks the intrinsic limit of this path: the angelic aspect implies liberation from lust, passionlessness, freedom from the flesh, but it leaves an ontological void as far as the body is concerned, for a body is proper to man and is given to him inalienably and permanently. The salvation of the body, its glorification, is given not by angelhood but by the perfect God-Man, resurrected from the dead and raising the dead in their glorified, spiritual bodies. It is for this reason that the least in the Kingdom of God is greater than John, the earthly angel, although in the Kingdom of God John is the greatest of all creatures, with the exception of the Mother of God, the Queen of heaven and earth, who is superior to all creation.

Seeking to attain the angelic state can have the negative significance of the ascetic diminution or simplification of the human nature through the renunciation of the flesh. But it also has a positive significance. We are faced here with a problem that cannot be fathomed within the confines of the present aeon but one that is nevertheless encompassed within this aeon: the problem of the nature and the place of the angelic world in relation to God, to man, and to the world.

Angels are closer to God than are human beings and all other creatures, with the exception of the Mother of God, who is closest of all to God. Angels are "second lights" that surround and radiate out from the first light, that of God. They are powers of God, rays of His glory, that receive hypostatic being. Although a choir of angels exists in the sense of a celestial army with its "celestial hierarchy," they do not have their own creaturely world, such as the one human beings have; and they do not have a personal life, although they have a creaturely one. The creatureliness of the angels consists in the fact that their hypostatic countenances are summoned by God to being from nonbeing, are *created*. But these hypostases are created as having the divine energies as their nature. They live, so to speak, in God Himself, constituting His surround: "incorporeal angels, standing before God's throne, illuminated by His rays and eternally shining with His irradiations, are second lights" (from the Office of the Angels). The "second lights" are, as it were, a creaturely hypostatic mirror of the First Light, "the beginning of creation." They are an image of God in the luminous reflection and surround.

Of course, this union of the creaturely and the divine, this communion of creaturely hypostases with the divine life, is a mystery that is unfathomable and incomprehensible for human beings in this aeon. There are iconographic hints concerning this mystery in the fact that angels are portrayed on icons either in human form, as warriors but with wings, for they are sent by God to human beings; or as belonging to the priestly order; or (which is more important for our purposes) only as faces, or as eyes, or wings, circles, and so on. In other words, this is a symbolic description of a hypostatic *being* that does not possess a body, its own nature. And it signifies the mysterious, terrible proximity of angels to God's throne, which they surround.

The idea that angels are created hypostatic energies of God, but without their own nature, finds confirmation in the Old Testament. It is well known that, in numerous manifestations to human beings (to Abraham, to Moses, and so on), either God is directly called an Angel (see Isa. 9:6) or the expressions "God" and "angel" alternate in the same narrative for no reason we can understand (e.g., in Exod. 3). One must conclude that, in this case, "God" and "Angel" have the same ontological meaning. This identification should not, of course, be understood to mean that an angel is God, that is, it should not be understood in a polytheistic sense. Rather, it means that God manifests Himself in the aspect of an angel, as an energy that belongs to Him, although it is endowed with independent created-hypostatic being.

Thus, a sort of ontological *pars pro toto*, part for the whole, is admitted here. This identification is rooted in the fact that, in a certain sense, angels participate in Divinity, are immanent in the Divine nature as "second lights" inseparable from the first. Their life consists in being "angels," God's messengers or agents, celebrators of God's will. Their nature is completely *transparent* for Divine life, is this life itself in a hypostatic consciousness. How this can be is a mystery of the angelic nature, unfathomable to human beings; but that this is so is attested to by Scripture and the whole of Church tradition: "[God] maketh his angels spirits; his ministers a flaming fire" (Ps. 104:4). Thus, they serve the human world, and this service results in their participation in this world. In the age to come, angels and human beings will rejoice in joint possession of this one, human world, in which angels ascend and descend by the ladder erected for our salvation (see Gen. 28:12) and unite the open heaven (see John 1:51) with the saved earth.

Nevertheless, the angels do not have their own creaturely life. Only the demons, as a result of their fall, desire to have their own life and their own world. They "kept not their first estate, but left their own habitation" (Jude 6). And for want of their own world, they have for a while gained by theft the human world. But the pretender, the illegitimate "prince of this world," will, with his angels, "be cast out" (John 12:31) by the true King of the tribe of David.

There is one more trait which distinguishes angels from human beings but which also makes them similar. Although it is proper to angels to be energies of God (whence the suffix "el," God, affixed to the names of angels known to us: Michael, Gabriel, Raphael, and so on), the fullness of the Divine image belongs only to man, according to his creation (see Gen. 1:27). In its fullness, the angelic world reflects the life of the Most Holy Trinity in its three hypostases. The totality of the angelic orders manifests the fullness of this life. Following Pseudo-Dionysius, the Church counts nine orders of angels, which, of course, may also contain many subdivisions that are unknown to us.

Each angel reflects only his own ray of Divinity, in privileged relation with one or another of the hypostases. Thus, is the Archangel Gabriel, the herald of the Annunciation, not the special messenger of the Holy Spirit? And does Michael not assist the feat of the incarnate Son of God?

Of determining significance here is the distinction made by the Church: the angels form an *assembly* (or an *army*), whereas human beings form the *human race*. The angelic world is a *hierarchy*, in which a single common nature is manifested by a mutual hierarchical teaching, by the revelation of the Divine mysteries from the superior to the inferior orders. This division into orders constitutes the very basis of the angelic assembly.

In this sense, one can say that the angelic world expresses the fullness of the divine life *hierarchically*, by differentiating and specifying each of its rays. Correlated amongst one another, these rays, taken together, prefigure the Divine *all* that is manifested in the creation; and in this sense they ontologically precede the creation. This is indicated by the first words of Genesis: "In the beginning God created the heaven and the earth," where heaven is usually taken to mean the angelic world, while the earth is usually taken to mean all the primordial elements out of which the world is created. The interdependence of the two worlds is thus understandable: angels are the messengers, agents, and guardians of creation. The foundation of the world is prefigured in angels, and all created things have their correlative in the angelic world. In particular, human hypostases, having their guardian angels in heaven, are ontologically correlated with these angels and represent in the human world an analogy to what exists in the angelic world.

Nevertheless, the fundamental difference between human beings and angels consists in the fact that *only* human beings possess the *fullness* of the image of God. Not only does a human being bear the image of God in a hierarchical union with all other human beings, but every human being has this image in himself. Therefore, humankind is not an "assembly," i.e., a hierarchical whole, but a "genus," i.e., a multi-unity, where every member possesses ontological fullness. A clear proof of this is the Incarnation: in His single person the Lord could assume perfect humanity, in which the fullness is present corporeally. And every human being is deified in Him: "For ye are all one in Christ Jesus" (Gal. 3:28). This means that every human being potentially possesses the fullness of the image of God and that it is manifested in Christ. Human beings can fall very low because of their sinful state. They can be completely ignorant of the riches of their nature, unlike the angels, who have full knowledge of their own nature. Human beings will become themselves only in the age to come. But they differ from the angels by the fact that they have their own creaturely nature, their world, in which they are placed in order to have dominion over it, and by the fact that they have their own life in this world. The human nature is the creaturely world formed by Divine Wisdom. Man is the hypostatic bearer of Divine Wisdom in creation: He is *sophianic* in his nature; and, in him, she is therefore "justified of her works."

The hierarchical differences that exist in the human race concern only the degree to which each person realizes the one and only path of sanctification, the path of clothing oneself in Christ, the path of "imaging Christ in oneself," of union with Christ. "There is neither Jew nor

On the Interrelationship of the Angelic and Human Worlds

Greek, there is neither bond nor free, there is neither male nor female: for ye are all one in Christ Jesus" (Gal. 3:28). It is this fullness of human sophianicity, the image of God implanted in man at the creation, that contains the ontological possibility of God's in-humanization, of the union of the divine and human natures. But this possibility does not exist for angels.

Thus, the angelic and human worlds are correlative and interdependent, for they are both equally grounded in the Divine Wisdom, the fullness of Divine life. But they are grounded in the Divine Wisdom in different ways. The angelic world is created out of nonbeing only with regard to its hypostases; its nature directly proceeds from the Divine light. In contrast, the human world is created out of nothing with regard both to its hypostases and to its nature. This means that, in contrast to angels, human beings are *not* fleshless: they have their own flesh.

Thus, both a correlation and an insurmountable difference exist between the human and angelic worlds. On the one hand, man would be ontologically diminished if the *fullness* of his sophianicity were replaced by the hierarchism proper to the angelic world. On the other hand, man does not have the power to attain the proximity to God's throne and the constant presence before it that, by nature, are proper to angels. But this distance between the two worlds was overcome by the Incarnation, in which God, having descended to earth, united in Himself the heavenly and the earthly, as the Holy Church sings: "You who ineffably united that which is of earth with that which is of heaven, and who formed a single church for angels and human beings, we glorify you without ceasing" (Canon of the Archangel, tone 3, ode 9, tr. 1).

The unification of the angelic and human worlds was realized by the Incarnation: According to His Divine nature, the Lord had the angelic world within His depths; and therefore, in and through Him, this world was united with the human nature, constituting "one Church," the Body of Christ. This body is the whole of creation, heavenly and earthly, united in Christ; and the angelic world thereby enters into an active relation with the human world. Therefore, in the Apocalypse the destinies of the Church are portrayed as being accomplished both in heaven and on earth, as is the battle with the "dragon."

As a consequence of the Incarnation, the Most Pure Mother of God, raised into heaven in Her glory, is "more venerable than the cherubim and incomparably more glorious than the seraphim." This is because, as the God-bearer, She is closer than the rest of creation to Her Son and, in Him, to the Holy Trinity. In Her, the human nature manifests its fullness. In

Her, the glorification of the human nature above that of the angels is accomplished, based on the fact that God the Word assumed not the angelic but the human nature.

Another consequence of the Incarnation is that the Lord's Forerunner and Baptist, who stood near the Lord at the Jordan and saw there a manifestation of the entire Holy Trinity, becomes equal to the angels or simply "an angel" (according to the Church hymn) while remaining a human being. This equi-angelic character of the Forerunner cannot signify a diminution of the human nature: the latter does not become a part of a whole, a link in a hierarchical structure. If the Forerunner is an angel, this is only in the sense that he is an all-angel, one who participates in all the orders of the angelic assembly. If, as an angel-man, as the Lord's Baptist, the Forerunner, is, according to the *Deisis*, closer (together with the Mother of God) to the Lord than any other created being, angelic or human, it necessarily follows that the greatest of those born of women is also the greatest, the first, among the angels. If this is the case, it is evident *what* place the Forerunner occupies in heaven: the place left vacant since time immemorial by the fallen first angel.[1] "How art thou fallen from heaven, O Lucifer, son of the morning!" (Isa. 14:12).

The place of the first angel is occupied by the friend of the Bridegroom, while the place of "the prince of this world," taken by theft, is occupied by the One to Whom it belongs, by the King of kings and the Lord of lords. In his human nature, the Forerunner reunites the whole angelic world with the human race. His human hypostasis participates in both the human and the angelic, i.e., the divine, nature. While preserving its identity, his nature enters the spiritual heaven, the divine world. In him is realized that union of angels and human beings that has its foundation in Christ's Divine-humanity. The Mother of God, as superior to the rest of creation, abides outside these two worlds, beyond this division, venerated equally by human beings and by angels.

The power and mystery of this union of the two natures in the Forerunner by his participation in the angelic nature and his entry into the angelic heaven, this power and mystery are, in the present aeon, mostly concealed from us. They are only hinted at, but we know that they are a

---

1. This comparison illuminates in a new way the fact that, immediately after the baptism, when the Lord revealed Himself to His Baptist and was recognized by him, He was led by "the Spirit into the wilderness to be tempted of the devil" (Matt. 4:1). Here He was approached by the fallen Lucifer, Satan, who earlier had occupied the place of a friend, as the first angel.

direct consequence of the Incarnation. When He came into the world, the Lord Jesus Christ had near Him not only His Most Pure Mother, who served this awesome mystery and attained perfect deification. Not only was He surrounded by angels, who "ministered unto him" (Matt. 4:11; also Mark 1:13; Luke 22:43), and who also served as messengers at the Annunciation, Birth, and Resurrection. He also had a "friend" at His side, an angel-man who represented the principle of angelic-human reunification. In and through him, the angelic nature played not only an external but also an inner part in the Incarnation, and thus received the fruits, both heavenly and earthly, of the Incarnation.

And in this sense, the Forerunner is, once again, the first angel, the mediator of the Incarnation in the angelic choir. The latter did not have need of redemption from sin, for sin had not gained power over it. However, the kenosis of God, who went so far in His self-diminution as to assume the human nature, signifies a certain elevation and glorification of all creation, including the angelic choir, not to mention the joy and triumph of the angels by virtue of their love for the human race.[2]

The union of angels and human beings in one Church as a consequence of the Incarnation is, for the angelic world as well, a kind of new creation, an expansion and enrichment of the angelic nature through its new convergence with the human nature. This convergence has a similar significance for the human nature, which finds its supreme expression in the Forerunner. By participating in the Divine life in the God-Man, man received access to angelic divinity, encompassing it as the lesser in the greater (for the Most Pure Mother of God is already superior to the angels). And the deification of man, which is also expressed in his communion with the angelic nature, is manifested in the Baptist. When, during the baptism of the Lord, they saw him "touch the head of the Most High, the heavenly powers were seized with fright in the presence of this most glorious mystery" (Office of Baptism, sticheron to "Glory").

The dignity of the angels is expressed in their presence before God's throne and in their unceasing praise of His magnificence. Their life con-

---

2. The fact that the angelic world united with the human world in the person of the Forerunner has a multifarious significance for the whole human race. If the feat of the Forerunner has not only an individual significance but also the general significance of a way of salvation, then the union with the angelic world too is prepared for all. Every man has his guardian angel, present before the throne of God, and in this angel receives his place and his point of attachment in the angelic world. This union lies beyond the limits of our personal experience, but it is marked out for us as a path by the glorification of the Forerunner.

sists in unceasing prayer and contemplation of the face of God. Man's approach to such angelic service is proportional to the intensity of his prayer and thought about God. The required intensity is indicated in the apostle Paul's words: "Rejoice evermore. Pray without ceasing. In every thing give thanks" (1 Thess. 5:16-18).

The Church attributes to angels a special participation in prayers and in liturgy, especially in the celebration of the sacrament of the Body and Blood of Christ. And the celebrants, present before the Lord's altar, are considered worthy of the angelic service: the priest who celebrates the liturgy is "an angel of the Lord." Priesthood represents an angelic order, although it does not have to be so in the course of an entire life. Its union with monasticism constitutes an exception. In entering into marriage, a priest sets out on the path not of the renunciation of the flesh but of its inner conquest. Monasticism, on the other hand, is an angelic condition not only in virtue of the ascetic renunciation of the flesh but also in virtue of the unceasing presence before God in prayer, which is the main spiritual task of the monk. Finally, the angelic condition is connected with leadership in the Church, which is why a bishop is usually called an "angel of the Church": like a guardian angel, he prays to God for the Church.

Thus, the angelic service includes priesthood, the presence before God in prayer and leadership in the Church. To the degree a person cannot and should not live without being present before God in prayer, he participates in the angelic ministry, while fully remaining human. Angels cannot encompass the human nature, whereas man is called to unite himself with the angelic order and to integrate it into himself. And the first of those present before God in prayer, in both the human and the angelic world, is Christ's Forerunner. Present in prayer before God's throne, he represents both the human race and the angelic choir as the first among both human beings and angels: he is "the earthly angel and the heavenly man." The Church therefore bears witness, in the *Deisis,* to his terrible and exclusive proximity to the Lord's throne. Only the Queen of heaven also stands so high and so near to the throne: the man-angel and the one who is "more venerable than the cherubim and incomparably more glorious than the seraphim" implore the Lord to be merciful to the human race. It is only behind them and a distance apart from them that the heavenly army and the earthly Church pray. Such is the Forerunner's stature and grandeur.

EXCURSUS 2

St. John the Forerunner and St. John the Divine

St. John the Divine was a disciple of St. John the Forerunner. Precisely the Gospel of John, that of an apostle and an eyewitness, tells the story of how two of the Forerunner's disciples were standing next to him. As is his custom, the Evangelist gives the name of only one of them, Andrew; while the other, he himself, was not named (John 1:40). When he saw Jesus Christ, the Forerunner repeated, *only for these two,* the words that he had pronounced the previous day (see John 1:29, 36): "Behold the Lamb of God."

And this was sufficient reason for the disciples, who had already heard this thunderous testimony, to follow Jesus (John 1:37). This marks a moment of extraordinary importance in the history of Christ's Church, in fact, its very beginning: The friend of the Bridegroom brings new *friends* to the Bridegroom — which is what the Lord Himself calls His disciples at the Last Supper (John 15:14-15). Christ's Forerunner "hands over" to the Lord disciples chosen and prepared for Him.

Who precisely these disciples were is, of course, of extreme importance for the Church. The first to be named in the Gospel is Andrew, the "First Called." It is he who marks the beginning of the apostolic vocation, although the synoptics only mention briefly that he was called together with Simon. Only the Gospel of John (1:40) records that Andrew was the first called. No explanation is given for this fact, but it must be supposed that this election somehow depended upon the spiritual qualities of the apostle Andrew.

The other disciple was the one who was to become the beloved disciple, the "adopted" son of the Mother of God, and, in virtue of this adoption, a brother of the Lord Himself[1] — the one whom the Lord honored with primacy in love and with the inner knowledge that flows from it. Both disciples *heard*, with their interior hearing, the words of the Forerunner and knew the Lord. About Andrew it is said that, having found his brother Simon, the future chief apostle, he announced to him: "We have found the Messias" (John 1:41) in this Lamb of God. The other disciple, as is his custom, does not speak explicitly about himself or about his secret knowledge; rather, his entire narrative indirectly attests to it.

Apart from all else, it is evident that the Lord's special love for the beloved disciple was requited by the disciple's love. And the beloved disciple's love flared up at the very first meeting; at least nowhere is it said that there was a time when this love did not exist. John is first called the disciple "whom Jesus loved," without any particular explanation, only at the Last Supper (John 13:23; cf. John 21:20). It was then that this secret side of the personal relations between John and the Lord became clear to all. All the apostles are *friends (philoi)* of the Lord (John 15:15), but John is the chosen, personal, beloved friend.

He alone is accorded the personal caress of the Divine Friend — he leans on Jesus' bosom: "Now there was leaning on Jesus' bosom one of his disciples, whom Jesus loved" (John 13:23). This was why Peter could discreetly beckon to him that he should ask Jesus who the betrayer was: "He then lying on Jesus' breast saith unto him, Lord, who is it?" (John 13:25).

The Evangelist is silent about the nature of the personal relations between the Forerunner and the two disciples, and in particular about the relations between the Forerunner and the future beloved disciple of Christ. Perhaps any inquiry into these relations is inappropriate. The Forerunner's ascesis of self-renunciation left no room for personal feelings and attachments. A single feeling, one that was suprapersonal, dominated the Forerunner's spiritual world: his love for the Messiah, the yearning of the friend of the Bridegroom for the Bridegroom. He did not have any *humanly* personal feelings if this is to be understood as a special attachment or particular closeness to one disciple or another for his personal qualities.

Here too, the Forerunner differs from Jesus. Besides His disciples, near and distant, and His entire "entourage," Jesus also had *personal* friends. Besides John the Divine, the Gospel mentions Martha and Mary

---

1. Office of the Theologian, 26 September, canon, ode 6, tr. 1: "Jesus, my Lord and my God, having recognized your purity and your perfect saintliness, O Theologian, received you like a brother."

and their brother Lazarus, whom Jesus loved (John 11:3, 5). Without doubt, this personal love was mutual and based on certain particular personal qualities of the Lord's friends: on a tenderness of great delicacy, implicitly suggested in John 11:11, 13. Once this tenderness is even underscored, namely in the narrative of the raising of Lazarus: "Jesus wept. Then said the Jews, Behold how he loved him!" (John 11:35-36). Nowhere else in the Gospels is it said that the Lord wept over someone: he wept neither at the raising of the daughter of Jairus nor at that of the widow's son. The only other time He wept was when He approached Jerusalem for the last time (Luke 19:41). But here He was saying farewell to and condemning the city of David, marking the sad end of Israel's election.

But His tears over Lazarus were an indication of His personal feeling, His personal sorrow for a friend. Having assumed the entire human nature except sin, the Lord had evidently also received the gift of personal love and friendship, divorced, to be sure, from all passion and sin. And in so doing, He had sanctified this gift. But on John the Forerunner's ascetic path of sacrifice, *all* human possibilities and faculties were consecrated to one love, one deed, one service. And in this sense it would be meaningless to speak of John's possible personal attachments to his disciples. However, this ascetic indifference does not prevent John from recognizing the personal traits of different people and from being guided by them when choosing his disciples. Nor does it prevent him, in a practical sense, from appreciating (or at least distinguishing) their qualities.

And of course it is not a coincidence that the Forerunner repeated his testimony concerning the Lamb of God precisely to Andrew and John and that, making a sacrificial offering of his chosen disciples to Christ, he told them, as it were, to follow Him. The friend of the Bridegroom chose and prepared the Bridegroom's best friend; and at this solemn hour, he "handed him over," silently sending him, as it were, into the circle of Jesus' disciples.

It is noteworthy that nothing is said about the relation of the other ten apostles to the Forerunner. His relations with Christ's disciples were limited to Andrew and John. On the other hand, it is precisely John the Divine who, in his Gospel, reveals the entire significance of the ministry of the Forerunner as a witness to Christ, as the first evangelist and the friend of the Bridegroom. And it is John the Divine who shows the supra-eternal connection between the Forerunner and Christ in the Incarnation. At the same time, the Forerunner's testimony concerning Christ is interwoven with the personal testimony of John the Divine, which is his Gospel as a whole. In a certain sense, the Gospel of John is an unfolding of the content of the Forerunner's Gospel. A certain mysterious spiritual unity of the two Johns is established in the prism of the Gospel of John. As a witness to Christ, John the Divine is, as it were, the New Testament successor and continuator of the Forerunner's work: the Forerunner stands at the boundary between the two Testaments, while John stands beyond him, on this side of the boundary.

This constitutes the main difference between the narrative about the Forerunner in the Gospel of John and that in the three synoptic Gospels. The synoptic narratives are histories that give us an external view of the Forerunner, as it were, describing him as preacher of repentance, prophet, and baptist. In contrast, the Gospel of John reveals the inner content of the evangelical accomplishments, and therefore portrays the Forerunner as a witness and an evangelist. The two approaches are different and even opposite, without contradicting each other or being incompatible in meaning. The teacher and the disciple, John the Forerunner and John the apostle, are co-evangelists, as it were: one of the Old Testament, the other of the New.

The Gospel of John is also that of the Mother of God, who made Her "adopted" son the guardian of the mystery of Her life and that of Her Son. In a special sense, it is the Gospel of the Holy Spirit and of the Holy Trinity, in contradistinction to that of Luke, which in this respect is the Gospel about the Mother of God. This underscores the connection between the Forerunner and John the Divine in a new aspect: in their relation to the Mother of God.

This relation is represented by two types of icons: by the *Deisis,* in which the Mother of God and the Forerunner stand before Christ; and by icons of the Crucifixion in which the Mother of God and John the Divine stand at the foot of the Cross. Both the Forerunner and John the Divine are particularly close to the Mother of God, but the closeness has a different origin and a different significance in the two cases. The Forerunner's closeness to the Mother of God refers wholly to the glorified Church, to their common glorification, grounded in their inner nature. But it has virtually no basis (or at least any we know of) in their earthly lives. In contrast, the closeness between the Mother of God and John the Divine refers to the life of the earthly Church and is grounded in the adoption of John, the Lord's beloved disciple, by the Mother of God, Who was received into his house.

One can say that John the Divine belongs to the life of the earthly Church, the militant Church, and even the mystery of his death attests to this.[2] It is true that, even while abiding in the earthly Church, he presents himself before the Lord and abides in the glorified Church. To become convinced of this, it is sufficient to mention his appearance, together with the Mother of God, on the day of Her Protection, to St. Andrew, the holy fool, as well as to St. Sergius and St. Seraphim.[3] Nevertheless, in contrast to Elias and Enoch, who were taken from the world, John the Divine abides, in some sense, in the world. His connection with the earthly Church is not broken even in his state of glorification. And this is not only by virtue of the communion in prayer of all the saints, but also by virtue of a special link with the earthly Church in the sense of a certain personal abiding in the latter.

But this signifies something wholly other than what is said with regard to the Mother of God: When She was resurrected, She was united with Her flesh, which did not remain on earth, but was raised to heaven. In contrast, no relics of John the Divine remain, because in a certain sense — largely unfathomable by us — he did not die (according to tradition, his tomb was empty). Not completely separated from him, his body abides on earth — though not in "relics" but in a certain other state, which cannot be defined precisely. Even at the present time the beloved disciple protects his Mother, the Church. By this act of protection, he is united with the protection of the Mother of God, the Queen of heaven and of earth, who leaves heaven in order to descend to earth (according to St. Andrew's vision).

The opposite can be affirmed about the Forerunner: Although his sacred relics are found on earth, he abides, in his equi-angelic nature, in heaven, standing, together with the Mother of God, before Christ's throne. He protects and watches over the earthly Church from the heavenly height, not from within it, like John the Divine. He abides in a glori-

---

2. See my essay, "Peter and John: The Two First-Apostles," 1926.

3. In Her appearances to human beings the Mother of God has appeared more than once accompanied by John the Forerunner and John the Divine, by John the Divine alone, or by one of the holy apostles. We read in the life of St. Gregory of Neo-Caesarea (17 November) that when, in the year 240, before being consecrated bishop, he was studying in solitude the dogmas of the holy faith and praying to God and the Mother of God, She appeared to him with the apostle John the Divine and told the latter to instruct him in the exposition of the Orthodox faith. We read in the life of St. Cyril of Alexandria that St. Cyriac (June 9) saw in a dream the Queen of heaven together with the Forerunner and John the Divine (*Saying on the Earthly Life of the Most Holy Mother of God*, 7th ed., Moscow, 1897, pp. 223 sq.). St. Sergius was found worthy of seeing the Mother of God together with two apostles, John the Divine and Peter (St. Seraphim was also judged worthy of such a vision).

fied state, in the heavenly Church. But he tasted death, which is why his relics remain on earth, and His separation from the earthly Church, for a fixed period of time, is the same as that of all the saints, among whom he is the greatest. Only the Mother of God overcomes this separation, for She "did not abandon the world, even in Her dormition" (office, troparion). The Forerunner watches over the Church by virtue of his presence in prayer before the Lord, in the *Deisis;* and he gathers his fellows into his synaxis. But he is not the director of the earthly Church. In a certain sense, John the Divine, who does not leave the earth "till I come" (John 21:22-23), is her director. Their ministries differ according to the proper nature of each of the two great Johns. But, to be sure, this difference clearly does not abolish the uniqueness of the Forerunner's ministry with regard to the whole human race.

It remains for us to note that these two "relatives" of the Mother of God according to the flesh are also close to Her according to the spirit of humility and love. The Church particularly underscores yet another trait common to the two: they are both *virgins*. That John the Forerunner is the virgin of virgins, we know. But John the Divine too is venerated by the Church for his virginity: "Who can describe your greatness, O Virgin?" (kontakion). And in the office consecrated to him it is underscored that only a virgin could have been entrusted to receive the Ever-Virgin into his home. Many saints are celebrated by the Church for the feat of virginity, but St. John the Divine is venerated as a virgin *par excellence,* for he acquired by his virginity the gift of a particular closeness to Christ and the Mother of God. Thus, the Ever-Virgin is surrounded by a luminous nimbus of virginity in the persons of the Forerunner and John the Divine.

EXCURSUS 3

St. John the Forerunner and St. Joseph the Betrothed

The Orthodox Church usually venerates the Forerunner and the Mother of God together, and unites them iconographically — in the *Deisis*. But in Catholicism the Forerunner's place next to the Mother of God is taken by St. Joseph the Betrothed, who is thus situated, after the Mother of God, higher than the rest of creation (it is true that this practice is of recent origin). Pope Pius IX, who is remembered for having introduced two new dogmas, that of the Immaculate Conception and that of the Vatican, proclaimed also the dogma of Joseph as the Patron (father) of the whole Church. But before considering this new dogmatic decree, let us examine the question of the true place of St. Joseph in the economy of our salvation. This place is indisputably high.

The Gospel of Matthew refers to Mary's betrothal to Joseph as a *fait accompli* (Matt. 1:18), but how it was accomplished we can learn only from the apocryphal proto-gospel of James. According to this proto-gospel, the high priest Zacharias (the Forerunner's father) was instructed by an angel to gather together all the unmarried men from the branch of Judah, the house of David, in order to find a betrothed for the Virgin Mary. They had to bring their rods to see if a sign would be manifested. Joseph's rod flowered, and out of it flew a dove, which descended upon his head. When Joseph protested that he was old and had adult sons, Zacharias threatened him with divine punishment. And so Joseph agreed, not to marry the Virgin, but to take Her under his protection and, with this aim in mind, to become her betrothed.

Excursus 3

The Church does not have a special feast of the betrothal,[1] and therefore we do not have a liturgical confirmation of this story (the way we do for some of the other apocryphal stories). Nor is it mentioned in the Office of St. Joseph. The Gospel knows him as the "husband of Mary" (Matt. 1:16) and the "supposed" father of Jesus (Luke 3:23). But if Christ's genealogy is identified with that of Joseph, this only means, of course, that, according to the Jewish custom, genealogies were not computed according to women's lines, and that marriages were confined to the same branch. Joseph's genealogy is therefore the same as that of the Virgin Mary. In the Gospel of Luke this genealogy is given in 3:23-38, after the narrative of the Annunciation, which says: "How shall this be, seeing I know not a man" (Luke 1:34). But then we find: "Jesus . . . [was] (as was supposed) the son of Joseph, which was the son of Heli, which was the son of Matthat . . ." etc. (Luke 3:23-24). This is why the "Godparents," Joachim and Anna, so piously venerated by the Church (and commemorated at the end of the matins and the vespers), do not figure in this genealogy.

Certain questions arise concerning Joseph's life before the betrothal: Had he been married previously and did he have children from this previous marriage? Or was he a virgin? We find no evidence for the state of virginity in the Old Testament, according to which Joseph lived his entire life before the betrothal with Mary. In this respect he cannot be compared with St. John the Divine, who was a youth when he became an apostle of Christ and who therefore led his entire mature life in a New Testament atmosphere. Nor is Joseph's virginity supported by the patristic tradition, with the exception of a single polemical allusion by St. Jerome. But this allusion is contradicted by a whole chorus of patristic voices, mainly Eastern, but also Western, which attest that the tradition of the ancient Church did not consider St. Joseph to be celibate or a virgin.

This question is posed in connection with the question — difficult to answer with precision — concerning *Jesus' brothers and sisters*, who are mentioned several times in the Gospel. Who were they? For our purposes, we have no need of a comprehensive examination of this question. We are interested in it only insofar as Joseph is concerned, and this not so much

---

1. In contrast, in Catholicism, simultaneously with the entire movement in favor of a new cult of Joseph, a special feast was consecrated to the betrothal or marriage of Joseph and Mary. The Pope Benedict XIII extended it to the whole Church in 1725 (this date shows sufficiently to what extent this cult represents an innovation). The feast that celebrates Joseph as the "patron" of the Church was introduced by the congregation of rites in 1680 and extended to the whole Catholic Church by Pius IX in 1847.

from a historical as from a *dogmatic* point of view. Could Joseph have been the father of Jesus' "brothers"? Three different answers were given to this question in the patristic literature.

The first answer, associated with the name Helvidius, a heretic who lived in Rome at the beginning of the fourth century, was that "Jesus' brothers" were children of Joseph and Mary. It is clear, with regard to the Mother of God, that this view (which even at present is widespread among rationalists) is an unbelieving and impious one. Of the writers of the Church, Tertullian, however strange this might seem, was inclined to share this opinion, although this was at the time of his heretical leanings. This view allows that, after the Annunication and the birth of Christ, the Virgin Mary could have become the wife of Joseph, and that Joseph, at his advanced age and after having witnessed all the events linked to the Nativity, could have been guilty of such an act. This idea is so absurd, monstrous, and blasphemous that it does not merit dogmatic examination. That Mary was a Virgin before, during, and after the birth of Christ is a firmly established doctrine of the Church. This opinion, therefore, does not even merit consideration. (It clearly contradicts the fact, mentioned by Jerome, that the Savior entrusted His Mother to John's care, which would be incomprehensible if She had had grown children.)

It was Jerome who undertook the task of disputing Helvidius's impious doctrine. For this purpose Jerome composed a special treatise (383) on Mary's ever-virginity: *De perpetua virginitate Mariae*. Refuting Helvidius's opinions by a strong and convincing critique, he was carried away to such a polemical extreme that he began to assert the virginity — "by virtue of Mary, *per Mariam*" — of Joseph himself.

This idea, which Jerome let fall in passing, has been taken up and is being developed now by Catholic theology, but it remains isolated in the patristic literature. Predominant here is an opinion expressed by St. Epiphanius of Cyprus and shared by a large number of Eastern and Western fathers, including Origen, Eusebius, St. Gregory of Nyssa, St. John Chrysostom, St. Cyril of Alexandria, St. Sophronius, Theophylact, Euthymius, St. Ambrose, St. Hilary, and Gregory of Tours. According to this opinion, prior to his betrothal to the Virgin Mary, at an age of at least eighty, Joseph had been married and had had four sons (James, Joshua, Simeon, and Jude) and two daughters (Mary and Salome). St. Epiphanius develops this view (in *Against Heresies*, no. 78) in his dispute with the ebionitic heresy of the antidicomarianites, who contested the veneration of Mary and approached Helvidius's false doctrine.

The history of this question makes clear, first of all, that it was never viewed as having dogmatic significance. All the mentioned Church fathers decisively reject as blasphemous the notion that the "brothers of Jesus" could be Mary's children, for this offends and denies Her ever-virginity and shakes the dogma of the Mother of God. But the same fathers freely admitted, and even suggested, that the "brothers of Jesus" were Joseph's children. Second, the notion that Joseph was not a virgin but had been married and had had children before his betrothal to the Virgin Mary, met with no opposition in the consciousness of the Church in the course of the centuries. In the view of the fathers, nearness to the Virgin Mary and to the Divine Infant did not require a state of celibacy. It was not required of the elder Simeon or of the prophetess Anna, a widow of the branch of Phanuel, or of the apostles.

The fact that, after the Crucifixion, the Most Holy Virgin was entrusted to John the Divine as a virgin has its special *New Testament* significance. But this does not mean that nothing that had to do with marriage could come into contact with the Mother of God. Examples of this, besides the marriage in Cana of Galilee, include the righteous Elisabeth, the female myrrh-bearers at the cross, the apostles, etc. The impossibility that Joseph, the Betrothed of the Virgin, could have been married, even in the past, did not appear obvious to the holy fathers; on the contrary, a married state seemed more appropriate. In contrast, recent Catholic literature has asserted that this impossibility is dogmatically self-evident, following, it is argued, from the dogma of the ever-virginity of the Mother of God.

This assertion is motivated by the desire to remove any shadow of impurity from Joseph. With regard to Christ, it is argued in favor of this thesis that the Lord, who loved virginity, would not have tolerated a "father" who was not crowned with its flower. With regard to Mary, it is argued that, since She was a virgin, the Betrothed given to Her also had to be a virgin. With regard to Joseph, it is argued that his love would have been divided if he had had other children, and thus he could not have devoted himself entirely to Mary and the Infant. It is also asserted that the Gospel does not contain any traces of other members of Joseph's family besides Mary and Jesus — although to this one can object that the appearance in the Gospel of Jesus' "brothers," together with His Mother, is a sufficient refutation of this assertion, for these "brothers" were certainly part of Mary's family after Joseph's death.

All these considerations, which, as we have seen, are foreign to the Church fathers, are totally unconvincing and are based on an aversion to marriage and on an excessive emphasis on physical purity and celibacy. The Church knows virginity not as celibacy (a Catholic invention) but only as monasticism, as one of numerous monastic vows and feats: as an assumption of the angelic "habit" and a separation from the world. Here the Catholics invent a celibate marriage from which the fleshly relation is banished — not only because of veneration directed at the Most Pure Virgin Mary and Joseph's advanced age, but also in the name of virginity itself. Therefore the first among marriages becomes an implicit condemnation of childbirth in marriage, an aversion to marriage within marriage itself. It must be noted that Catholic theology considers Joseph to have been in the prime of life (30-40 years old), virile and handsome, when he entered into his union with Mary; and accordingly his death is considered to have occurred nearly at the time of the baptism of the Lord.

By no means do we dispute that, in Christianity, virginity is superior to marriage (this was not the case in Judaism, which did not know monasticism). But by no means can a legitimate marriage (or, more generally, the absence of virginity) in the past be considered to contaminate a man to the point where he is unworthy of being the protector of the Most Holy Virgin. Should we not also extend this to the "Godparents," Joachim and Anna, in whose parental care Mary remained until Her Presentation at the temple?

The assertion of Joseph's celibacy indirectly reflects the Catholic bias in the dogma of the Mother of God, who is removed here from the human race by the fact of Her "immaculate conception" and supposed freedom from original sin. Thus, Catholic theology wishes to remove Joseph too from the genealogy of Christ the Savior, not letting it continue through him in the human race.

But the Gospel, as if responding to future conjectures, *assures* us of the contrary. For Christ's humanity it is important not only that He have *ancestors* but also that He have *relatives* in the human race. And these relatives by blood are as close to Him as possible — the most glorious of them being the Forerunner, who is considered by tradition to be the Lord's cousin, for Elisabeth, Mary's "cousin" (Luke 1:36), is considered to be a sister of the righteous Anna.

On His Mother's side, the Lord could not have had first cousins, for She was the only child of Her parents. His *closest* relatives, then, could only have been Joseph's children. This supports the hypothesis that Jesus' brothers were Joseph's children. It is for this reason that the Gospel (which is usually so spare in details, especially concerning Jesus' childhood and family) repeatedly and specifically refers to Jesus' brothers — not, certainly, as rationalists think, to attribute to Jesus a fleshly origin, but to make us perfectly conscious of the fullness and authenticity of his humanity: "Is not this the carpenter's son? is not his mother called Mary? and his brethren, James, and Joses, and Simon, and Judas? And his sisters, are they not all with us?" (Matt. 13:55-56; also Mark 6:3). Do these words not refer directly to Joseph's family, to which Jesus Himself belongs? And this family is needed precisely to bring Jesus fully into the human family. Therefore, contra the Catholics, for Christ's humanity and for the fulfillment of His genealogy, it was necessary for Joseph to have a family and for Jesus' "brothers and sisters" to be not distant relations but close relatives, even if stepsisters and stepbrothers, children of His father from another mother.

On the other hand, it was precisely Joseph's situation as the Betrothed, the protector of Mary's virginity and the "nominal" father of the Divine Infant, that required him to be truly a *father*. And fatherhood, certainly, cannot be proper to a virgin monk who renounces the world; and it is incomprehensible why it should be proper to a celibate husband, who for some reason would be allowed all the capacities of a father in marriage except procreation. It is here that we can find the difference between the situations of Joseph and John the Divine, even though Catholic theology likes to bring the two of them together as virgins in proximity to the Most Holy Virgin: John the Divine was only a *son*, whereas Joseph was a father and a husband, a protector of virginity.

Of course, the object of marriage and fatherhood is not limited to procreation, which can even be absent (as in the case of adopted children and stepchildren). There remains the spiritual and moral foundation of the family, which is superior to and, to a certain degree, even independent of the physical relation. It is for this reason that Joseph is the husband of Mary (Matt. 1:19; Luke 1:27) and the father of Jesus (Luke 2:48).

But the fact that Joseph had previously been married does not contradict but even befits Joseph's place near the Holy Family. The qualities of father and husband that were then prepared in him are now revealed in their purest form. And there was nothing unclean in this lawful marriage of long ago, for the Virgin Mary was conceived in a similar marriage. To be sure, sexual intercourse had receded into the distant past and even had become impossible owing to Joseph's advanced age; and in this sense, Joseph can be considered a spouse who leads a monastic life. It should be mentioned that to have been married in the past has never been an obstacle to becoming a monk or, consequently, of entering the choir of virgins. Therefore, again contrary to the opinion of the Catholics, Joseph was betrothed to Mary at an age so advanced that there could have been no thought of conjugal relations; the protective role of father and husband would have been more appropriate.

Strictly speaking, it is even imprecise to speak of the *marriage* of Joseph and Mary; in fact, the Gospel speaks only of betrothal (Matt. 1:18; Luke 1:27). According to tradition, the betrothed was intended to be not a husband but a guardian of virginity, though he is called a husband and father. By contrast, Catholic theology gives great emphasis to his fatherhood in relation to the Savior and to his husbandhood in relation to the Mother of God. It derives Joseph's heavenly glorification from this *familial* proximity of Joseph to the Mother of God and the Divine Infant. But Joseph's relationship with Mary does not constitute such a familial proximity: when he first learned that She was great with child, he wanted to send Her away, so weak was familial feeling in him at that time. Also, the angel speaks to him about the Mother and the Infant in an impersonal manner, as it were: "Arise, and take the young child and his mother" and "when he arose, he took the young child and his mother" (Matt. 2:13-14; cf. 2:20-21).

On the other hand, when Mary found Jesus in the temple and addressed to Him the reproach, "Son, why has thou thus dealt with us? behold, thy father and I have sought thee sorrowing" (Luke 2:48), He told them: "How is it that ye sought me? wist ye not that I must be about my Father's business? And they understood not the saying which he spake unto them. And he went down with them, and came to Nazareth, and was subject unto them: but his mother kept all these sayings in her heart" (Luke 2:49-51). Does the Lord's answer not imply, in a mild form, a radical distinction between His nominal father and His true Father in heaven, as well as a clear rejection of family ties, which was fully manifested later, at the time of his preaching? It is said only that He "was subject unto them," but only "his mother kept all these sayings in her heart." In other words, Joseph the Betrothed is not so much a father as a guardian and protector. It is therefore incorrect to conceive these relations as familial ones (the "Holy Family" is a Western expression), where Joseph is considered the father and Jesus, who is "subject" to him, is the son, as Catholic theology emphasizes with such exaggeration.

One should certainly not diminish the greatness of Joseph's service and vocation; but it is necessary to recognize that, in a certain sense, his position is *external,* and that the ordinary norms and categories of a human family, fatherhood, sonhood, marriage, are inapplicable here. Nevertheless, such anthropomorphism, as applied to the Holy Family, serves as the basis of the whole Catholic doctrine of Joseph. This relatively external character of Joseph's service is confirmed by the fact that the revelations of the angel have no other purpose than to move him to some decision or action.

In relation to the Divine Infant, Joseph is a representative of the entire human race: he personally embodies the Infant's genealogy, both *before* and *after* His birth. Is this not what the Church has in mind when she links the commemoration of Joseph with that of King David, a forebear of the Lord, and with that of James, a brother of the Lord? The union of elderly spouses takes on the character of the lives of saints, spiritual and *virginal*; but this is even more true for a prolonged widowhood, such as that, according to tradition, of Joseph. Time erased all memory and all traces of fleshly relations, which Catholic theology always considers so degrading. It is appropriate to recall here the fact, so underscored by Luke 2:36-37, that the prophetess Anna (who, together with Simeon, was deemed worthy to receive the Lord in the temple) was a widow who, having spent seven years with her husband, the rest of her life (living to the age of eighty-four) "departed not from the temple, but served God with fastings and prayers night and day," manifesting an authentic monasticism. This should be compared to what the apostle Paul said about true widows (1 Tim. 5:3-16).

St. Joseph completes the Lord's genealogy. He closes this series of forefathers and fathers that is celebrated by the Church over the two weeks preceding Christmas. He therefore belongs to the Old Testament; and although he stands at the very cradle of the Divine Infant and is His father according to the law, he does not understand the mystery of what is being accomplished. The mystery of the Annunciation is unknown to him, as is clear from Matthew 1:18-19, which says that Joseph "was minded to put [Mary] away privily" because "she was found with child."

This reminds us to compare him to the one who truly stands at the threshold between the Old and the New Testament, and who "leaped" in his mother's womb when the Mother of God approached. In Joseph the discovery that Mary was with child unleashed "a storm of doubting thoughts" (Acathistus of the Mother of God, kontakion 4), which abated only when the angel appeared to him in the dream. And this storm, the temptation of Joseph, recurs (according to the Church's liturgical and iconographic testimony) on the very night of Christ's birth.

Joseph was a witness of the virginal birth, of the adoration of the shepherds and the magi, of the presentation in the temple; and for this he is venerated by the Church. It is he who accompanied the Mother and the Infant on the flight to Egypt, and he protected them in his house after their return. But there is no evidence that, knowing the mystery of the virginal birth, he was also initiated into the mystery of the Incarnation. Thus, Luke says the following about what the shepherds reported concerning the appearance of the angels: "And all they that heard it [and certainly not Joseph alone] wondered at those things which were told by the shepherds. But Mary kept all these things, and pondered them in her heart" (Luke 2:18-19). This is said about Mary alone.

On the occasion of the prophecy of the righteous Simeon during the presentation in the temple, it is said only: "Joseph and his mother marvelled at those things which were spoken of him" (Luke 2:33). And then, on the occasion of what the boy Jesus said during His conversation with the doctors in the temple, it is noted: "They understood not the saying which he spake unto them" (Luke 2:50). And then, on the subject of Mary alone, it is observed: "his mother kept all these sayings in her heart" (Luke 2:51).

In none of this is there any indication that the mystery of the Incarnation was revealed to Joseph, although he knew that the "light to lighten the Gentiles" (Luke 2:32), born of the Virgin, had been specially sent by God. And what makes most clear that Joseph did not know Jesus as the Son of God is the fact that, according to Church tradition, Joseph died before the Lord's baptism, the Theophany, and the testimony of John; the fact that Joseph is not mentioned after the initial chapters of the Gospel is further confirmation of this. Before the Baptism the Messiah was not yet manifested to the world and was not yet anointed by the descent of the Holy Spirit upon His human nature. If the Baptism can be considered the completion of the Incarnation and the fulfillment of the Annunciation, then, before the Baptism, it was not possible to know the Son of God, Whom the Forerunner was called to meet. Therefore, one can say that Joseph knew only the human, not the divine, or Divine-human, nature of Christ. In this sense, the elder Joseph remains, together with the righteous Simeon and Anna, in the Old Testament whose light is fading. He remains on that side of the New Testament.

This is indirectly confirmed by the fact that, according to all the Evangelists, the Forerunner belongs to the Gospel, whereas St. Joseph remains at its threshold. He is present only in the Gospel of Matthew, whose aim is to reveal the Judaic origin and the human nature of Christ; and in the prologue to the Gospel of Luke, which mentions a number of persons associated with the events described. But he is completely absent in Mark, who, as we know, opens his Gospel with the story of the Forerunner and does not mention Joseph. Likewise, the Gospel of John speaks of the Forerunner but is completely silent about Joseph.

In fact, St. Joseph's significance in the Gospel narratives consists in the fact that, as a patriarch and a representative of the Old Testament humanity under the law, he was called to serve *humanly* the *human* needs of the Mother of God and of the God-Man. His role is limited to this. Therefore, Joseph has a direct relation neither to the Gospel of the Lord Jesus Christ nor to His preaching and ministry; and consequently he is called from this world when his human guardianship becomes unnecessary. His mission ends precisely when that of the Forerunner begins, the latter attesting already in his mother's womb to the divinity of the Savior.

This defines Joseph's relation to the Forerunner, as well as his relation to the Mother of God. The relations between the Forerunner and the Mother of God depend entirely on their glorified state (the *Deisis*), whereas Joseph's relation to the Mother of God is determined by their human and earthly intimacy. One should not, of course, diminish Joseph's importance in the economy of our salvation, nor his "righteousness," purity, and humility, which are necessary for his particular mission. God prepared a number of persons who were worthy of receiving and serving the Savior: St. Joseph, Simeon and Anna, the holy apostles, not to mention the Forerunner, whose coming was announced by the prophets, instructed by the Holy Spirit.

But Joseph's place, however significant it may be, remains *among* these persons, and of course does not justify the attribution to him of the title *co-redeemer*. And by no means can his place be equated with that of the Forerunner, who directly participated in the work of the Incarnation. Generally speaking (and this is the most interesting aspect of the recent Catholic dogma concerning Joseph), Catholic devotion has assigned to Joseph the place that, in Orthodoxy, belongs to the Forerunner. Thus, the veneration of the Forerunner has been diminished in Catholic theology, which even explicitly affirms that Joseph's saintliness surpasses that of all the saints, including the Forerunner, as well as that of the angels. Accordingly, the Lord's declaration that no one born of a woman is greater than John (Matt. 11:11) is attributed by Catholic interpreters solely to the Old Testament, not to the New. And so, St. Joseph, who died before the Theophany, is considered to be more New Testamental in character than the Forerunner. This, of course, greatly contradicts the reality. Generally speaking, Catholicism does not fully understand the Forerunner's significance and, conversely, greatly exaggerates that of Joseph.

In particular, Catholicism asserts Joseph's absolute infallibility, at least from the time of his "virginal marriage." In the opinion of certain authors, Joseph was sanctified in his mother's womb and received the gracious gift of total infallibility that would last his entire life. By virtue of his position and "privilege" of grace, "he surpasses all the saints and all the angels in grace and glory" (Lepicier: *Tractatus de St. Joseph*). Only the Mother of God is superior to him.

Catholicism also applies to him all manner of honorific titles, some of which are grounded in reality, some of which are not: *corona martyrum, corona doctorum, corona virginum*. Joseph is called a *co-redeemer* and placed just behind Mary, who is the *co-redemptrix* par excellence. Physical beauty is attributed to him and he is considered to have been in the prime of life (30 to 40 years old) at the time of his betrothal to Mary. He is also thought to have been free of illness and, finally, it is believed that he was resurrected at the moment of the Savior's death on the cross. Moreover, in the opinion of many, the resurrected Christ called Joseph to eternal life and took him up to heaven in glory, which ascent is confirmed by the absence of his visible relics (as if this could be established). Gerson therefore applies Hebrews 11:35 ("women received their dead raised to life again") to the Virgin Mary, who, besides Christ, also received Her husband, Joseph. In 1870, Pius IX proclaimed Joseph the patron of the whole Church (the foundations and characteristics of this *patrocinium* were developed in the encyclical of Leo XIII, 1889).

The motives behind this new dogma, as well as those behind that of 1854 (the "Immaculate Conception"), are certainly pious, suggested as they are by a desire to celebrate worthily the Most Pure Virgin and Her betrothed. But the new dogma is a typical expression of that anthropomorphism which generally marks Catholicism, i.e., an excessive predominance of the natural-human element in the reception of Christ. This has resulted in a cult of Joseph based on the fact of his physical proximity to the Savior's cradle. And this provides a basis for glorifying him as more venerable than all other human beings and more glorious than the cherubim and seraphim. When Jesus was told that His mother and brothers had come to speak with Him, He answered: "Who is my mother? and who are my brethren? And he stretched forth his hand toward his disciples, and said, Behold my mother and my brethren!" (Matt. 12:47-48). It would seem that with these words the Lord eliminated for good the possibility of dogmatic hypotheses based on human intimacy with Him. But it is precisely this feature that characterizes the Catholic dogma concerning Joseph and constitutes its entire content.

For us, this dogma is interesting and instructive as a symptom, in the Catholic consciousness, of indifference to the Forerunner, of an obscuring of his role. The main reason for this is the anthropopathism mentioned above. If it is at all possible to speak of a "patron of the Church" among men (although such an application of the notion of fatherhood is inappropriate in the Church, where the sole "patron" is our Heavenly Father), such a one could only be the greatest of those born of women, who, together with the Mother of God, is present before the Lord's throne: the Baptist and Forerunner. If there is a man who is superior to the angels, as both an angel and a man in one person, it is the Forerunner. In other words, Catholicism attributes to Joseph all the honor and glory that belong to the Forerunner. And the new dogma concerning Joseph therefore has the same relationship to the Orthodox doctrine of the Forerunner as the concave side of a body has to the convex side. The Catholic dogma repeats the Orthodox doctrine, but applies it wrongly. And so, the main significance of this dogma for us is that it serves as an indirect confirmation of the Orthodox doctrine. At the very least, a characteristic separation is exhibited here between the spirit of Orthodox piety and the spirit of Catholic piety. That is why two different, mutually exclusive answers are given to the same dogmatic question: Which created being, after the Mother of God, stands highest and in the closest proximity to God — St. Joseph the Betrothed or St. John, the Forerunner and Baptist of the Lord?

By their prayers, O Lord, save our souls!

Index

Abandonment by God, 93-95, 97, 99
Agony: of Christ, 93-98; of the Forerunner, 93, 98-102; of Mother of God, 99
Ambrose of Milan, 72n.1
Andrew the Apostle, 171-173
Angels, 83-84, 130-134, 140, 157-159, 163-169; and priesthood, 170
Antonii, Metropolitan, 95n.4

Baptism: of Jesus' disciples, 49; of John, 46-47, 50, 66, 72-76, 112; of the Lord, 51-53, 56-58, 60, 62, 68-69, 111, 126, 185; with Spirit and fire, 76; and washing of feet, 76-77
Bulgakov, Sergius: biography, viii-ix; "The Burning Bush," xi, 38, 144n.5, 150n.7; "The Holy Grail," 76n.4; "Peter and John: The Two First-Apostles," 175n.2

Cana of Galilee, 76-77, 160
Christ: agony of, 93-95; baptism of, 51-53, 56-58, 60, 69; brothers of Jesus, 178-180, 182; His friends, 172-173; Lamb of God, 66-67, 70, 78, 86, 173; testimony about the Forerunner, 10, 64, 90, 104-106, 108-113, 151; temptation by Satan, 96; and women, 122-123
Chrysostom, John, 109, 116

"Deisis," ix-x, xi, 1-2, 39, 107n.1, 126, 129, 130, 149, 153n.9, 154-155, 168, 174, 177, 186; doctrine of, 137-138, 141-144

Elias (Elijah), 111-112, 115-118, 130-132, 175
Elisabeth, 27-28
Epiphany, 53-54
Eucharist, 135-136

Helvidius, 179
Herod, 115, 121-123, 128
Herodias, 119, 121, 123

Jerome, 178-179
Job, 92-93
John of Damascus, 75n.3
John the Divine, 2, 70, 172; and John the Forerunner, 171, 173-174, 182; and Mother of God, 174-176, 180; and virginity, 176
John the Forerunner (John the Baptist): agony of, 93, 98-102; angelic nature of, vii, 83-84, 130-134, 136, 139-142, 148, 156-157, 162-163, 168-170; annunciation of conception, 30-31; as Baptist, 12, 46, 51-52, 59-62, 68-69, 72-73, 111, 126; birth of, 18, 23-24, 35; death of, 92, 119, 121-122, 126-127, 130; decapitation of, 127-128, 130, 134-135; and Elias, 111-112, 115, 117-118, 131; and Eucharist,

Index

135-136; as friend of the Bridegroom, vii, 3, 8-10, 15, 62, 74, 78-80, 84, 91-92, 120, 142, 159, 171-172; glorification of, 98, 102, 113, 119, 129, 131, 139, 147-149; hermitage of, 36-38; icons of, 129-130, 131n.2, 134-137, 156-157; imprisonment, 85; and John the Divine, 171, 173-174; and Joseph the Betrothed, 186, 188; and Last Judgment, 144-148; and Mother of God, 2, 4, 18-20, 29, 32, 37-40, 99, 107, 125-126, 132, 137-138, 141, 143, 145, 149, 155, 174, 176, 177; as preacher of repentance, 42-44; prophecies about, 6, 33-35, 130-131, 135; as prophet, 65; question about Christ, 86-91, 98, 100-102, 105, 151; relics of, 175-176; and Sophia (Wisdom), 152-153; synaxis of, 1, 16, 54; testimony about Christ, 63, 66-67, 69-71, 78-84, 87, 105, 119, 173; testimony about himself, 64, 74; virginity of, 38-40, 125-126

Joseph the Betrothed: Catholic dogma of, 177, 187-188; and John the Forerunner, 186, 188; and Mother of God, 177-178, 184, 186

Josephus Flavius, 85n.1

Last Judgment, 144-148

Monasticism: and the angelic habit, vii, 158-159, 161, 163, 181; and Christ, 160

Mother of God, ix, 1-4, 13, 18-20, 29, 32, 37-40, 57, 84, 99, 107, 120, 125-126, 133-134, 142-147, 152-155, 160-162, 167, 169, 174-176, 180-182, 184, 187-188; and angelic world, 132, 138-139; crowning of, 137; and Joseph, 177-178, 186

Nestorius, 57

Origen, 27

Pseudo-Dionysius, 165

Relics, 138-139, 175; of John the Forerunner, 175-176

Salome, 120, 123-124
Seraphim of Sarov, Saint, 139, 175
Sergius, Saint, 175
Song of Songs, 78-79
Sophia (Wisdom), 113-114, 149-150, 152, 154, 166-167; icons of, 1, 39, 129, 130, 137, 153-154; and Mother of God, 138

Tertullian, 179
Transfiguration, 57, 116

Zacharias, 7, 22, 25-28, 30-35, 177

www.ingramcontent.com/pod-product-compliance
Lightning Source LLC
Chambersburg PA
CBHW030403250426
43670CB00049B/172